KB054189

직독직해로 읽는

이솝우화

Aesop's Fables

직독직해로 읽는

이솝우화
Aesop's Fables

개정판 4쇄 발행   2021년 10월 20일
초판 1쇄 발행   2011년 8월 10일

원작	이솝
역주	더 콜링(김정희, 박윤수)
디자인	DX
일러스트	정은수
발행인	조경아
발행처	랭귀지북스
주소	서울시 마포구 포은로2나길 31 벨라비스타 208호
전화	02.406.0047 **팩스** 02.406.0042
이메일	languagebooks@hanmail.net
MP3 다운로드	blog.naver.com/languagebook
등록번호	101-90-85278 **등록일자** 2008년 7월 10일
ISBN	979-11-5635-036-1 (13740)
가격	12,000원

ⓒ LanguageBooks 2011

blog.naver.com/languagebook에서 MP3 파일을 다운로드할 수 있습니다.

직독직해로 읽는

이솝우화
Aesop's Fables

이솝 원작
더 콜링 역주

Language Books

머리말

"어렸을 때 누구나 갖고 있던 세계명작 한 질.
그리고 TV에서 하던 세계명작 만화에 대한 추억이 있습니다."

"친숙한 이야기를 영어 원문으로 읽어 봐야겠다고 마음 먹고 샀던 원서들은
이제 애물단지가 되어 버렸습니다."

"재미있는 세계명작 하나 읽어 보려고 따져 보는 어려운 영문법,
모르는 단어 찾느라 이리저리 뒤져 봐야 하는 사전.
몇 장 넘겨 보기도 전에 지칩니다."

영어 독해력을 기르려면 술술 읽어가며 내용을 파악하는 것이
중요합니다. 현재 수능 시험에도 대세인 '직독직해' 스타일을 접목시
킨 〈직독직해로 읽는 세계명작 시리즈〉는 세계명작을 영어 원작으
로 쉽게 읽어갈 수 있도록 안내해 드릴 것입니다.

'직독직해' 스타일로 읽다 보면, 영문법을 들먹이며 따질 필요가
없으니 쉽고, 끊어 읽다 보니 독해 속도도 빨라집니다. 이 습관
이 들여지면 어떤 글을 만나도 두렵지 않을 것입니다.

명작의 재미를 즐기며 영어 독해력을 키우는 두 마리의 토끼
를 잡으세요!

    〈직독직해로 읽는 세계명작 시리즈〉의 나의 소중한 파트너 오랜 친구 윤수와 늘 성실한 모습으로 함께하는 일러스트레이터 은수 씨, 좋은 동역자인 디자인 DX, 그리고 이 책이 출판될 수 있도록 늘 든든하게 지원해 주시는 랭귀지북스에 감사의 마음을 전합니다.

    마지막으로 내 삶의 기쁨이 되시는 하나님께 영광을 올려 드립니다.

더 콜링 김정희

목차

C O N T E N T S

mini test 5

1

The Aethiop
이디오피아 인

THE PURCHASER of a black servant / was persuaded
흑인 노예를 사려는 사람이   설득당했다

/ that the color of his skin / arose from dirt / contracted
노예의 검은 피부색은   먼지 때문이라고

through the neglect of his former masters.
전 주인의 게으름에서 비롯된.

On bringing him home / he resorted to every means of
노예를 집으로 데려오자마자   그는 모든 방법을 동원하여 씻겼고,

cleaning, / and subjected the man to incessant scrubbings.
             계속해서 북북 문질렀다.

The servant caught a severe cold, / but he never changed /
노예는 심한 감기에 걸렸지만,   결코 바꾸지 못했다

his color or complexion.
피부색을.

What's bred in the bone / will stick to the flesh.
뼈 속에서 야기된 본질은   그 겉모습을 고수하는 법이다

Key Expression

on –ing : ~하자마자
on –ing는 '~하자마자'라는 의미로, as soon as를 사용한 절로 바꿔 쓸 수 있습니다.

▶ on –ing : ~하자마자 (=as soon as)
▶ in –ing : ~할 때 (=when)

ex) On bringing him home he resorted to every means of cleaning.
  (=As soon as he brought him home, he resorted to every means of cleaning.)
  그 노예를 집으로 데려오자마자 그는 씻기기 위해 모든 방법을 동원했다.

The Ant and the Dove
개미와 비둘기

AN ANT went to the bank of a river / to quench its
개미 한 마리가 강둑으로 갔다가   갈증을 해소하려고,

thirst, / and being carried away / by the rush of the
               휩쓸려서   거센 물살에,

stream, / was on the point of drowning.
           물에 빠져 죽을 위험에 처했다.

A Dove / sitting on a tree / overhanging the water /
비둘기 한 마리가 나무 위에 앉아 있던   강물 위에 튀어나온

plucked a leaf / and let it fall / into the stream / close to
나뭇잎을 떼어   떨어뜨렸다   물로   개미 근처의.

her. The Ant climbed onto it / and floated in safety / to
    개미는 나뭇잎에 올라타서   안전하게 떠내려갔다

the bank.
강둑으로.

Shortly afterwards / a birdcatcher came and stood /
곧 이어   새잡이가 다가와 멈춰서더니

under the tree, / and laid his lime-twigs / for the Dove, /
나무 아래,   끈끈이를 바른 장대를 뻗었다   비둘기를 향해,

which sat / in the branches.
앉아 있던   나뭇가지에.

The Ant, / perceiving his design, / stung him in the foot.
개미는,   새잡이의 계획을 알아채고,   그의 발을 물었다.

In pain / the birdcatcher threw down the twigs, / and the
아파서   새잡이는 장대를 떨어뜨렸고,

noise made the Dove take wing.
그 소리에 비둘기는 날아갔다.

---

servant 하인 | persuade 설득하다, 납득시키다 | arise from ~로 인하다, 말미암다 | dirt 먼지 | contract
계약하다, 관계맺다 | neglect 방치, 소홀 | resort to (어떤 방법에) 기대다, 의지하다 | incessant 끊임없는 |
scrubbing 북북 문지름 | severe 심각한 | complexion 안색 | breed 기르다, 야기하다 | stick to ~을 계속하다,
(바꾸지 않고) 고수하다 | flesh 살, 피부 | bank 둑, 제방 | quench (갈증을) 풀다 | thirst 갈증 | carry away
운반해 가다, (파도·바닷물이) 휩쓸어 가다 | stream 개울, 물의 흐름 | overhang 돌출하다, 쑥 나오다 | pluck 뽑다
| float 떠가다, 뜨다 | afterwards 나중에 | birdcatcher 새 잡는 사람 | lime-twig 끈끈이를 바른 나뭇가지 |
branch 나뭇가지 | perceive 알아차리다 | sting (곤충이나 식물이) 쏘다, 찌르다

The Ants and the Grasshopper
개미와 베짱이

THE ANTS were spending a fine winter's day / drying
개미들이 겨울을 보내고 있었다　　　　　　　　곡식을 말리며

grain / collected in the summertime. A Grasshopper, /
　　　여름 동안 수확한.　　　　　　　　　베짱이 한 마리가,

perishing with famine, / passed by / and earnestly begged /
배고픔으로 죽을 것 같은,　　　　지나가다가　　간절히 부탁했다

for a little food.
음식을 조금 달라고.

The Ants inquired of him, / "Why did you not treasure up
개미들이 베짱이에게 물었다.　　　　　"왜 넌 음식을 모아두지 않았니

food / during the summer?" He replied, / "I had not leisure
　　　여름 동안?"　　　　베짱이가 대답했다.　"난 여유가 없었어.

enough. I passed the days / in singing."
　　　　　　　시간을 보냈거든　　노래하면서."

They then said / in derision: / "If you were foolish / enough
그러자 개미들이 말했다　조롱하며:　　"네가 바보라면　　　노래할 만큼

to sing / all the summer, / you must dance supperless to bed
노래하려고　여름 내내,　　　　굶은 채 춤을 추다가 잠들겠구나

/ in the winter."
　　겨울에는."

The Apes and the Two Travelers
침팬지와 두 여행자

TWO MEN, / one who always spoke the truth / and the
두 사람이,　　　진실만 말하는 사람과

other who told nothing but lies, / were traveling together /
거짓말만 말하는 사람,　　　　　　함께 여행하고 있었는데

and by chance / came to the land of Apes.
우연히　　　　침팬지의 나라에 도착했다.

One of the Apes, / who had raised himself to be king, /
침팬지 한 마리가　　　왕이 되도록 길러진,

commanded / them to be seized / and brought before him, /
명령했다　　　그들을 잡아서　　　앞에 데려오라고.

that he might know / what was said of him / among men. He
왕은 알고 있었다   자신에 대해 뭐라고 하는지   인간들이.

ordered / at the same time / that all the Apes be arranged /
왕은 명령했다   동시에   모든 침팬지들에게 늘어서라고

in a long row / on his right hand / and on his left, / and that
긴 줄로   오른편과   왼편에,

a throne be placed for him, / as was the custom among men.
그리고 왕좌가 준비됐다,   인간 세계의 관습처럼.

After these preparations / he signified / that the two men
준비가 끝나자   왕은 지시했다   두 사람을 데려오라고

should be brought / before him, / and greeted them / with
    자신의 앞에,   그리고 그들에게 인사했다

this salutation: / "what sort of a king / do I seem to you to
이런 인사말로: "어떤 왕처럼   내가 당신들에게 보이는가,

be, / O strangers?"
낯선 이들이여?"

The Lying Traveler replied, / "You seem to me / a most
거짓말쟁이 여행자가 대답했다,   "당신은 보입니다

mighty king." "And / what is your estimate / of those you
가장 강력한 왕처럼."   "그러면   뭐라고 생각하는가

see around me?"
내 주위에 서 있는 이들은?"

Key Expression

시간을 보내다

'시간을 보내다'라는 말을 표현할 때에는 spend나 pass를 사용하며 동명사가 뒤따릅니다.

▶ spend/pass time   + (in) -ing : ~하면서 시간을 보내다
                + with ~ : ~와 시간을 보내다
▶ waste time   + (in) -ing : ~하면서 시간을 낭비하다
▶ kill time   + (in) -ing : ~하면서 시간을 죽이다

ex) I passed the days in singing.
    나는 노래하면서 시간을 보냈어.

---

grasshopper 메뚜기, 베짱이 | grain 곡식 | perish 죽다 | famine 기근 | earnestly 진정으로 | beg 간청하다,
구걸하다 | inquire 묻다 | treasure up 모아두다, 저장하다 | leisure 여가, 여유 | derision 조롱 | supperless
저녁 식사를 하지 않은 | ape 유인원(오랑우탄, 침팬지 등) | command 명령하다, 지시하다 | seize 체포하다, 붙잡다
| arrange 배열하다 | throne 왕좌, 옥좌 | preparation 준비 | signify 나타내다, 보여 주다 | greet 환영하다 |
salutation 인사말 | mighty 강력한 | estimate 추정, 평가

19

"These," / he made answer, / "are worthy companions of
"이들은," 그는 대답했다, "훌륭한 동료들입니다,

yourself, / fit at least / to be ambassadors / and leaders of
적어도 대사이거나 군대의 지도자에 알맞은."

armies." The Ape and all his court, / gratified with the
침팬지 왕과 모든 대신들은, 이 거짓말에 만족하여,

lie, / commanded / that a handsome present be given / to
명령했다 멋진 상을 내리라고

the flatterer.
아첨꾼에게.

On this / the truthful Traveler thought to himself, / "If
이를 보고 진실한 여행자는 생각했다,

so great a reward be given / for a lie, / with what gift /
"저렇게 멋진 보상을 받는다면 거짓말에 대해, 어떤 선물도

may not I be rewarded, / if, / according to my custom, /
받지 못할지도 모르는 일인가, 만약, 내가 하던 대로,

I tell the truth?" The Ape quickly turned to him. "And
진실을 말하면?" 침팬지는 그에게 돌아섰다.

pray how / do I and these my friends around me seem /
"그러면 어떻게 나와 내 주위의 친구들이 보이는가

to you?" "Thou art," / he said, / "a most excellent Ape,
당신에게?" "당신은," 그는 말했다, "가장 훌륭한 침팬지이죠,

/ and all these thy companions / after thy example / are
그리고 친구들도   당신의 본보기를 따르는

excellent Apes / too."
훌륭한 침팬지이고요   역시."

The King of the Apes, / enraged at hearing these truths, /
침팬지의 왕은,   이 진실을 듣고 화를 내며,

gave him over / to the teeth and claws of his companions.
그에게 넘겨버렸다   동료들은 이빨과 발톱에.

The Ass and the Frogs
당나귀와 개구리

AN ASS, / carrying a load of wood, / passed through a
당나귀가,   나뭇짐을 지고 가던,   연못을 건너게 되었다.

pond. As he was crossing through the water / he lost his
                물을 건너고 있을 때

footing, / stumbled and fell, / and not being able to rise /
발을 헛디며,   비틀거리면서 넘어졌고,   일어날 수 없게 되어

on account of his load, / groaned heavily.
짐 때문에,   신음 소리를 심하게 냈다.

Some Frogs frequenting the pool / heard his lamentation,
그 연못을 자주 다니던 개구리들이   당나귀의 탄식을 듣고,

/ and said, / "What would you do / if you had to live here
말했다,   "어떡할 거니   만약 네가 이곳에 살아야 한다면

/ always / as we do, / when you make such a fuss / about a
항상   우리처럼,   그렇게 법석을 떨다니

mere fall into the water?"
물에 겨우 한 번 빠진 것 정도로?"

Men often bear little grievances / with less courage / than
사람들은 종종 작은 불만을 참아내곤 한다   작은 용기가 필요한   견디기

they do / large misfortunes.
보다는   큰 불행을.

worthy (주로 명사 앞에서) 훌륭한 | companion 동행, 친구 | ambassador 대사, 사신 | gratify 만족시키다 |
flatterer 아첨꾼 | reward 보상 | enrage (주로 수동태로 쓰임) 격분하게 만들다 | claw (동물이나 새의) 발톱 | ass
당나귀(=donkey)의 고어형 | stumble 발을 헛디디다, 비틀거리다 | groan 신음 소리를 내다 | frequent 자주 다니다 |
lamentation 애통, 한탄, 통탄 | fuss 호들갑, 법석 | grievance 불만

21

The Ass Carrying the Image
조각상을 운반하는 당나귀

AN ASS once carried / through the streets of a city /
한번은 당나귀가 운반했다   도시의 거리를 통과하며

a famous wooden Image, / to be placed / in one of its
유명한 나무 조각상을,   놓일 예정인   그 도시의 사원에.

Temples. As he passed along, / the crowd made lowly
당나귀가 지나가자,   사람들이 낮게 엎드렸다

prostration / before the Image.
조각상 앞에서.

The Ass, / thinking / that they bowed their heads / in
당나귀는,   생각하면서   사람들이 절을 하고 있다고

token of respect for himself, / bristled up with pride, /
자신에게 경의를 표하기 위해,   자만심으로 털을 세우고,

gave himself airs, / and refused to move another step.
잘난 척 하며,   더 이상 움직이기를 거부했다.

The driver, / seeing him thus stop, / laid his whip lustily /
당나귀 주인은,   당나귀가 멈춘 것을 보고,   힘껏 채찍질 하며

about his shoulders / and said, / "O you perverse dull-
어깨에   말했다,   "이런 심술궂은 멍청이!

head! It is not yet come to this, / that men pay worship
그런 게 아니란 말이다,   사람들이 당나귀에게 경의를 표하는

to an Ass."
것이."

They are not wise / who give to themselves the credit /
현명하지 않은 사람들이다   자신을 칭찬하는 사람은

due to others.
다른 사람 때문에.

---

temple 신전, 사원 | prostration (예배를 위해) 엎드림 | in token of ~의 표시로 | bristle 발끈하다, 털이
곤두서다 | lay 놓다, (부담을) 지우다 | whip 채찍 | lustily 힘차게 | perverse 비뚤어진, 심술궂은 | dull-head
바보, 멍청이 | worship 숭배 | credit 칭찬 | due to ~ 때문에

The Ass, the Cock, and the Lion
당나귀와 수탉과 사자

AN ASS and a Cock were / in a straw-yard / together /
당나귀와 수탉이   우리에 있었다   함께

when a Lion, / desperate from hunger, / approached the
그때 사자가,   무척 굶주린,   그곳으로 다가왔다.

spot. He was about to spring / upon the Ass, / when the
사자는 달려들려고 했다   당나귀에게,   그러자 수탉이

Cock / (to the sound of whose voice the Lion, / it is said,
          (사자가 내는 소리를 듣고,   흔히 말하길,

/ has a singular aversion) / crowed loudly, / and the Lion
이상한 혐오감을 주는)   크게 울었고,   사자는 달아났다

fled away / as fast as he could.
                최대한 빨리.

The Ass, / observing his trepidation / at the mere
당나귀는,   두려움을 알아채고   수탉의 울음 소리에

crowing of a Cock / summoned courage / to attack him, /
                        간신히 용기를 내어   사자를 공격하며,

and galloped after him / for that purpose. He had run no
전속력으로 쫓아갔다   그 때문에.   당나귀는 그리 멀리 가지

long distance, / when the Lion, / turning about, / seized
못했다.   사자가,   방향을 바꿔,   당나귀를 잡

him / and tore him to pieces.
아서   갈기갈기 찢어놓았기 때문에.

False confidence / often leads into danger.
잘못된 자신감은   종종 위험을 부르는 법이다.

Key Expression

not ~ when… 구문의 해석

not ~ when… 구문은 '…할 때까지는 ~하지 않다', 즉 '~하지 않았을 때 …하
다'의 의미로 해석합니다. 주절이 끝나는 시점과 종속절의 시작이 일치한다는 것
이죠. 이때 주절의 시제는 when절보다 앞선 시제를 사용합니다.

ex) He had run no long distance, when the Lion, turning about, seized him and
tore him to pieces.
그가 멀리 가지 못했을 때 사자가 몸을 돌려 그를 잡아 갈기갈기 찢어놓았다.

The Ass and His Shadow
당나귀와 그림자

A TRAVELER hired an Ass / to convey him to a distant
여행자가 당나귀를 빌렸다　　　　　　　　　먼 곳으로 타고 가기 위해.

place. The day being intensely hot, / and the sun shining
날은 너무 더웠고,　　　　　　　　　태양은 강하게 빛나고 있어서,

in its strength, / the Traveler stopped to rest, / and sought
　　　　여행자는 휴식을 취하려 멈춰 서서,　　　쉴 곳을 찾았다

shelter / from the heat / under the Shadow of the Ass.
더위를 피해　　　당나귀의 그림자 밑에.

As this afforded only protection for one, / and as the
이 그림자는 한 명 몫밖에 안 되어,

Traveler and the owner of the Ass / both claimed it, /
여행자와 당나귀 주인은　　　　　　모두 그림자에 대해 주장했고,

a violent dispute arose / between them / as to which
폭력적인 논쟁이 일어났다　　　둘 사이에

of them had the right / to the Shadow. The owner
어느 쪽이 권리를 가졌는가에 대해　그림자를 사용할.　당나귀 주인은 주장했다

maintained / that he had let the Ass only, / and not his
　　　　자신은 당나귀만 빌려 줬고,　　　　그림자는 빌려 주지

Shadow. The Traveler asserted / that he had, / with the
않았다고.　여행자는 주장했다　　　자신은,　　　당나귀를 빌리면서,

hire of the Ass, / hired his Shadow also.
　　　　그림자까지 빌린 거라고.

The quarrel proceeded / from words to blows, / and while
논쟁은 진행되었고　　　말싸움에서 몸싸움으로,

the men fought, / the Ass galloped off.
두 사람이 싸우는 동안,　당나귀는 달아나 버렸다.

In quarreling about the shadow / we often lose the
그림자에 대한 싸움 속에서　　　　우리는 종종 본질을 잃곤 한다.

substance.

---

straw-yard 짚을 깐 가축의 겨울 우리 | approach 다가오다 | spring 뛰어오르다 | singular 뛰어난, 특이한 |
aversion 혐오감 | crow 수탉이 울다 | trepidation 두려움 | summon (용기를 어렵게) 내다 | gallop 전속력으로
달리다 | for that purpose 그 (목적) 때문에 | confidence 자신감 | hire 빌리다, 고용하다 | convey 운반하다 |
distant 먼, (멀리) 떨어져 있는 | intensely 몹시 | protection 보호 | claim 권리를 주장하다 | dispute 논쟁 |
maintain 주장하다 | assert 주장하다 | blow 세게 때림 | substance 본질, 중요한 것

25

The Ass and the Lapdog
당나귀와 애완견

A MAN had / an Ass, / and a Maltese Lapdog, / a very
한 사람이 갖고 있었다 당나귀와, 말티즈 애완견을,

great beauty. The Ass was left / in a stable / and had
매우 아름다운. 당나귀는 남겨졌고 마구간에

plenty of oats and hay to eat, / just as any other Ass
귀리와 건초를 먹었다, 다른 당나귀처럼.

would. The Lapdog knew many tricks / and was a great
애완견은 수많은 비결을 알고 있었고

favorite with his master, / who often / fondled him / and
주인에게 매우 사랑받았다, 주인은 종종 애완견을 아주 귀여워 하여

seldom went out to dine / without bringing him home /
식사하러 가지 않았다 강아지를 데려 가지 않고서는

some tidbit to eat.
맛있는 것을 먹으러.

The Ass, / on the contrary, / had much work to do / in
당나귀는, 반대로, 일을 많이 했다

grinding the corn-mill / and in carrying wood from the
옥수수를 빻거나 숲에서 땔감을 옮기거나

forest / or burdens from the farm. He often lamented his
농장에서 짐을 나르며. 당나귀는 종종 자신의 힘든 운명을

own hard fate / and contrasted it / with the luxury and
한탄했고 비교했다 애완견의 화려하고 할일 없는 운명과,

idleness of the Lapdog, / till at last / one day / he broke
마침내 어느 날

his cords and halter, / and galloped into his master's
당나귀는 목줄과 고삐를 끊고, 주인의 집으로 돌진했고,

house, / kicking up his heels / without measure, / and
뒷발을 차며 격렬하게,

frisking and fawning / as well as he could.
뛰어다니고 아양을 떨었다 최대한.

lapdog 애완용 소형견 | stable 마구간 | oats (복수형) 귀리 | trick 비결, 요령 | fondle 쓰다듬어 귀여워하다,
애지중지하다 | dine 식사를 하다 | tidbit 맛있는 가벼운 음식 | on the contrary 그와 반대로 | grind 갈다, 빻다
| corn-mill 제분기 | fate 운명 | contrast 대조하다, 대비시키다 | cord 줄 | halter 고삐 | without measure
굉장히, 과도하게 | frisk 뛰놀다, 뛰어 다니다 | fawn 아양떨다 | smash to atoms 가루가 되게 산산이 부수다 |
lick 핥다 | hubbub 왁자지껄한 소리 | club 곤봉 | cuff (손바닥으로) 때림 | stall 마구간

He next tried to jump / about his master / as he had seen
당나귀는 또 다시 뛰어들려고 했다   주인에게   애완견이 하는 것을 봤던

the Lapdog do, / but he broke the table / and smashed all
대로,   하지만 탁자를 부수고

the dishes upon it to atoms. He then attempted to lick his
탁자 위의 접시들을 박살내고 말았다.   그리고 나서 주인을 핥으려 하며,

master, / and jumped upon his back.
주인의 등에 뛰어올랐다.

The servants, / hearing the strange hubbub / and
하인들은,   왁자지껄한 소리를 듣고

perceiving the danger of their master, / quickly relieved
주인이 위험하다고 생각하여,   재빨리 주인을 구했고,

him, / and drove out the Ass to his stable / with kicks
당나귀를 마구간으로 쫓아버렸다

and clubs and cuffs.
발로 차고 주먹과 곤봉으로 때려.

The Ass, / as he returned to his stall / beaten nearly to
당나귀는,   마구간으로 돌아오자   죽을 듯이 맞은 채,

death, / thus lamented: / "I have brought it all on myself!
이렇게 한탄했다: "자업자득이구나!

Why could I not have been contented / to labor with my
왜 난 만족하지 못했을까   동료들과 함께 일하는 것에,

companions, / and not wish to be idle / all the day / like
빈둥거리기를 바라지 않고   하루종일

that useless little Lapdog!"
저 쓸모없는 애완견처럼!"

The Bald Man and the Fly
대머리 남자와 파리

A FLY bit the bare head of a Bald Man / who, /
파리가 대머리 남자의 민머리를 물었고   남자는,

endeavoring to destroy it, / gave himself a heavy slap.
파리를 잡으려다가,   자신을 세게 치고 말았다.

Escaping, / the Fly said mockingly, / "You who have
달아나면서,   파리가 조롱하듯이 말했다,   "복수하려고 하더니,

wished to revenge, / even with death, / the Prick of a tiny
                              죽여서,   작은 벌레가 따끔거리게 한 것을,

insect, / see / what you have done to yourself / to add
          보세요   자신에게 한 짓을

insult to injury?"
상처를 더했군요?"

The Bald Man replied, / "I can easily make peace with
대머리 남자가 대답했다,   내 자신은 쉽게 용서할 수 있어,

myself, / because I know / there was no intention to hurt.
왜냐하면 알고 있으니까   다치게 할 의도는 없었다는 것을.

But you, / an ill-favored and contemptible insect / who
하지만 넌,   불쾌하고 경멸 받아 마땅한 곤충은

delights in sucking human blood, / I wish that I could have
사람의 피를 빨며 즐거워 하는,   죽여 버릴 수 있으면 좋겠어

killed you / even if I had incurred a heavier penalty."
                더 무거운 벌을 받게 되더라도."

The Bat And The Weasels
박쥐와 족제비

A BAT / who fell upon the ground / and was caught by
박쥐가　　　땅에 떨어져　　　　　　　족제비에게 잡힌

a Weasel / pleaded to be spared his life. The Weasel
목숨을 살려 달라고 애원했다.　　　　　　족제비는 거절했다.

refused, / saying / that he was by nature / the enemy of
말하면서　　자신은 천성적으로　　　　모든 새들의 적이라고.

all birds. The Bat assured him / that he was not a bird, /
박쥐는 단언했고　　　　자신은 새가 아니라.

but a mouse, / and thus was set free.
쥐라고,　　　그렇게 해서 풀려났다.

Shortly afterwards / the Bat again fell to the ground /
얼마 후　　　　그 박쥐는 다시 땅으로 떨어져서

and was caught by another Weasel, / whom he likewise
다른 족제비에게 잡히게 되었고,　　　　똑같이 간청했다

entreated / not to eat him. The Weasel said / that he had
잡아먹지 말라고.　　　족제비는 말했다

a special hostility to mice. The Bat assured him / that he
자신은 쥐에게 특별한 적개심을 갖고 있다고. 박쥐는 단언했다

was not a mouse, / but a bat, / and thus / a second time
자신은 쥐가 아니라,　　박쥐라고,　　그리고 그렇게

escaped.
다시 한 번 풀려났다.

It is wise / to turn circumstances / to good account.
현명한 일이다　환경을 바꾸는 것은　　좋은 구실로.

---

bite 물다 | bare 벌거벗은, 맨~ | endeavor 노력하다, 시도하다 | destroy 파괴하다 (동물을) 죽이다 | slap (
손바닥으로) 철썩 때리기 | escape 달아나다, 탈출하다 | mockingly 조롱하듯, 희롱하여 | revenge 복수 | prick
찌르다, 따끔거리게 하다 | tiny 아주 작은 | insect 곤충, 벌레 | insult 모욕하다 | injury 상처 | intention 의도
| ill-favored 불쾌한, 싫은 | contemptible 경멸 받을 만한 | delight 기쁨, 즐거움 | suck 빨아 먹다 | incur
초래하다, 발생시키다 | penalty 처벌 | weasel 족제비 | plead 애원하다 | spare 피하게 해 주다, 면하게 해 주다
| by nature 선천적으로, 본래 | assure 단언하다, 확신시키다 | entreat 간청하다 | hostility 적대감, 증오 |
circumstance 환경 | account 설명

The Bear and the Two Travelers
곰과 두 여행자

TWO MEN were traveling together, / when a Bear
두 사람이 함께 여행하고 있었다.   그때 곰이 갑자기 그들과

suddenly met them / on their path.
맞닥뜨렸다   가는 길에.

One of them / climbed up quickly into a tree / and
한 명은   나무 위로 재빨리 올라가

concealed himself / in the branches. The other, / seeing
몸을 숨겼다   나뭇가지 속에.   다른 사람은,

that he must be attacked, / fell flat on the ground, / and
공격 당할 것을 알고,   땅바닥에 바짝 엎드렸다.

when the Bear came up / and felt him with his snout, /
그리고 곰이 다가와   그를 코로 건드리며,

and smelt him all over, / he held his breath, / and feigned
냄새를 샅샅이 맡자,   그는 숨을 멈추고,   죽은 척 했다

the appearance of death / as much as he could. The Bear
          최대한.

soon left him, / for it is said / he will not touch a dead
곰은 곧 떠났다,   왜냐하면 말이 있어서   곰은 시체를 건드리지 않는다는.

body.

When he was quite gone, / the other Traveler descended
곰이 가 버리자,   다른 여행자가 나무에서 내려와,

from the tree, / and jocularly inquired of his friend / what
          친구에게 익살스럽게 물어봤다

it was / the Bear had whispered / in his ear. "He gave me
뭐였는지   곰이 속삭인 것이   그의 귀에.

this advice," / his companion replied. "Never travel / with
"내게 충고를 했네,"   친구가 대답했다.   "여행하지 말라고 하더군

a friend / who deserts you / at the approach of danger."
친구와는   사람을 저버리는   위험이 다가올 때."

Misfortune tests / the sincerity of friends.
불행은 시험하곤 한다   친구의 정직을.

path 길 | conceal 감추다, 숨기다 | flat 평평하게, 낮게 | snout (동물의) 코 | feign 가장하다, ~인 척하다 |
appearance 겉모습 | descend 내려오다 | jocularly 우스꽝스럽게 | desert 버리다, 저버리다 | approach 접근 |
sincerity 성실, 정직

The Bee and Jupiter
벌과 제우스

A BEE from Mount Hymettus, / the queen of the hive, /
히메투스 산에서 온 벌이,　　　　　　　　벌집의 여왕인,

ascended to Olympus / to present Jupiter / some honey
올림포스 산에 올라갔다　　　　제우스에게 선물하려고

fresh from her combs. Jupiter, / delighted with the
자신의 벌집에서 딴 신선한 꿀을.　제우스는,　꿀 선물에 기뻐하며,

offering of honey, / promised to give / whatever she
　　　　　　　　　주겠다고 약속했다

should ask.
여왕벌이 원하는 것은 무엇이든.

She therefore besought him, / saying, / "Give me, / I
그러자 여왕벌이 간청했다,　　　　　말하면서,　　"주십시오,

pray thee, / a sting, / that if any mortal shall approach /
바라건대,　　침을,　　　치명적인 위협이 다가오면

to take my honey, / I may kill him." Jupiter was much
제 꿀을 빼앗으려는,　　죽일 수 있도록."　제우스는 매우 불쾌했지만,

displeased, / for he loved the race of man, / but could not
　　　　　　인간을 매우 사랑했기에,

refuse the request / because of his promise.
그 요청을 거절할 수 없었다　약속이기 때문에.

He thus answered the Bee: / "You shall have your
그래서 그는 벌에게 대답했다 :　　"네 소원을 이루게 될 것이다,

request, / but it will be / at the peril of your own life. For
하지만 그 침은　　　네 목숨을 위험에 빠뜨릴 것이다.

if you use your sting, / it shall remain in the wound you
왜냐하면 네가 침을 사용하면,　　스스로 만들어낸 상처를 남길 것이고,

make, / and then you will die / from the loss of it."
　　　그리고 넌 죽게 될 것이다　　그 상처로 인해 잃은 것 때문에."

Evil wishes, / like chickens, / come home to roost.
사악한 소원은,　　닭처럼,　　　다시 되돌아 오는 법이다.

Jupiter 로마 신화 속 최고의 신, 그리스 신화에서의 제우스와 같은 신 | Mount Hymettus 히메투스 산(아테네 동쪽에 있는 산) | hive 벌집 | ascende 올라가다 | Olympus 올림포스 산(그리스 북부의 높은 산으로 그리스 신화 속 신들이 사는 산) | comb 벌집(=honeycomb) | beseech 간청하다 | mortal 치명적인, 심각한 | displease 불쾌하게 만들다 | peril 위험 | roost (닭이나 새가 올라앉아 쉬는) 홰

The Bitch and Her Whelps
어미개와 강아지

A BITCH, / ready to whelp, / earnestly begged a
어미개가,   새끼를 낳으려는,   목동에게 간절히 애원했다

shepherd / for a place where she might litter. When her
어지럽힐 만한 장소를.

request was granted, / she besought permission / to
요청이 받아들여지자,   어미개는 허락을 구했다

rear her puppies / in the same spot. The shepherd again
강아지를 기르게 해 달라고   같은 장소에서.   목동은 다시 한 번 허락했다.

consented.

But / at last / the Bitch, / protected by the bodyguard of
하지만   마침내   어미개는,   강아지들의 호위를 받아,

her Whelps, / who had now grown up / and were able to
성견으로 자라나   스스로를 지킬 수 있게 된,

defend themselves, / asserted her exclusive right to the
그 공간에 대한 자신만의 권리를 주장했고

place / and would not permit / the shepherd to approach.
허락하지 않았다   목동이 다가오는 것을.

Key Expression ✏

come home to roost : 자업자득

come home to roost는 '남에게 한 나쁜 일은 결국 자신에게 더 큰 피해로
돌아온다'는 뜻으로, '누워서 침뱉기', '자업자득'에 해당하는 표현입니다.
이는 원래 Chickens come home to roost에서 나온 말인데, 닭이 전에 있
던 자리로 돌아와 둥지를 트는 습성에서 유래된 속담입니다.

ex) Evil wishes, like chickens, come home to roost.
    사악한 소원은, 닭처럼, 다시 되돌아 오는 법이다.

---

bitch 암개 |whelp 강아지, 개가 새끼를 낳다 |shepherd 양치기 |litter 어지럽히다 |grant 승인하다 |
permission 허가 |rear 기르다, 교육하다 |consent 동의하다, 허락하다 |exclusive 배타적인, 독점적인

The Blind Man and the Whelp
장님과 강아지

A BLIND MAN was accustomed/ to distinguishing
장님은 익숙했다 동물을 구별하는 것에

different animals / by touching them with his hands. The
손으로 만져서.

whelp of a Wolf was brought him, / with a request / that
늑대 새끼를 그에게 데려갔다. 요청으로

he would feel it, / and say what it was. He felt it, / and
그것을 만져보고, 무엇인지 말하라는. 장님은 만져보고,

being in doubt, / said: / "I do not quite know / whether it
의심하며, 말했다: "잘 모르겠어요

is the cub of a Fox, / or the whelp of a Wolf, / but this / I
여우 새끼인지, 아니면 늑대 새끼인지, 하지만 이것만은

know full well. It would not be safe / to admit him to the
잘 알겠습니다. 안전하지 않을 겁니다 이 동물이 들판에 나가도록 허락

sheepfold"
하면."

Evil tendencies are shown / in early life.
사악한 성향은 나타나는 법이다 어린 시절부터.

The Boy and the Filberts
소년과 개암열매

A BOY put his hand into a pitcher/ full of filberts. He
한 소년이 물주전자에 손을 집어 넣었다 개암열매로 가득 찬. 소년은

grasped/ as many as he could possibly hold, / but when
움켜쥐었지만 가능한 한 많이.

he tried to pull out his hand, / he was prevented from
손을 빼려고 하자, 할 수 없었다

doing so / by the neck of the pitcher. Unwilling to lose his
병의 목에 걸려서. 열매를 놓고 싶지 않았지만,

filberts, / and yet unable to withdraw his hand, / he burst
손을 뺄 수 없어서, 소년은 울음을

into tears / and bitterly lamented his disappointment.
터뜨렸고 몹시 실망했다.

A bystander said to him, / "Be satisfied with half the
지나가던 행인이 소년에게 말했다.   "절반만큼의 양에 만족하렴,

quantity, / and you will readily draw out your hand."
          그러면 손을 뺄 수 있을 거야."

Do not attempt too much / at once.
너무 많이 시도하지 말라   한 번에.

The Boy and the Nettles
소년과 쐐기풀

A BOY was stung by a Nettle. He ran home / and told
한 소년이 쐐기풀에 찔렸다.   소년은 집으로 달려가   엄마에게 이야기

his Mother, / saying, / "Although it hurts me very much,
했다,   이렇게 말하며,   "많이 아프지만,

/ I only touched it gently."
살짝 건드렸을 뿐이었어요."

"That was just why it stung you," / said his Mother. "The
"바로 그래서 풀이 널 쏜 거란다,"   엄마가 말했다.

next time / you touch a Nettle, / grasp it boldly, / and it
"다음 번에   쐐기풀을 건드리게 되면,   꽉 잡거라,

will be soft as silk / to your hand, / and not in the least
그러면 실크처럼 부드럽게 되어   네 손에,   절대 해치지 않을 거야."

hurt you."

Whatever you do, / do with all your might.
무슨 일을 하든지,   온 힘을 다해서 하라.

---

be accustomed to -ing~에 익숙해지다 | distinguish구별하다 | in doubt의심하며 | cub(곰, 사자, 여우
등의) 새끼 | admit인정하다 | sheepfold양을 치는 들판 | tendency성향 | filbert개암 | pitcher물주전자 |
grasp꽉 잡다, 움켜쥐다 | prevent막다, 예방하다 | withdraw빼내다, 뒤로 물러나다 | burst into(갑자기)
터뜨리다 | bitterly몹시 | bystander행인 | quantity양 | nettle쐐기풀 | gently부드럽게 | boldly대담하게

The Boy Bathing
목욕하는 소년

A BOY bathing in a river / was in danger of being
강에서 목욕하던 소년이 　　　　　물에 빠질 위험에 빠졌다.

drowned. He called out to a passing traveler / for help, / but
소년은 지나가던 여행자에게 소리쳤다 　　　　　도와달라고,

instead of holding out a helping hand, / the man stood by
하지만 도움의 손길을 뻗는 대신, 　　　　　그 사람은 태연히 멈춰 서서,

unconcernedly, / and scolded the boy / for his imprudence.
　　　　　소년을 꾸짖었다 　　　　　경솔함을.

"Oh, sir!" / cried the youth, / "Pray help me now / and scold
"아, 아저씨!" 　소년이 소리쳤다, 　　　"지금은 제발 저를 도와주세요 　그리고 꾸중하

me / afterwards."
세요 　나중에."

Counsel without help / is useless.
도움 없는 조언은 　　　쓸모없는 법이다.

The Brother and the Sister
형제와 자매

A FATHER had one son and one daughter, / the former
아버지에게는 아들 하나와 딸 하나가 있었는데,

remarkable for his good looks, / the latter for her
전자(아들)는 외모가 출중했고, 　　　　　후자(딸)는 굉장한 추녀였다.

extraordinary ugliness.

While they were playing one day / as children, / they
어느 날 그들이 놀고 있을 때   어린 시절에,

happened by chance to look / together / into a mirror /
우연히 보게 되었다   함께   거울 속을

that was placed on their mother's chair.
어머니의 의자에 걸려 있던.

The boy congratulated himself / on his good looks; / the
소년이 자축하자   자신의 외모에 대해;

girl grew angry, / and could not bear / the self-praises of
소녀는 화가 나서,   참을 수 없었다   오빠의 자화자찬을,

her Brother, / interpreting all he said / (and how could
그가 말하는 모든 얘기를 해석하며

she do otherwise?) / into reflection on herself.
(아니면 어떻게 할 수 있었을까?) 자신에 대한 반영으로.

She ran off to her father, / to be avenged on her Brother,
소녀는 아버지에게 달려갔다,   오빠에게 복수하기 위해,

/ and spitefully accused him of having, / as a boy, / made
그리고 악의를 담아 비난했다,   소년이,

use of that / which belonged only to girls.
놀렸다고   소녀만 갖고 있는 것을.

The father embraced them both, / and bestowing his
아버지는 둘을 함께 껴안고,   입맞춤과 애정을 표하며

kisses and affection / impartially on each, / said, / "I
각자에게 똑같이,   말했다,

wish you both would look into the mirror / every day: /
"너희 둘 다 거울을 보았으면 좋겠구나   매일;

you, my son, / that you may not spoil your beauty / by
아들아, 너는,   아름다움을 망치지 말아야 한다

evil conduct; / and you, my daughter, / that you may
나쁜 행동으로;   그리고 딸아, 너는,

make up for your lack of beauty / by your virtues."
부족한 아름다움을 보충하거라   덕을 갖춤으로써."

unconcernedly태연하게, 무관심하게 | imprudence경솔, 조심성 없음, 무모함 | counsel조언 | remarkable
놀라운, 주목할 만한 | extraordinary보기 드문, 대단한 | self-praises자화자찬, 자기 자랑 | interpret해석하다
| reflection반영 | avenge복수하다 | spitefully독살스럽게, 악의적으로 | accuse비난하다 | embrace껴안다
| bestow수여하다 | affection애정 | impartially편견 없이 | spoil망치다 | make up for보충하다 | lack
부족, 결핍 | virtue선, 미덕

The Buffoon and the Countryman
어릿광대와 시골 농부

A RICH NOBLEMAN / once / opened the theaters /
부유한 귀족이　　　　　　한 번은　 극장을 무료로 개방하고

without charge to the people, / and gave a public notice
사람들에게,　　　　　　　　공지를 냈다

/ that he would handsomely reward / any person who
큰 상금을 주겠다고

invented a new amusement / for the occasion .
새로운 오락거리를 만들어내는 사람에게　 그 기간동안.

Various public performers contended / for the prize. Among
다양한 공연자들이 경쟁했다　　　　　　상을 두고.

them / came a Buffoon / well known among the populace /
그들 중　 한 어릿광대가 와서　　사람들에게 유명한

for his jokes, / and said / that he had a kind of entertainment
농담으로,　　　　　말했다　　 자신에게는 오락거리가 있다고

/ which had never been brought out / on any stage / before.
보여진 적 없는　　　　　　　어느 무대에서도　 전에.

This report being spread about / made a great stir, / and the
이 소식이 퍼지자　　　　　　　큰 동요가 일어났고,

theater was crowded / in every part.
극장은 붐볐다　　　　　구석구석.

Key Expression

부사구 도치 구문

장소나 방향의 부사 혹은 부사구가 문장 맨 앞에 나왔을 때, 뒤따르는 주어 동사의
위치가 바뀌는 도치가 일어납니다. 단 동사를 수식하는 부사일 때, 자동사가 쓰인
경우에만 도치가 일어납니다.
또한 부사구 뒤에 콤마가 쓰이거나 주어가 대명사일 경우에는 도치가 일어나
지 않습니다.

ex) Among them came a Buffoon well known among the populace for his jokes.
　　그들 중에서 사람들에게 농담으로 유명한 한 어릿광대가 다가왔다.

The Buffoon appeared alone / upon the platform, /
어릿광대가 홀로 나타나자   단 위에,

without any apparatus or confederates, / and the very
아무런 장치나 동료들도 없이,   기대감으로 인해

sense of expectation / caused an intense silence. He
    강한 정적이 흘렀다.

suddenly bent his head / towards his bosom / and
그가 갑자기 고개를 숙이고   가슴 쪽으로

imitated the squeaking of a little pig / so admirably /
새끼 돼지의 꿀꿀 소리를 흉내 내자   매우 훌륭하게

with his voice / that the audience declared / he had a
자신의 목소리로   관중들은 주장하며   그가 돼지를 숨기고

porker / under his cloak, / and demanded / that it should
있다고   망토 속에,   요구했다

be shaken out. When that was done / and nothing was
망토를 열어 보라고.   요구대로 행해졌고   아무것도 발견되지 않자,

found, / they cheered the actor, / and loaded him with the
    관중들은 배우에게 환호하며,   큰 박수갈채를 보냈다.

loudest applause.

A Countryman in the crowd, / observing all that has
군중 속에 있던 한 시골 농부가,   이 모든 것을 지켜보다가,

passed, / said, / "So help me, Hercules, / he shall not beat
말했다,   "저런, 맙소사,   그는 날 이기지 못할 거예요

me / at that trick!" / and at once / proclaimed / that he
그 속임수로!"   그리고 즉시   선언했다

would do the same thing / on the next day, / though in a
자신도 같은 공연을 하겠다고   다음 날,

much more natural way.
훨씬 더 자연스러운 방식으로.

---

buffoon 어릿광대 |countryman 주민, 시골 사람 |nobleman 상류층, 귀족 |charge 요금 |handsomely
훌륭하게 |amusement 재미 |occasion 때, 기회 |contend 경쟁하다 |populace 대중들, 서민들 |stir 동요
|platform 단, 연단 |apparatus 기구, 장치 |confederate 공범 |intense 강렬한 |bosom 가슴 |imitate
모방하다 |squeak 끽(찍) 하는 소리를 내다 |admirably 훌륭하게 |declare 선언하다 |porker 살찐 새끼 돼지
|cloak 망토 |demand 요구하다 |cheer 환호하다 |applause 박수 |Hercules 헤라클레스 (그리스 신화 속
제우스 신의 아들인 영웅), 'oh my god'과 같은 의미로 쓰임 |proclaim 선언하다

On the morrow / a still larger crowd assembled / in the
다음 날　　　　　　　더 많은 관중이 모여들었다

theater, / but now / partiality for their favorite actor / very
극장에,　　하지만 이번에는　자신들이 좋아하는 배우만을 위해서였고

generally prevailed, / and the audience came / rather to
매우 유명한,　　　　　　관중들은 왔다

ridicule the Countryman / than to see the spectacle
농부를 조롱하기 위해　　　그의 공연을 보기 위해서라기보다.

Both of the performers appeared / on the stage. The
두 공연자가 모두 나타났다　　　　　무대 위에.

Buffoon grunted and squeaked away / first, / and
어릿광대가 꿀꿀거리며 흉내 냈고　　　먼저,

obtained, / as on the preceding day, / the applause
받았다,　　그 전 날처럼,　　　　　관중들의 박수와 환호를.

and cheers of the spectators Next the Countryman
다음으로 농부가 시작했다,

commenced, / and pretending that he concealed a little
새끼 돼지를 감추지 않은 척 가장하며

pig / beneath his clothes / (which in truth he did, / but not
옷 속에　　　　　　　　(실제로 그는 그렇게 했지만,

suspected by the audienc) / contrived to take hold of and
관중들에게 의심 받지 않았다)　돼지 귀를 잡아당겨

to pull his ear / causing the pig to squeak.
꿀꿀 소리를 내게 했다.

The Crowd, / however, / cried out / with one consent /
관중들은,　　하지만,　　소리 질렀다　한 목소리로

that the Buffoon had given / a far more exact imitation, /
어릿광대가 보여 주었다고　　훨씬 정확한 흉내를,

and clamored / for the Countryman / to be kicked out of
그리고 떠들어댔다　농부를 쫓아 내라고　　극장 밖으로.

the theater.

morrow그 다음 날, 내일(=tomorrow) ┃ assemble모이다, 모으다 ┃ partiality~을 아주 좋아함 ┃ prevail
유행하다, 만연하다 ┃ ridicule조롱 ┃ spectacle구경거리 ┃ performer연기자, 연주자 ┃ grunt꿀꿀거리다 ┃
preceding이전의, 앞선 ┃ spectator관중, 구경꾼 ┃ commence시작하다 ┃ beneath아래에 ┃ suspect의심하다
┃ contrive to용케 ~하다 ┃ consent동의, 일치 ┃ clamore떠들어 대다

On this / the rustic produced the little pig / from his cloak
이 광경을 보고   농부는 새끼 돼지를 꺼내어   망토 속에서

/ and showed / by the most positive proof / the greatness of
보여 줬다   가장 결정적인 증거로   군중들의 실수에 대한.

their mistake. "Look here," / he said, / "This shows / what
"여기를 보시오,"   그가 말했다,   "이 돼지는 보여 줍니다

sort of judges you are."
여러분이 어떤 판단 실수를 하고 있는지."

The Bull and the Goat
황소와 염소

A BULL, / escaping from a Lion, / hid in a cave / which
황소 한 마리가,   사자로부터 달아나던,   동굴 안에 숨었다

some shepherds had recently occupied As soon as he
최근에 목동들이 살고 있던.   황소가 들어가자 마자,

entered, / a He-Goat left in the cave / sharply attacked him
동굴에 있던 숫염소가   황소를 강하게 공격했다

/ with his horns
뿔로.

The Bull quietly addressed him: / " Butt away / as much as
황소는 조용히 염소에게 말했다: "들이받게나   네가 원하는 만큼.

you will. I have no fear of you, / but of the Lion. Let that
나는 네가 전혀 무섭지 않지만,   사자는 무서워.

monster go away / and I will soon let you know / what is
저 괴물을 물러가게 하고 나서 곧 네게 보여 주겠어

the respective strength / of a Goat and a Bull."
각자 얼마나 힘이 센지   염소와 황소가."

It shows / an evil disposition / to take advantage of a friend
이 우화는 보여 준다 나쁜 성격을   친구를 이용하려는

/ in distress.
고통에 빠진.

rustic시골 사람 | proof증거 | judge판단 | bull황소 | cave동굴 | occupy차지하다, 거주하다 | He-Goat
숫염소 | horn뿔 | address말하다, 진술하다 | butt들이받다 | respective각각의 | disposition기질 | take
advantage of이용하다 | distress고통

mini test 1

A. 다음 문장을 해석해 보세요.

(1) The King of the Apes, / enraged at hearing these truths, / gave him over to the teeth / and claws of his companions.
→

(2) He had run no long distance, / when the Lion, turning about, / seized him and tore him to pieces.
→

(3) His master often fondled him and seldom went out to dine without bringing him home some tidbit to eat.
→

(4) The audience came / rather to ridicule the Countryman / than to see the spectacle.
→

B. 다음 주어진 문장이 되도록 빈칸에 써 넣으세요.

(1) 논쟁은 말싸움에서 몸싸움으로 진행되었다.

The quarrel proceeded _____.

(2) 박쥐는 자신은 새가 아니라 쥐라고 단언했다.

The Bat assured him that _____.

(3) 그 침은 네 목숨을 위험에 빠뜨릴 것이다.

It will be _____.

(4) 무슨 일을 하든지, 온 힘을 다해서 하라.

→

A. (1) 침팬지의 왕은 이 진실을 듣고 화를 내며, 그를 동료들에게 넘겨 이빨로 물어뜯고 발톱으로 할퀴게 했다. (2) 그가 멀리 가지 못했을 때, 사자가 몸을 돌려, 그를 잡아 갈기갈기 찢어놓았다. (3) 주인은 종종 애완견을 귀여워 했고 식사하러 나갈 때마다 맛있는 음식을 가져다 주곤 했다. (4) 관중들은 농부의 공

42   Aesop's Fables

C. 다음 주어진 문구가 알맞은 문장이 되도록 순서를 맞춰 보세요.

(1) 그 노예를 집으로 데려오자마자 그는 노예를 씻기기 위해 모든 방법을 동원했다.
(him / On / home / bringing)

_____ he resorted to every means
of cleaning.

(2) 나는 노래하면서 시간을 보냈어.
(singing / passed / in / I / the days)
→

(3) 자업자득이구나!
(all / myself / brought / it / have / on / I)
→

(4) 바로 그래서 그것이 널 쏜 거란다.
(why / stung / That / just / it / you / was)
→

D. 다음 단어에 대한 맞는 설명과 연결해 보세요.

(1) incessant ▶ ◀ ① quality of being important or significant

(2) estimate ▶ ◀ ② make an approximate judgment or calculation

(3) lamentation ▶ ◀ ③ without stopping

(4) substance ▶ ◀ ④ expression of great sorrow

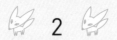

2

The Camel
낙타

WHEN MAN first saw the Camel, / he was so frightened
사람이 낙타를 처음 보았을 때,   매우 겁을 먹고

/ at his vast size / that he ran away. After a time, /
어마어마한 크기에   도망쳤다.   얼마 후,

perceiving the meekness and gentleness / of the beast's
온순함과 상냥함을 깨닫고   그 짐승의 성질의,

temper, / he summoned courage / enough to approach him.
            사람은 용기를 내어   낙타에게 다가갔다.

Soon afterwards, / observing / that he was an animal
곧 이어,   알게 되자   낙타는 완전히 모자라는 동물이라는 것을

altogether deficient / in spirit, / he assumed such boldness
                     지능적으로,   사람은 대담한 용기를 내서

/ as to put a bridle / in his mouth, / and to let a child drive
굴레를 씌웠다   낙타의 입에,   그리고 어린 아이에게 몰게 했다.

him.

Use serves to overcome dread.
쓸모는 두려움을 이겨내는 법이다.

Key Expression

전치사 into

into는 공간과 움직임이 결합된 전치사로, '안으로'라는 공간의 이동, 혹은 변화(의
결과)를 나타내는 의미로 쓰입니다.
변화의 의미로 쓰이는 into는 주로 다음과 같은 동사와 짝을 이루어 쓰입니다.

▶ change into ~ : ~으로 바꾸다
▶ transform into ~ : ~으로 변화시키다
▶ translate into ~ : ~으로 번역하다
▶ be made into ~ : ~으로 만들다

ex) A CAT fell in love with a handsome young man, and entreated Venus to
change her into the form of a woman.
고양이가 잘생긴 청년과 사랑에 빠져서, 자신을 여자의 모습으로 바꿔 달라고
비너스 여신에게 간청했다.
Venus consented to her request and transformed her into a beautiful damsel.
비너스는 그 요청을 받아들여 고양이를 아름다운 처녀로 탈바꿈 시켰다.

The Cat and Venus
고양이와 비너스

A CAT fell in love / with a handsome young man, /
고양이 한 마리가 사랑에 빠져서 잘생긴 청년과,

and entreated Venus / to change her / into the form of a
비너스 여신에게 간청했다 자신을 바꿔 달라고 여자의 모습으로.

woman. Venus consented to her request / and transformed
비너스는 고양이의 요청을 받아들여 탈바꿈 시켰다

her / into a beautiful damsel, / so that the youth saw her /
아름다운 처녀로, 그러자 그 청년은 그녀를 보고

and loved her, / and took her home / as his bride.
사랑에 빠져, 집으로 데려갔다 신부로 삼으려고.

While the two were reclining / in their chamber, / Venus
두 사람이 편안하게 누워 있을 때 침실에서,

wishing to discover / if the Cat in her change of shape /
비너스는 알아내고 싶어서 겉모습이 바뀐 고양이가

had also altered her habits of life, / let down a mouse / in
생활 습관도 바꾸었는지, 쥐를 풀어놓았다

the middle of the room.
방 한가운데에.

The Cat, / quite forgetting her present condition, / started
고양이는, 자신의 현재 상태를 완전히 잊어버리고,

up from the couch / and pursued the mouse, / wishing to
소파에서 뛰어올라 쥐를 쫓기 시작했다, 잡아먹으려고.

eat it. Venus was much disappointed / and again caused
비너스는 매우 실망하여 그녀를 다시 되돌려놓았다

her to return / to her former shape.
원래의 모습으로.

Nature exceeds nurture.
본성은 훈련으로 바꾸지 못하는 법이다.

---

frightened 겁먹은, 무서워하는 | vast 어마어마한 | meekness 온순함 | gentleness 상냥함 | temper 성질 |
altogether 완전히 | deficient 부족한, 모자라는 | assume (성질, 양상을) 띠다, 취하다 | bridle 굴레 | dread
두려움 | Venus 비너스 여신, 로마 신화 미의 여신으로 그리스 신화의 아프로디테와 같은 신 | transform 완전히
바꿔 놓다 | damsel 처녀 | bride 신부 | recline 편안하게 눕다, 비스듬히 기대다 | chamber 침실, 방 |
discover 발견하다, 알아내다 | alter 바꾸다 | couch 긴 의자 | pursue 뒤쫓다, 추격하다 | exceed 초월하다 |
nurture 양육, 훈련

45

The Cat and the Mice
쥐와 고양이

A CERTAIN HOUSE was overrun with Mice. A Cat, /
어느 집에 쥐가 들끓었다.   고양이가,

discovering this, / made her way into it / and began to
이를 발견하고,   집 안으로 들어가서   쥐를 쫓아 잡아먹기 시작했다

catch and eat them / one by one. Fearing for their lives, /
한 마리씩.   생명의 위기를 느끼고,

the Mice kept themselves close / in their holes.
쥐들은 머물렀다   쥐구멍 안에.

The Cat was no longer / able to get at them / and
고양이는 더 이상   쥐를 잡을 수 없게 되자

perceived / that she must tempt them forth / by some
알아차렸다   쥐를 꾀어내겠다고   장치를 사용하여.

device. For this purpose / she jumped upon a peg, / and
이를 위해   고양이는 말뚝 위로 뛰어 올라,

suspending herself from it, / pretended to be dead.
말뚝에 자신을 매달고,   죽은 척 했다.

One of the Mice, / peeping stealthily out, / saw her and
쥐 한 마리가,   몰래 엿보다가,   고양이를 보고 말했다,

said, / "Ah, my good madam, / even though you should
"어머나,   당신이 식량 주머니로 변한다 해도,

turn into a meal-bag, / we will not come near you."
우리는 가까이 가지 않을 거예요."

The Cat and the Cock
고양이와 수탉

A CAT caught a Cock, / and pondered / how he might find
고양이가 수탉을 잡고,   생각했다   어떻게 하면 적당한 이유를 찾

a reasonable excuse / for eating him. He accused him / of
을 수 있을지   그 닭을 먹기 위한.   고양이는 수탉을 비난했다

overrun 급속히 퍼지다, 들끓다 | tempt 유혹하다, 유도하다 | peg 못, 말뚝 | suspend 매달다. 걸다 | peep
훔쳐보다 | stealthily 몰래 | ponder 곰곰이 생각하다 | excuse 변명, 이유 | nuisance 골칫거리 | benefit 혜택,
이득 | abound 아주 많다, 풍부하다 | specious 허울만 그럴 듯한 | charcoal-burner 제탄공(製炭工), 숯 굽는
사람 | fuller (천의 올을 배게 하는) 축융공(縮絨工); 천을 바래고 다듬는 직공 | housekeeping 살림 | lessen
줄이다 | arrangement (처리) 방식, 배치 | as far as I am concerned 나로서는, 내 생각에는 | blacken 검어지다
| Like will draw like 유유상종(類類相從), 끼리끼리 모인다

being a nuisance to men / by crowing / in the nighttime
사람들에게 폐가 된다고　　시끄럽게 울어서　밤 시간에

/ and not permitting them to sleep. The Cock defended
잠을 자지 못하게 해서.　　　　수탉은 자신을 변호했다

himself / by saying / that he did this / for the benefit of
말하면서　자신이 우는 것은　　사람들을 위한 것이라고,

men, / that they might rise / in time / for their labors.
사람들이 일어날 수 있도록　제 시간에　일하러 가기 위해.

The Cat replied, / "Although you abound in specious
고양이는 대답했다.　"네게 그럴듯한 변명거리가 아무리 많아도,

apologies, / I shall not remain supperless;" / and he made a
나는 굶은 채로 있지 않겠어,"　　그리고 고양이는 수탉을

meal of him.
먹이로 삼았다.

The Charcoal-Burner And The Fuller
숯 굽는 사람과 직공

A CHARCOAL-BURNER carried on his trade / in his
숯 굽는 사람이 사업을 시작했다

own house.
자신의 집에서.

One day / he met a friend, / a Fuller, / and entreated him
어느 날　그는 친구를 만나,　직공인,　부탁했다

/ to come and live with him, / saying / that they should be
자신과 같이 살자고,　　말하면서　그들은 더 좋은 이웃이 될 것이며

far better neighbors / and that their housekeeping expenses
생활비를 줄일 수 있을 것이라고.

would be lessened

The Fuller replied, / "The arrangement is impossible / as
직공이 대답했다.　"그 방식은 불가능해

far as I am concerned, / for whatever I should whiten, / you
내 생각에는,　왜냐하면 내가 뭐든 하얗게 만들어도,

would immediately blacken again / with your charcoal."
네가 바로 다시 검게 만들 테니까　네 숯으로."

Like will draw like.
끼리끼리 모이는 법이다.

The Cobbler Turned Doctor
의사가 된 구두 수선공

A COBBLER / unable to make a living / by his trade
구두 수선공이   생활할 수 없어서   자신의 사업으로는

/ and made desperate by poverty, / began to practice
가난으로 죽을 것 같아,   의사 노릇을 했다

medicine / in a town / in which he was not known. He
마을에서   자신이 알려지지 않은.

sold a drug, / pretending that it was an antidote / to all
그는 약을 팔았다,   그것이 해독제인 척 하면서

poisons, / and obtained a great name for himself / by
모든 독약의,   그리하여 엄청난 명성을 얻었다

long-winded puffs and advertisements .
장황한 찬사와 선전으로.

When the Cobbler happened to fall sick himself / of a
구두 수선공 자신이 아프게 되자

serious illness, / the Governor of the town / determined
심각한 병으로,   그 마을의 총독이   그의 기술을 시험하기

to test his skill. For this purpose / he called for a cup,
로 결정했다.   이를 위해   그는 컵을 가져오게 해서,

/ and while filling it with water, / pretended to mix /
컵에 물을 채우고,   섞은 척 한 후

poison with the Cobbler's antidote, / commanding him to
독약과 구두 수선공의 해독제를,   그에게 그것을 마시라고 명령했다

drink it / on the promise of a reward.
보상금을 걸고.

The Cobbler, / under the fear of death, / confessed / that
구두 수선공은,   죽음이 두려워서,   고백했다

he had no knowledge of medicine, / and was only made
자신에게는 의학적 지식이 없음을,   그리고 단지 유명해진 것이라고

famous / by the stupid clamors of the crowd.
군중들의 어리석은 소란 때문에.

The Governor then / called a public assembly / and
그러자 총독은   대중 집회를 소집하여

addressed the citizens: / "Of what folly / have you been
시민들에게 연설했다;   "어떤 어리석은 행동을   여러분은 저질러 왔는가?

guilty? You have not hesitated / to entrust your heads / to a
여러분은 주저하지 않고   목숨을 맡겼네

man, / whom no one could employ to make even the shoes /
사람에게,   구두 제작도 맡기지 못한 사람에게

for their feet."
발에 맞는."

The Fighting Cocks and the Eagle
싸움닭과 독수리

TWO GAME COCKS were fiercely fighting / for the
싸움닭 두 마리가 맹렬히 싸우고 있었다

mastery of the farmyard. One at last / put the other to flight.
농장의 지배권을 놓고.   마침내 한 마리가   싸움에서 이겼다.

The vanquished Cock skulked away / and hid himself / in
패한 닭은 몰래 달아나   몸을 숨겼다

a quiet corner, / while the conqueror, / flying up to a high
조용한 구석에,   반면 승리한 닭은,   높은 담 위로 날아올라,

wall, / flapped his wings / and crowed exultingly / with all
날개를 퍼덕이며   기쁘게 울었다

his might. An Eagle sailing through the air / pounced upon
자신의 힘으로. 하늘을 날아가던 독수리가   그 닭에게 갑자기 달려

him / and carried him off / in his talons. The vanquished
들어   채어 가 버렸다   발톱으로.   패한 수탉은

Cock / immediately came out of his corner, / and ruled
즉시 구석에서 나와,   그 이후로 죽 지배했다

henceforth / with undisputed mastery.
모두 인정하는 지배자로서.

Pride goes before destruction.
자만은 파멸을 부르는 법이다.

cobbler 구두 수선공 | practice (의사, 변호사 등으로) 일하다, 개업하다 | antidote 해독제 | long-winded 길고
지루한, 장황한 | puff 잔뜩 부풀린 칭찬 | advertisement 광고, 선전 | Governor 총독, 주지사 | determine
결정하다 | call for 요청하다, 가져오게 하다 | on the promise of ~을 조건으로 | confess 고백하다 | assembly
집회 | folly 어리석음, 어리석은 행동 | guilty 유죄의, 책임이 있는 | hesitate 망설이다 | entrust 맡기다 |
employ 고용하다, 이용하다 | game cock 싸움닭 | fiercely 맹렬하게 | mastery 지배 | farmyard 농장 안
마당 | vanquished 패배한 | skulk 몰래 숨다 | conqueror 정복자 | flap 퍼덕이다 | exultingly 크게 기뻐하여
| pounce 갑자기 달려들다, 와락 덤벼들다 | talon (특히 맹금류의 갈고리 모양의) 발톱 | henceforth 이후로 (죽) |
undisputed 반박의 여지가 없는, 모두가 인정하는 | destruction 파괴, 파멸

The Crab and Its Mother
게와 엄마 게

A CRAB said to her son, / "why do you walk so one-
게가 아들에게 말했다,   "넌 왜 옆으로 걷니,

sided, / my child? It is far more becoming to go /
아들아?   걸어야 하는 거야

straight forward." The young Crab replied: / "Quite true,
똑바로 앞으로."   아들 게가 대답했다: "맞아요,

/ dear Mother; / and if you will show me / the straight
엄마;   엄마가 보여 주시면   똑바로 걷는 것을,

way, / I will promise to walk / in it."
저도 걷겠다고 약속할게요   그 선을 따라."

The Mother tried in vain, / and submitted / without
엄마 게가 시도했지만 성과가 없었고,   포기했다   불평없이

remonstrance / to the reproof of her child.
아들을 나무라는 것을.

Example is more powerful than precept.
모범이 교훈보다 더 강한 법이다.

The Crab and the Fox
게와 여우

A CRAB, / forsaking the seashore, / chose a neighboring
게가,   해변을 저버리고,   근처의 푸른 초원을 선택했다

green meadow / as its feeding ground. A Fox came
먹이를 구할 곳으로.   여우가 게에게 다가와서,

across him, / and being very hungry / ate him up.
매우 배가 고파서   게를 먹어 버렸다.

Just as he was on the point of being eaten, / the Crab
막 잡혀 먹히려는 순간,   게가 말했다,

said, / "I well deserve my fate, / for what business / had
"난 당해도 싸지,   뭘 하려고

I on the land, / when by my nature and habits / I am only
이 땅에 있는 건가,   타고난 본성과 습관으로

adapted for the sea?"
난 바다에만 알맞은데?"

Contentment with our lot / is an element of happiness.
가진 것에 만족하는 것이   진정한 행복의 조건이다.

The Crow and the Raven
까마귀와 갈까마귀

A CROW was jealous of the Raven, / because he was
까마귀는 갈까마귀를 질투했다.　　　　　　　　왜냐하면 갈까마귀는 여겨져서

considered / a bird of good omen / and always attracted
길조로　　　　　　　　　항상 끌었기 때문이다

/ the attention of men, / who noted / by his flight / the
인간들의 주목을,　　　사람들은 알아차렸다　그것의 나는 모습으로

good or evil course of future events.
미래에 행운나 불행이 올지.

Seeing some travelers approaching, / the Crow flew up
여행자들이 다가오는 것을 보면서,　　　　　까마귀는 나무 위로 날아올라,

into a tree, / and perching herself on one of the branches,
나뭇가지 위에 앉아,

/ cawed as loudly as she could.
되도록 큰 소리로 울었다.

The travelers turned / towards the sound / and wondered
여행자들은 고개를 돌리며　　　소리가 나는 쪽으로　　　궁금해 했다

/ what it foreboded, / when one of them said / to his
그 소리가 무엇을 예언하는지,　한 여행자가 말했다

companion, / "Let us proceed on our journey, / my
동료에게,　　　　　"여행을 계속하지,

friend, / for it is only the caw of a crow, / and her cry, /
친구여,　　　그것은 까마귀 울음 소리일 뿐이고,　　　까마귀의 울음은,

you know, / is no omen."
자네도 알다시피,　아무 징조도 아니라네."

Those who assume a character / which does not belong
캐릭터를 가장하는 이는　　　　　　자신이 속하지 않은,

to them, / only make themselves ridiculous.
어리석을 뿐이다.

---

crab 게 |one-sided 한쪽으로 치우친 |submit 굴복하다 |remonstrance 항의, 불평 |reproof 책망, 나무람 |
precept 교훈 |forsake 저버리다, 그만두다 |seashore 해안 |neighboring 이웃의, 근처의 |meadow 목초지 |
feeding 먹이 주기 |deserve ~을 받을 만하다, 누릴 자격이 있다 |adapted 알맞은 |contentment 만족,
자족 |element 요소 |crow 까마귀 |raven 까마귀과에 속하지만 까마귀보다 몸집이 큰 품종. 한국어로는 보통
갈가마귀라고 번역한다 |jealous 질투하는 |consider 여기다, 생각하다 |omen 징조, 조짐 |attention 주의,
주목 |caw 까악까악 |forebode ~의 전조가 되다. (나쁜 일을) 예언하다 |proceed 진행하다, 계속해서 하다 |
ridiculous 말도 안 되는, 어리석은

The Crow and the Pitcher
까마귀와 물 항아리

A CROW perishing with thirst / saw a pitcher, / and
목마름에 죽어가는 까마귀가 　　　　　　 물 항아리를 보고,

hoping to find water, / flew to it / with delight. When he
물을 발견하기를 바라며, 　　 날아갔다 　 기뻐하며. 　　　　 항아리에 도착

reached it, / he discovered to his grief / that it contained
했을 때, 　　 까마귀는 슬펐다 　　　　　　　 항아리에 물이 거의 들어

so little water / that he could not possibly get at it. He
있지 않아서 　　 마실 수 없었기 때문에. 　　　　　　　　 까마귀는

tried everything / he could think of / to reach the water, /
모든 것을 시도했다 　 생각해 낼 수 있는 　　 물에 닿기 위해,

but all his efforts were / in vain.
하지만 모든 노력은 　　　　　 허사였다.

At last / he collected / as many stones as he could carry /
마침내 　 까마귀는 모아서 　 옮길 수 있는 최대한 많은 돌을

and dropped them / one by one / with his beak / into the
떨어뜨렸다 　　　　 하나씩 　　　　 부리로

pitcher, / until he brought the water / within his reach /
항아리에, 　 그리하여 물이 올라와서 　　　　　 닿을 수 있는 거리에

and thus saved his life.
그렇게 목숨을 구할 수 있었다.

Necessity is the mother of invention.
필요는 발명의 어머니이다.

The Mischievous Dog
말썽꾸러기 개

A DOG used to run up quietly / to the heels of everyone
개 한 마리가 조용히 뛰어올라   모든 사람의 발꿈치로

/ he met, / and to bite them / without notice. His master
만나는,   물곤 했다   갑자기.

suspended a bell / about his neck / so that the Dog might
개 주인이 종을 매달았다   개의 목에   개가 나타나는 것을 알려 주도록

give notice of his presence / wherever he went. Thinking
        어디로 가든지.

it a mark of distinction, / the Dog grew proud of his bell /
그 종을 특별함의 표시라고 생각해,   개는 종을 자랑스러워하며

and went tinkling it / all over the marketplace.
딸랑거렸다   온 시장을 돌아다니며.

One day / an old hound said to him: / "Why do you make
어느 날   늙은 사냥개가 말했다: "너는 왜

/ such an exhibition of yourself? That bell / that you
   그토록 자신을 자랑하는 거니?   그 종은

carry is not, / believe me, / any order of merit, / but on
네가 달고 있는,   확신하건대,   아무 가치도 없는데다가,

the contrary a mark of disgrace, / a public notice to all
반대로 치욕의 표시란다,   모든 사람들에게 알리는 거야

men / to avoid you / as an ill mannered dog."
   널 피하라고   버릇없는 개인."

Notoriety is often mistaken for fame.
악명은 종종 유명세로 오해되곤 한다.

---

containe 들어있다 |collect 모으다, 수집하다 |beak (새의) 부리 |necessity 필요 |invention 발명 |
mischievous 말썽꾸러기의 |without notice 예고 없이, 갑자기 |mark 표시하다 |distinction 뛰어남, 특별함
|tinkle 딸랑 소리를 내다 |marketplace 시장 |hound 사냥개 |exhibition 표현, 드러냄 |merit 가치, 장점 |
contrary ~와 반대되는 |disgrace 수치, 치욕 |avoid 방지하다, 피하다 |notoriety 악명

The Two Dogs
두 마리의 개

A MAN had two dogs: / a Hound, / trained to assist him
한 사람이 개 두 마리를 기르고 있었다: 사냥개와, 그를 돕도록 훈련된

/ in his sports, / and a Housedog, / taught to watch the
사냥할 때, 집 지키는 개였다, 집을 지키도록 훈련된.

house. When he returned home / after a good day's sport,
주인이 집에 돌아오면 성공적인 사냥을 마치고,

/ he always gave the Housedog / a large share of his spoil.
언제나 집 지키는 개에게 주었다 전리품 중 큰 몫을.

The Hound, / feeling much aggrieved at this, / reproached
사냥개는, 이를 보고 매우 억울해 하며,

his companion, / saying, / "It is very hard to have / all
동료를 비난했다, 말하면서, "힘들게 얻었어

this labor, / while you, / who do not assist in the chase, /
이 모든 것을. 반면 너는, 사냥감 추격을 돕지도 않았는데,

luxuriate on the fruits of my exertions."
내가 노력한 성과를 즐기는구나."

The Housedog replied, / "Do not blame me, / my friend,
집 지키는 개가 대답했다, "날 비난하지 말고, 친구여,

/ but find fault with the master, / who has not taught me /
주인을 탓하렴, 그는 내게 사냥 일을 가르치지 않고,

to labor, / but to depend for subsistence / on the labor of
생활하도록 가르쳤으니까 다른 일로."

others."

Children are not to be blamed / for the faults of their
아이들을 비난해서는 안 된다 부모의 잘못 때문에.

parents.

---

assist 돕다 | housedog 집에서 기르는 개, 집 지키는 개 | spoil 전리품, 성과 | aggrieved 분개한, 억울해 하는
| reproach 비난하다 | chase 추격 | luxuriate 사치스럽게 지내다, 즐기다 | exertion 노력 | subsistence 최저
생활, 호구 | doe 암토끼 | press 괴롭히다, 궁지에 몰아넣다 | refuge 피난 | woe is me (옛글투) 아, 슬프도다 |
exclaim 소리치다, 외치다

The Doe and the Lion
암토끼와 사자

A DOE hard pressed / by hunters / sought refuge / in a
심하게 궁지에 몰린 암토끼가   사냥꾼에 의해   피신했다   동굴

cave / belonging to a Lion.
안으로   사자가 살고 있는.

The Lion concealed himself / on seeing her approach, /
사자는 모습을 감췄다가   토끼가 다가오는 것을 보고,

but when she was safe / within the cave, / sprang upon
토끼가 안전해지자   동굴 안에서,   토끼에게 뛰어올라

her / and tore her to pieces. "Woe is me," / exclaimed
산산조각을 냈다.   "아, 슬프도다,"   토끼가 소리쳤다,

the Doe, / "who have escaped from man, / only to throw
"사람을 피하려다.   나를 내던지고 말다니

myself / into the mouth of a wild beast?"
맹수에 입 속에?"

In avoiding one evil, / care must be taken / not to fall
악마를 피하려거든,   주의해야 한다

into another.
다른 악마에게 떨어지지 않도록.

The Dog and the Hare
개와 토끼

A HOUND / having started a Hare / on the hillside /
사냥개 한 마리가   토끼를 놀라게 한   산비탈에서

pursued her / for some distance, / at one time biting her
추격하다가   어느 정도의 거리를 두고,   한 번은 물려고 하다가

/ with his teeth / as if he would take her life, / and at
이빨로   토끼를 죽일 듯이,

another fawning upon her, / as if in play with another dog.
다음 순간 꼬리를 쳤다,   다른 개와 장난치는 듯이.

The Hare said to him, / "I wish you would act sincerely by
토끼가 개에게 말했다,   네가 나를 진심으로 대해 주고

me, / and show yourself in your true colors. If you are a
진정한 모습을 보여 주었으면 좋겠어.   네가 친구라면,

friend, / why do you bite me so hard? If an enemy, / why
왜 그렇게 심하게 물려고 한 거니?   적이라면,

do you fawn on me?"
왜 내게 꼬리를 치는 거니?"

No one can be a friend / if you know not / whether to trust
누구도 친구가 될 수 없다   알지 못한다면

or distrust him.
믿을 만한 사람인지 아닌지를.

The Dog, the Cock, and the Fox
개와 수탉과 여우

A DOG and a Cock being great friends, / agreed to travel
개와 수탉이 친한 친구가 되어,   함께 여행하기로 했다.

together.

At nightfall / they took shelter / in a thick wood. The Cock
해질녘에   그들은 쉴 곳을 마련했다   울창한 숲 속에.

flying up, / perched himself on the branches of a tree, /
수탉은 날아올라,   나뭇가지에 앉아 쉬었고,

while the Dog found a bed / beneath in the hollow trunk.
반면 개는 잠자리를 찾았다   비어 있는 나무 둥걸 속에.

When the morning dawned, / the Cock, / as usual, /
아침이 밝아오자,   수탉은,   평소처럼,

crowed very loudly / several times. A Fox heard the
크게 울었다 몇 번이나. 여우가 그 소리를 듣고,

sound, / and wishing to make a breakfast on him, / came
수탉을 아침 식사로 삼고자,

and stood / under the branches, / saying / how earnestly
다가와 서서 나뭇가지 아래에, 말했다

he desired to make the acquaintance / of the owner of so
진정으로 친구가 되고 싶다고

magnificent a voice.
그토록 훌륭한 목소리의 주인공과.

The Cock, / suspecting his civilities, / said: / "Sir, / I
수탉은, 여우의 예의바른 칭찬을 의심하며, 말했다: "여우님,

wish you would do me the favor / of going around / to
제 부탁을 들어주셨으면 좋겠어요 근처로 가서

the hollow trunk / below me, / and waking my porter, /
비어 있는 나무 등걸 제 아래에 있는, 제 짐꾼을 깨워 주세요,

so that he may open the door / and let you in."
그래서 그가 문을 열고 당신을 들어오게 하도록."

When the Fox approached the tree, / the Dog sprang out /
여우가 나무로 다가가자, 개가 뛰어 나와

and caught him, / and tore him to pieces.
여우를 잡았고 갈기갈기 찢어버렸다.

The Dogs and the Fox
개와 여우

SOME DOGS, / finding the skin of a lion, / began to tear
개 몇 마리가, 사자의 가죽을 발견하고, 그것을 찢어버렸다

it in pieces / with their teeth. A Fox, / seeing them, / said,
이빨로. 여우가, 개들을 보고, 말했다,

/ "If this lion were alive, / you would soon find out / that
"사자가 살아있다면, 너희들도 곧 알게 될 텐데

his claws were stronger / than your teeth."
사자의 발톱이 훨씬 강하다는 걸 너희들의 이빨보다."

hare 토끼 | hillside 산비탈 | sincerely 진심으로 | trust 신뢰하다 | nightfall 해질녘 | hollow 빈 | trunk
나무의 몸통 | dawn 날이 밝다 | acquaintance 아는 사람, 친분 | magnificent 훌륭한 | civilities (복수형)
예의상 하는 말 | porter 짐꾼 | skin 피부, (동물의) 껍질

It is easy / to kick a man that is down.
쉬운 법이다   넘어진 사람을 차는 것은.

The Dogs and the Hides
개와 가죽

SOME DOGS famished with hunger / saw a number
심하게 굶주린 개 몇 마리가   많은 소가죽을 발견했다

of cowhides / steeping in a river. Not being able to
강물 속에 잠겨 있는.   가죽에 닿을 수 없어서,

reach them, / they agreed to drink up the river, / but it
개들은 물을 마시기로 했다,

happened / that they burst themselves with drinking /
하지만   배가 터져 버렸다

long before they reached the hides.
가죽에 닿기에 한참 남았는데.

Attempt not impossibilities.
불가능한 일은 시도하지 말라.

The Dog and the Oyster
개와 굴

A DOG, / used to eating eggs, / saw an Oyster and, /
어느 개가,   달걀을 먹는데 익숙했던,   굴을 발견하고,

opening his mouth / to its widest extent, / swallowed it
입을 벌려   최대한 크게,   삼켜 버렸다

down / with the utmost relish, / supposing it to be an egg.
매우 기뻐하며,   그것이 달걀이라고 생각하고.

Soon afterwards / suffering great pain in his stomach, /
잠시 후   배가 너무 아파서,

he said, / "I deserve all this torment, / for my folly / in
말했다,   "이 모든 고통을 받아도 싸지,   어리석은 짓을 했으니

thinking that everything round must be an egg."
둥근 것은 모두 달걀이라고 생각해 버리는."

They who act / without sufficient thought, / will often
행동하는 사람은   충분히 생각하지 않고,

fall into unsuspected danger.
종종 예상치 못한 위험에 빠지곤 한다.

kick a man when he's down 넘어진 사람을 차다, 약점을 악용하여 나쁜 짓을 하다 | famished 배가 고파 죽을
지경인 | cowhide 소가죽 | steep 적시다, 담그다 | attempt 시도 | oyster 굴 | extent 정도, 규모 | swallow
삼키다 | utmost 최고의, 극도의 | relish 즐기다, 좋아하다 | stomach 위(胃),복부, 배 | torment 고통, 고뇌 |
sufficient 충분한

The Dog and the Cook
개와 요리사

A RICH MAN gave a great feast, / to which he invited /
어느 부자가 성대한 잔치를 열고,   잔치에 초대했다

many friends and acquaintances.
많은 친구와 지인들을.

His Dog availed himself of the occasion / to invite a
부자의 개는 이때를 이용하여

stranger Dog, / a friend of his, / saying, / "My master
낯선 개를 초대했다,   친구의 친구인,   말하면서,   "주인이 큰 잔치를 열었는데,

gives a feast, / and there is always much food remaining; /
항상 음식이 많이 남으니까;

come and sup with me / tonight."
와서 나랑 같이 먹자   오늘 밤에."

The Dog thus invited went / at the hour appointed, / and
초대 받은 개는 도착하여   약속한 시간에,

seeing the preparations / for so grand an entertainment, /
준비된 음식을 보고   성대한 연회를 위해,

said in the joy of his heart, / "How glad I am that I came!
기뻐하며 말했다,   "오게 되어서 정말 기뻐!

I do not often get such a chance / as this. I will take care
기회가 별로 없거든   이와 같은. 충분히 먹어야지

and eat enough / to last me both today and tomorrow."
오늘과 내일까지 견딜 수 있도록."

While he was congratulating himself / and wagging his
개가 기뻐하며   꼬리를 흔들자

tail / to convey his pleasure / to his friend, / the Cook
기쁨을 전하려고   친구에게,

saw him moving about / among his dishes and, / seizing
요리사는 개가 돌아다니는 것을 보고   음식 주변에서,

him by his fore and hind paws, / bundled him / without
개의 네 다리를 잡아   몰아내 버렸다

ceremony / out of the window.
무지막지하게   창문 밖으로.

He fell with force upon the ground / and limped away,
개는 정원으로 떨어져   절뚝거리며 달아났다,

/ howling dreadfully. His yelling soon attracted / other
몹시 짖어대며.   개의 짖는 소리가 곧 주의를 끌었고,

street dogs, / who came up to him / and inquired / how
다른 길거리 개들의, 개들은 다가와서 물어봤다

he had enjoyed his supper.
저녁 만찬이 어땠는지.

He replied, / "Why, / to tell you the truth, / I drank so
개는 대답했다, "맙소사, 사실은 말이지,

much wine / that I remember nothing. I do not know /
와인을 너무 마셔서 아무것도 기억이 나지 않아. 모르겠어

how I got out of the house."
내가 어떻게 집 밖으로 나왔는지도."

The Dog and the Shadow
개와 그림자

A DOG, / crossing a bridge over a stream / with a piece
개 한 마리가, 시냇물에 놓인 다리를 건너다가

of flesh in his mouth, / saw his own shadow / in the
살코기 한 점을 입에 물고, 자신의 그림자를 보고는 물에 비친

water / and took it for that of another Dog, / with a piece
그것을 다른 개라고 착각했다, 고기를 물고 있는

of meat / double his own in size. He immediately let go
자신보다 두 배나 큰. 개는 즉시 자신의 고기를 버리고,

of his own, / and fiercely attacked the other Dog / to get
다른 개를 맹렬하게 공격했다

his larger piece from him.
그 개의 더 큰 고기를 빼앗으려고.

He / thus / lost both: / that which he grasped / at in
개는 그렇게 하여 둘 다 잃었다: 자신이 잡은 고기는

the water, / because it was a shadow; / and his own, /
물 속에 있었고, 그림자였기 때문에; 그리고 자신의 고기는,

because the stream swept it away.
시냇물에 떠내려가 버렸기 때문이다.

feast연회, 잔치 | avail oneself of이용하다 | sup홀짝홀짝 먹다, 마시다 | appointed정해진, 약속된 | last견디다 | congratulate (oneself on)~을 기뻐하다 | wag(개가 꼬리를) 흔들다 | fore앞쪽의 | hind뒤쪽의 | bundle 마구 밀어 넣다 | without ceremony무지막지하게 | limp절뚝거리다 | howl울다, 울부짖다 | dreadfully몹시, 끔찍하게 | yell소리치다 | flesh살코기 | take A for B A를 B라고 착각하다 | sweep휩쓸고 가다

mini test 2

A. 다음 문장을 해석해 보세요.

(1) Fearing for their lives, / the Mice kept themselves close / in their holes.
→

(2) The Cock defended himself / by saying / that he did this / for the benefit of men, / that they might rise / in time / for their labors.
→

(3) Children are not to be blamed / for the faults of their parents.
→

(4) Woe is me, / who have escaped from man, / only to throw myself / into the mouth of a wild beast?
→

B. 다음 주어진 문장이 되도록 빈칸에 써 넣으세요.

(1) 당신이 식량 주머니로 변한다 해도, 우리는 가까이 가지 않을 거예요.

_____, we will not come near you.

(2) 유유상종.

→

(3) 까마귀는 가능한 한 큰 소리로 울었다.

The Crow cawed _____.

(4) 모든 노력은 허사였다.

→

A. (1) 생명의 위기를 느껴서, 쥐들은 쥐구멍 안에 머물렀다. (2) 수탉은 자신이 우는 것은 사람들이 일하러 가기 위해 제 시간에 일어날 수 있도록 하기 위한 것이라고 말하면서 자신을 변호했다. (3) 부모의 잘못 때문에 아이들이 비난 받아서는 안 된다. (4) 아, 슬프도다, 사람을 피하려다 결국 나를 맹수의 입 속에 내던

C. 다음 주어진 문구가 알맞은 문장이 되도록 순서를 맞춰 보세요.

(1) 난 당해도 싸지.
(fate / deserve / I / my / well)

→

(2) 날 비난하지 말고 주인을 탓하렴.
(the master / with / find / Do / not / but / blame / fault / me)

→

(3) 넘어진 사람을 차는 것은 쉬운 법이다.
(easy / is / It is / to / down / kick / that / a man)

→

(4) 오게 되어서 정말 기뻐!
(came / glad / I / How / I / am / that)

→

D. 의미가 비슷한 것끼리 서로 연결해 보세요.

(1) suspend   ▶   ◀ ① be reluctant

(2) entrust   ▶   ◀ ② hang

(3) hesitate   ▶   ◀ ③ enjoy

(4) relish   ▶   ◀ ④ assign

Answer

지고 만 것인가? | B. (1) Even though you should turn into a meal-bag (2) Like will draw like, (3) as loudly as she could (4) All his efforts were in vain. | C. (1) I well deserve my fate. (2) Do not blame me but find fault with the master. (3) It is easy to kick a man that is down. (4) How glad I am that I came! | D. (1) ② (2) ④ (3) ① (4) ③

3

The Eagle and the Jackdaw
독수리와 갈까마귀

AN EAGLE, / flying down / from his perch on a lofty
독수리 한 마리가, 날아 내려와서 높은 바위 위에 앉아 있다가,

rock, / seized upon a lamb / and carried him aloft / in his
새끼 양을 잡아채어 하늘 높이 데려갔다

talons.
발톱으로.

A Jackdaw, / who witnessed the capture of the lamb, /
갈까마귀가, 양을 포획하는 장면을 목격한,

was stirred with envy / and determined to emulate / the
부러워하며 따라 하기로 결심했다

strength and flight of the Eagle. He flew around / with a
독수리의 강력한 힘과 비행을. 갈까마귀는 날아 다니다가

great whir of his wings / and settled upon a large ram,
날개를 크게 퍼덕이며 커다란 숫양 위에 앉았다,

/ with the intention of carrying him off, / but his claws
잡아가려는 생각으로,

became entangled / in the ram's fleece / and he was not
하지만 발톱이 얽혀 버려서 양의 털 속에 벗어날 수 없게 되었다.

able to release himself, / although he fluttered with his
날개를 퍼덕거렸지만

feathers / as much as he could.
최대한으로.

The shepherd, / seeing what had happened, / ran up / and
양치기가, 일어난 일을 보고, 달려와서

caught him. He / at once / clipped the Jackdaw's wings, /
갈까마귀를 잡았다. 그는 즉시 갈까마귀의 날개를 붙잡아,

and taking him home / at night, / gave him to his children.
집으로 가져가서 밤에, 아이들에게 주었다.

---

jackdaw 갈까마귀(=daw) | lofty 아주 높은 | lamb 어린 양, 새끼 양 | aloft 하늘 높이 | witness 목격하다 |
capture 포획하다 | envy 부러워하다 | emulate 모방하다 | whir 씽 소리내며 날다, 회전하다 | settle 정착하다,
앉다 | ram (거세하지 않은) 숫양 | entangle 얽어매다 | fleece 양털 | release 풀어주다, 날려 보내다 | flutter
흔들다, 펄럭이다 | feather 깃털 | clip 고정하다

On their saying, / "Father, / what kind of bird is it?" / he
아이들이 말하자,　　　"아빠,　　　그건 무슨 새인가요?"

replied, / "To my certain knowledge / he is a Daw; / but
그는 대답했다,　"내가 아는 바로는　　　　그건 갈까마귀란다:

he would like you to think an Eagle."
하지만 자신을 독수리라고 생각해 주길 바라고 있구나."

The Eagle, the Cat, and the Wild Sow
독수리와 고양이, 그리고 야생 암퇘지

AN EAGLE made her nest / at the top of a lofty oak; / a
독수리가 둥지를 지었다   높은 참나무 꼭대기에;

Cat, / having found a convenient hole, / moved into the
고양이는; 편안한 구멍을 발견하고,

middle of the trunk; / and a Wild Sow, / with her young,
나무둥걸 속으로 들어갔다;   그리고 야생 암퇘지는,   새끼를 데리고,

/ took shelter / in a hollow at its foot.
쉴 곳을 만들었다   나무 밑둥에 있는 구멍 안에.

The Cat cunningly resolved to destroy / this chance-
고양이는 교활하게도 파괴하고자 결심했다   우연히 결성된 이 집단을.

made colony. To carry out her design, / she climbed
자신의 계획을 실행하고자,

to the nest of the Eagle, / and said, / "Destruction is
고양이는 독수리 둥지로 기어 올라가서, 말했다,   "파괴하려고 해요

preparing / for you, and for me too, / unfortunately. The
당신과 저를,   유감스럽게도.

Wild Sow, / whom you see / daily digging up the earth,
저 암퇘지가,   당신도 보다시피   매일 땅을 파고 있는

/ wishes to uproot the oak, / so she may on its fall / seize
나무를 뿌리채 뽑으려고 해요,   그래서 나무가 쓰러지면

our families / as food / for her young."
우리 가족을 잡아서 먹이로 삼으려고요 자신의 새끼들을 위한."

Key Expression

접속사 for의 해석

전치사로 주로 쓰이는 for가 접속사로서 절을 동반할 경우에는 '왜냐하면(그 이유
는) ~이니까'의 의미로 해석합니다. 이때 접속사 for는 쉼표 뒤에 위치합니다.
접속사 for는 회화체에서는 거의 쓰이지 않고 문학작품에 주로 등장합니다.

ex) Your children are in great danger; for as soon as you go out with your litter
to find food, the Eagle is prepared to pounce upon one of your little pigs.
당신 새끼들이 위험에 처해 있어요; 왜냐하면 당신이 새끼들을 데리고 먹이를 찾
으러 굴을 나서자마자 독수리가 덮치려고 하니까요.

Having thus frightened the Eagle out of her senses, / she
그렇게 독수리를 까무러칠 듯이 놀라게 하고,   고양이

crept down / to the cave of the Sow, / and said, / "Your
는 기어 내려와   암퇘지의 동굴에 가서,   말했다,

children are / in great danger; / for as soon as you go out
"당신 새끼들이   위험에 처해 있어요;   왜냐하면 당신이 굴을 나서자마자

/ with your litter / to find food, / the Eagle is prepared to
새끼들을 데리고   먹이를 찾으러,   독수리가 덮칠 준비를 하고 있거든요

pounce upon / one of your little pigs."
               새끼 돼지들을."

Having instilled these fears / into the Sow, / she went
이렇게 공포를 심어주고   암퇘지에게,

and pretended to hide herself / in the hollow of the tree.
고양이는 몸을 숨기는 척 했다   나무 구멍 속에.

When night came / she went forth / with silent foot / and
밤이 다가오자   고양이는 밖으로 나와   발소리를 죽인 채

obtained food / for herself and her kittens, / but feigning
식량을 구했다   자신과 새끼 고양이들을 위해,   하지만 두려워 하는

to be afraid, / she kept a lookout / all through the day.
척 하며,   고양이는 망을 봤다   하루 종일.

Meanwhile, / the Eagle, / full of fear of the Sow, / sat still
그 동안,   독수리는,   암퇘지에 대한 두려움으로,   나뭇가지 위

on the branches, / and the Sow, / terrified by the Eagle, /
에 가만히 앉아 있었고,   암퇘지는,   독수리가 두려워서

did not dare to go out from her cave.
동굴 밖으로 나오려 하지 않았다.

And thus they both, / along with their families, /
이렇게 둘 모두,   가족들과 함께,

perished from hunger, / and afforded ample provision /
굶어 죽어 버려서,   충분한 식량을 제공해 주었다

for the Cat and her kittens.
고양이와 새끼 고양이들에게.

sow 암퇘지 |nest (새의) 둥지 |oak 오크, 참나무 |convenient 편리한 |cunningly 교활하게 |resolve
결심하다 |colony (동식물의) 군집 |design 설계, 계획 |dig 파다 |uproot 뿌리째 뽑다 |frighten 겁먹게
만들다, 놀라게 만들다 |out of one's senses 분별이 없는 |litter 한 배에서 난 새끼들 |instill (생각을) 불어넣다,
심어 주다 |forth ~에서 멀리, 밖으로 |kitten 새끼 고양이 |feign 가장하다, ~인 척하다 |lookout 망보는 곳 |
terrified 두려워하는, 겁먹은 |ample 충분한 |provision 공급, 식량

The Eagle and the Fox
독수리와 여우

AN EAGLE and a Fox / formed an intimate friendship / and
독수리와 여우가   친한 친구가 되어

decided to live / near each other. The Eagle built her nest /
살기로 결정했다   서로 가까운 곳에.   독수리는 둥지를 지었고

in the branches of a tall tree, / while the Fox crept into the
높은 나뭇가지에,   여우는 덤불에 들어가

underwood / and there produced her young.
            그곳에서 새끼를 낳았다.

Not long after they had agreed upon this plan, / the Eagle, /
그들이 이 계획에 합의한 지 얼마 지나지 않아,   독수리는,

being in want of provision / for her young ones, / swooped
먹을 것이 부족하여   새끼들에게 줄,   급강하 하여

down / while the Fox was out, / seized upon one of the
down   여우가 밖에 나간 사이,   새끼 여우 한 마리를 잡아서,

little cubs, / and feasted herself and her brood. The Fox on
새끼들과 함께 먹었다.   집에 돌아온 여우가,

her return, / discovered what had happened, / but was less
무슨 일이 일어났는지 알게 되었지만,

grieved for the death of her young / than for her inability / to
새끼를 잃은 슬픔보다.   자신의 무능함에 더 슬퍼했다

avenge them.
복수하지 못하는.

A just retribution, / however, / quickly fell upon the Eagle.
적절한 천벌이,   그러나,   곧 독수리에게 내려졌다.

While hovering near an altar, / on which some villagers were
제단 주위를 맴돌다가,   마을 사람들이 염소를 제물로 바치고 있던,

sacrificing a goat, / she suddenly seized a piece of the flesh, /
독수리는 갑자기 고기 한 점을 물고,

and carried it, / along with a burning cinder, / to her nest.
가지고 갔다,   불기가 남아있는 재와 함께,   둥지로.

underwood(큰 나무 밑에 자라는) 덤불 | swoop급강하하다, 위에서 덮치다 | brood알을 품다 | inability
무능, 불능 | retribution응징 | hover맴돌다 | villager(시골) 마을 사람 | sacrifice 희생하다, 제물을 바치다
| cinder재 | fan바람이 불다 | spark(작은) 불꽃, 불똥 | eaglet새끼 독수리 | unfledged아직 깃털이 다 나지
않은 | roast굽다, 태우다 | gobble게걸스럽게 먹다 | overwhelmed압도된 | rueful후회하는, 슬퍼하는 |
mate 친구, 짝 | suitable적합한, 알맞은 | secure보장하다 | a means of living생활의 방편, 생계 | plunder약탈
| ostrich타조

A strong breeze soon fanned / the spark into a flame, /
곧이어 강한 바람이 불어와   재에 남은 불꽃을 활활 타게 만들었고,

and the eaglets, / as yet unfledged and helpless, / were
새끼 독수리들은,   깃털이 채 자라지 않아 무력했기에,

roasted / in their nest / and dropped down dead / at the
불에 타서   둥지 안에서   떨어져 죽고 말았다

bottom of the tree. There, / in the sight of the Eagle, / the
나무 아래로.   그곳에서,   독수리가 보는 앞에서,

Fox gobbled them up.
여우는 새끼들을 먹어 치웠다.

The Eagle and the Kite
독수리와 솔개

AN EAGLE, / overwhelmed with sorrow, / sat upon the
독수리 한 마리가,   슬픔에 잠긴 채,

branches of a tree / in company with a Kite.
나뭇가지에 앉아 있었다   솔개와 함께.

"Why," / said the Kite, / "do I see you with such a rueful
"왜,"   솔개가 말했다,   "그렇게 슬픈 표정을 하고 있니?"

look?"

"I seek," / she replied, / "a mate suitable for me, / and am
"난 찾고 있어," 독수리가 대답했다.   "내게 맞는 짝을,

not able to find one."
그런데 찾을 수 없어."

"Take me," / returned the Kite, / "I am much stronger
"날 짝으로 삼으렴," 솔개가 대답했다,   "난 너보다 힘이 훨씬 세거든."

than you are."

"Why, / are you able to secure the means of living / by
"그럼,   넌 생계를 보장해 줄 수 있니

your plunder?"
약탈로?"

"Well, / I have often caught and carried away / an ostrich
"글쎄,   난 종종 잡아서 가져오곤 했어   타조를

/ in my talons."
발톱으로."

The Eagle, / persuaded by these words, / accepted him /
독수리는,   이 말에 설득되어,   솔개를 받아들였다

as her mate.
짝으로.

Shortly after the nuptials, / the Eagle said, / "Fly off / and
짝짓기가 끝난 직후,   독수리가 말했다,   "날아가서

bring me back / the ostrich you promised me."
내게 가져다 줘   네가 약속한 타조를."

The Kite, / soaring aloft into the air, / brought back / the
솔개는,   하늘 높이 날아올랐다가,   가지고 돌아왔다

shabbiest possible mouse, / stinking / from the length of
초라한 쥐 한 마리를,   냄새가 고약한   오랫동안

time / it had lain about the fields.
       들판에 방치되어.

"Is this," / said the Eagle, / "the faithful fulfillment / of
"이것이,"   독수리가 말했다,   "제대로 지킨 거니

your promise to me?"
네가 한 약속을?"

The Kite replied, / "That I might attain your royal hand, /
솔개가 대답했다,   "네 마음을 얻기 위해서는,

there is nothing that I would not have promised, / however
약속하지 못할 게 없지,   아무리 내가

much I knew / that I must fail in the performance."
알고 있더라도   약속을 지키지 못할 것을."

The Farmer and His Sons
농부와 아들

A FATHER, / being on the point of death, / wished to be
한 아버지가,   거의 죽어가는,   확실히 하고 싶었다

sure / that his sons would give the same attention / to his
       아들들이 관심을 가져 주기를   to his

farm / as he himself had given it. He called them to his
농장에   자신이 쏟았던 것처럼.   그는 아들들을 침대맡으로 불러

bedside / and said, / "My sons, / there is a great treasure
       말했다,   "얘들아,   엄청난 보물이 숨겨져 있단다

hid / in one of my vineyards."
포도밭에는."

The sons, / after his death, / took their spades and
아들들은,   아버지가 돌아가신 후   삽과 곡괭이를 들고

mattocks / and carefully dug over / every portion of their
              열심히 땅을 팠다   포도밭 구석구석을.

land. They found no treasure, / but the vines repaid their
그들은 아무 보물도 발견하지 못했다,   그러나 포도밭은 그들의 수고에 보답해 주

labor / by an extraordinary and superabundant crop.
었다   엄청나게 풍부한 수확을 안겨줌으로써.

The Farmer and the Stork
농부와 황새

A FARMER placed nets / on his newly-sown plowlands
한 농부가 그물을 치고   새로 씨를 뿌린 밭에

/ and caught a number of Cranes, / which came to
두루미를 많이 잡았다,   씨앗을 먹으려고 다가온.

pick up his seed. With them / he trapped a Stork / that
                두루미들과 함께   황새 한 마리도 잡았는데

had fractured his leg / in the net / and was earnestly
다리가 부러진   그물에 걸려   황새는 농부에게 간절히 애원했다

beseeching the Farmer / to spare his life.
                목숨을 살려 달라고.

"Pray save me, / Master," / he said, / "and let me go free
"제발 살려 주세요,   주인님,"   황새가 말했다,   "그리고 저를 놓아 주세요

/ this once. My broken limb should excite your pity.
이번 한 번만.   다리가 부러졌으니 불쌍히 여겨 주세요.

nuptial 결혼식 | soaring 날아오르는 | shabby 다 낡은, 초라한 | stinking 악취가 나는, 지독한 | lain lie
의 과거분사 | faithful 충실한 | fulfillment 수행, 실천 | attain 이루다 | royal 성대한, 위풍당당한 | bedside
침대 옆, 머리맡 | treasure 보물 | vineyard 포도밭 | spade 삽 | mattock 곡괭이 | portion 부분, 몫 | vine
포도나무 | repay 갚다, 보답하다 | labor 노동, 수고 | superabundant 너무 많은, 과잉의 | crop 농작물, (한
철에 거둔) 수확량 | stork 황새(사람에게 아기를 데려다 준다는 전설이 있는 새) | newly-sown 새로 씨 뿌린 |
plowland 경작지, 논밭 | cranes 학, 두루미 | seed 씨앗 | trap 덫으로 잡다 | fracture 골절되다 | limb 팔
다리, (새의) 날개 | excite 자극하다, 불러일으키다 | pity 연민, 동정심

Besides, / I am no Crane, / I am a Stork, / a bird of
게다가, 저는 두루미가 아니라, 황새잖아요,

excellent character; / and see / how I love and slave / for my
훌륭한 모습의 새인; 아시잖아요 얼마나 사랑하고 헌신하는지

father and mother. Look too, / at my feathers / — they are
우리 부모님을 위해. 또 보세요, 제 깃털을

not the least like those of a Crane."
— 두루미 깃털과는 전혀 다르잖아요."

The Farmer laughed aloud / and said, / "It may be all as
농부는 크게 웃으며 말했다. "네 말이 모두 옳을지도 몰라,

you say, / I only know this: / I have taken you with these
하지만 이것만은 알고 있지: 이 도둑놈들과 함께 너를 잡았으니,

robbers, / the Cranes, / and you must die in their company."
두루미들과, 너도 같이 죽어야 한다는 것이지."

Birds of a feather flock together.
끼리끼리 몰려다니는 법이다.

The Farmer and the Snake
농부와 뱀

ONE WINTER / a Farmer found a Snake / stiff and frozen
어느 겨울 한 농부가 뱀 한 마리를 발견했다 추위로 뻣뻣하게 얼어버린.

with cold. He had compassion on it, / and taking it up, /
농부는 뱀을 불쌍히 여겨, 집어 들어서,

placed it in his bosom. The Snake was quickly revived /
가슴 속에 넣었다. 뱀은 곧 회복하여

by the warmth, / and resuming its natural instincts, / bit its
온기 때문에, 타고난 본능을 발휘하여,

benefactor, / inflicting on him a mortal wound.
은인을 물었고, 농부에게 치명적인 상처를 입혔다.

slave 고되게 일하다, 헌신하다 |robber 강도 |stiff 뻣뻣한 |compassion 연민, 동정심 |bosom 가슴 |revive
활기를 되찾다, 회복하다 |warmth 온기 |instinct 본능 |benefactor 후원자, 은인 |inflict (괴로움을) 가하다 |
mortal 치명적인, (죽을 정도로) 심각한 |scoundrel 악당 |ungrateful 은혜를 모르는, 배은망덕한 |wheat 밀 |
brandish (무기를) 휘두르다 |sling 고무총 |terror 두려움 |inspire 불러 일으키다 |swing 흔들리다 |cease
그치다 |forsake 저버리다 |Liliput 릴리펏(걸리버 여행기에 등장하는 가공의 소인국 섬나라) |suffice 충분하다

"Oh," / cried the Farmer / with his last breath, / "I am
"아,"　농부가 소리쳤다　마지막 숨을 거두며,

rightly served / for pitying a scoundrel."
"당연한 대가를 받았구나　악당을 불쌍히 여겼으니."

The greatest kindness will not bind the ungrateful.
지극한 친절은 배은망덕한 자들을 감싸진 못한다.

The Farmer and the Cranes
농부와 두루미

SOME CRANES made their feeding grounds / on some
두루미 몇 마리가 먹이를 구할 땅으로 삼았다　몇몇 밭을

plowlands / newly sown with wheat.
새로 밀 씨앗을 뿌린.

For a long time / the Farmer, / brandishing an empty
오랫동안　농부는,　빈 고무총을 쏘아대며,

sling, / chased them away / by the terror he inspired; /
새들을 쫓았다　공포를 조성하며;

but when the birds found / that the sling was only swung
하지만 새들은 알게 되자　고무총이 단지 흔들리고 있을 뿐이라는 사실을

/ in the air, / they ceased to take any notice of it / and
허공에서,　그 총에 주의를 기울이는 것을 그만두고

would not move. The Farmer, / on seeing this, / charged
밭에서 나가려 하지 않았다. 농부는,　이를 보고,

his sling with stones, / and killed a great number.
고무총에 돌을 장전하여,　많은 새들을 죽여 버렸다.

The remaining birds / at once / forsook his fields, /
살아남은 새들은　즉시　그 밭을 떠나며,

crying to each other, / "It is time for us to be off to
서로에게 소리쳤다,　"릴리펏으로 떠나야 할 때구나;

Liliput: / for this man is / no longer content to scare us, /
이 사람은　더 이상 겁주는 것에만 만족하지 않고,

but begins to show us / in earnest / what he can do."
보여 주기 시작했으니　진정으로　자신이 뭘 할 수 있는지."

If words suffice not, / blows must follow.
말로 충분하지 않다면,　폭력이 따라오는 법이다.

The Father And His Sons
아버지와 아들

A FATHER had a family of sons / who were perpetually
한 아버지에게 아들들이 있었다 · 서로 끊임없이 싸우기만 하던.

quarreling among themselves. When he failed to heal their
아들 간의 싸움을 말리는데 실패하자

disputes / by his exhortations, / he determined to give them
훈계로, · 아버지는 보여 주기로 결심했다

/ a practical illustration / of the evils of disunion; / and
실제적인 예를 · 분열의 해악을 보여 주는;

for this purpose / he one day told / them to bring him / a
이를 위해 · 어느 날 그는 말했다 · 아들들에게 가져오라고

bundle of sticks.
나뭇가지 한 묶음을.

When they had done so, / he placed the faggot / into the
그들이 가져오자, · 아버지는 나무 한 단을 쥐어 주고

hands of each of them / in succession, / and ordered them
각자의 손에 · 차례로, · 명령했다

/ to break it in pieces. They tried / with all their strength, /
부러뜨려 보라고. · 아들들은 시도했지만 · 있는 힘을 다해,

and were not able to do it. He next opened the faggot, / took
부러뜨릴 수 없었다. · 다음으로 아버지는 나무단을 풀러서,

the sticks separately, / one by one, / and again / put them
따로따로 분리한 후, · 하나씩, · 그리고 다시

into his sons' hands, / upon which / they broke them easily.
아들들의 손에 쥐어 주었다, · 그러자 · 쉽게 부러뜨릴 수 있었다.

He then addressed them / in these words: / "My sons, / if
그러자 아버지는 말했다 · 다음과 같이: · "애들아,

you are of one mind, / and unite to assist each other, / you
너희들이 한마음이 되어, · 서로 힘을 합쳐 돕는다면,

will be as this faggot, / uninjured by all the attempts of
이 나무단처럼, · 적들의 어떤 공격에도 상처 입지 않을 것이다;

your enemies; / but if you are divided among yourselves, /
하지만 너희들 사이에 분열이 일어난다면,

you will be broken / as easily as these sticks."
너희들은 부러져 버릴 것이다 · 이 나뭇가지처럼 쉽게."

The Father and His Two Daughters
아버지와 두 딸

A MAN had two daughters, / the one married to a gardener,
한 남자에게 두 딸이 있었는데,　　　한 명은 정원사에게 시집을 갔고,

/ and the other to a tilemaker.
다른 한 명은 벽돌공과 결혼했다.

After a time / he went to the daughter / who had married the
얼마 후　　　그는 딸에게 가서　　　정원사와 결혼한,

gardener, / and inquired / how she was / and how all things
물어봤다　　　잘 지내는지　　그리고 일은 잘 되는지.

went with her. She said, / "All things are prospering with
딸이 대답했다.　　"다 잘되고 있어요.

me, / and I have only one wish, / that there may be a heavy
그런데 소원이 하나 있어요.　　비가 많이 왔으면 좋겠어요,

fall of rain, / in order that the plants may be well watered."
정원의 나무들에게 물을 충분히 줄 수 있도록."

Not long after, / he went to the daughter / who had married
얼마 후,　　　그는 다른 딸에게 가서　　　벽돌공과 결혼한,

the tilemaker, / and likewise inquired of her / how she
똑같이 물어봤고　　　잘 지내는지;

fared; / she replied, / "I want for nothing, / and have only
딸이 대답했다.　　"원하는 건 없지만,　　단 한 가지 소원이 있어요.

one wish, / that the dry weather may continue, / and the sun
맑은 날씨가 계속 되어,

shine hot and bright, / so that the bricks might be dried."
햇볕이 쨍쨍했으면 좋겠어요,　　벽돌이 잘 마를 수 있도록."

He said to her, / "If your sister wishes for rain, / and you
그는 딸에게 말했다,　　"네 언니는 비를 바라고,

for dry weather, / with which of the two / am I to join my
넌 맑은 날을 바라니,　　둘 중에 어떤 소원을

wishes?"
내가 빌어야겠니?"

---

perpetually 끊임없이, 일년 내내 | heal 치료하다 | dispute 논쟁 | exhortation 경고, 훈계 | practical
실제적인 | illustration 삽화, 실례 | disunion 분리, 분열 | bundle 꾸러미 | stick 찌르다 | faggot (땔감용) 나무
한 단 | in succession 잇달아, 계속하여 | separately 따로따로 | unite 합치다. 연합하다 | uninjured 다치지
않은 | gardener 정원사 | prospering 번창하다 | fare (특정 상황에서) 잘하다, 잘못하다 | brick 벽돌

The Fawn and His Mother
새끼 사슴과 어미 사슴

A YOUNG FAWN / once / said to his Mother, / "You
새끼 사슴 한 마리가   어느 날   어미에게 말했다,

are larger than a dog, / and swifter, / and more used to
"엄마는 개보다 크고,   더 빠르고,   달리기도 잘하고,

running, / and you have your horns as a defense; / why, /
몸을 지킬 수 있는 뿔도 있잖아요;   왜,

then, / O Mother! Do the hounds frighten you so?"
그런데,   엄마!   사냥개를 그렇게 무서워하는 건가요?"

She smiled, / and said: / "I know full well, / my son,
어미가 웃으며,   대답했다: "나도 잘 알고 있단다,   애야,

/ that all you say is true. I have the advantages / you
네가 말하는 건 다 옳아.   내게는 장점이 있지

mention, / but when I hear even the bark of a single dog /
네가 말했듯이,   하지만 한 마리라도 개가 짖는 소리를 들으면

I feel ready to faint, / and fly away / as fast as I can."
까무러치듯 놀라서,   달아나 버리는구나   최대한 빨리."

No arguments will give courage to the coward.
겁쟁이에게는 어떤 말도 용기를 주지 못하는 법이다.

Key Expression

for the sake of ~ : ~을 위해서

sake는 동기, 이익, 목적, 원인 등의 뜻을 가진 명사인데, 일반적으로 for the sake of ~, 혹은 for one's sake와 같은 형태로 사용되며 '~을 위해서'라고 해석합니다.
또한 for Christ's[God's, goodness', heaven's, pity's, mercy's] sake와 같이 쓰일 때에는 '제발, 하느님 맙소사, 아무쪼록'이라는 의미가 됩니다.

ex) O foolish creatures that we are, for the sake of a little pleasure we have destroyed ourselves.
우리는 얼마나 어리석었던가, 작은 즐거움을 위해서 우리 자신을 망치고 말았으니.

---

fawn 새끼 사슴 |swift 빠른 |defense 방어 |mention 언급하다 |faint 기절하다 |argument 주장 |
coward 겁쟁이 |fir-tree 전나무 |bramble 검은딸기나무(=blackberry) |boastingly 자랑스럽게 |axe 도끼
|saw 톱 |hew 자르다 |jar 병 |overturned 뒤집히다 |greedily 게걸스럽게 |smeared 마구 바르다 |
suffocated 질식사하다

The Fir-Tree and the Bramble
전나무와 검은딸기나무

A FIR-TREE said boastingly / to the Bramble, / "You are
전나무가 자랑스럽게 말했다   검은딸기나무에게,

useful for nothing at all; / while I am everywhere used /
"넌 아무 쓸모 없구나;   난 모든 곳에 쓰이는데

for roofs and houses."
지붕이나 집을 짓는.

The Bramble answered: / "You poor creature, / if you
검은딸기나무가 대답했다: "불쌍한 것,

would only call to mind the axes and saws / which are
만약 네가 도끼나 톱을 만나게 되면

about to hew you down, / you would have reason to wish
널 쓰러뜨리려는,   바라게 될 걸

/ that you had grown up a Bramble, / not a Fir-Tree."
검은딸기나무로 자랐으면 좋았을 거라고,   전나무가 아니라."

Better poverty without care, / than riches with.
걱정 없는 가난한 삶이 더 나을 수도 있다,   걱정 많은 부자의 삶보다.

The Flies and the Honey-Pot
파리와 꿀단지

A NUMBER of Flies were attracted / to a jar of honey
수많은 파리떼가 매혹되어   꿀단지에

/ which had been overturned / in a housekeeper's room,
엎어져 있던   가정부의 방 안에,

/ and placing their feet in it, / ate greedily. Their feet, /
바닥에 발을 디디고   게걸스럽게 먹어 치웠다. 파리의 발은,

however, / became so smeared / with the honey that they
그러나,   꿀로 범벅이 되어서   날갯짓을 할 수도,

could not use their wings, / nor release themselves, / and
빠져나갈 수도 없게 되었고,

were suffocated.
결국 질식해 죽어 버렸다.

Just as they were expiring, / they exclaimed, / "O foolish
숨을 거두려는 순간,   파리들은 소리쳤다,

creatures that we are, / for the sake of a little pleasure /
"우리는 얼마나 어리석었던지,   작은 즐거움을 위해서

we have destroyed ourselves."
우리 자신을 망쳐버리고 말았으니."

Pleasure bought with pains, hurts.
즐거움은 고통이나 상처를 동반하기 마련이다.

The Fox and the Woodcutter
여우와 나무꾼

A FOX, / running before the hounds, / came across a
여우 한 마리가, 사냥개에게 쫓겨 달아나던,

Woodcutter / felling an oak / and begged him / to show
나무꾼과 마주치자   떡갈나무를 베고 있던   간청했다

him a safe hiding-place. The Woodcutter advised him /
숨을 장소를 알려 달라고.   나무꾼은 여우에게 조언했고

to take shelter / in his own hut, / so the Fox crept in / and
숨으라고   자신의 오두막 안에,   여우는 기어들어가

hid himself / in a corner.
몸을 숨겼다   구석에.

The huntsman soon came up / with his hounds / and
곧 사냥꾼이 다가와서   사냥개와 함께

inquired of the Woodcutter / if he had seen the Fox. He
나무꾼에게 물었다   여우를 봤는지.   나무꾼

declared / that he had not seen him, / and yet pointed, /
은 대답했지만   보지 못했다고,   손으로 가리켰다,

all the time he was speaking, / to the hut / where the Fox
말하는 내내   오두막 쪽을   여우가 숨어있는.

lay hidden. The huntsman took no notice of the signs, /
           사냥꾼은 그 신호를 눈치채지 못한 채,

but believing his word, / hastened forward in the chase.
그의 말을 믿고,   서둘러 추격을 계속했다.

As soon as they were well away, / the Fox departed /
사냥꾼과 사냥개가 떠나자마자,　　　　　　여우도 떠났다

without taking any notice of the Woodcutter: / whereon
나무꾼에게 아무 인사도 없이:　　　　　　　　　　그것에 대해

he called to him / and reproached him, / saying, / "You
나무꾼이 여우를 불러　　꾸짖으며,　　　　말했다,

ungrateful fellow, / you owe your life to me, / and yet you
"은혜를 모르는 녀석이구나,　　내게 목숨을 빚졌는데,　　　　떠나다니

leave me / without a word of thanks."
　　　　고맙다는 말도 없이."

The Fox replied, / "Indeed, / I should have thanked you
여우가 대답했다,　　　"맞아요,　　　진심으로 고맙다는 인사를 했어야겠죠

fervently / if your deeds had been / as good as your words,
　　　　만약 당신의 행동이　　　　　말과 같았다면,

/ and if your hands had not been / traitors to your speech."
　그리고 당신의 손짓이　　　　　　　말을 배신하지 않았다면."

Key Expression

as good as : ~와 다름 없는
as good as는 '~와 다름없는, ~와 같은'이라는 의미를 가진 표현입니다.

ex) I should have thanked you fervently if your deeds had been as good as your
words.
만약 당신의 행동이 말과 같았다면 진심으로 고맙다는 인사를 했어야겠죠.

---

expiring 숨을 거두려고 하는 | woodcutter 나무꾼 | come across 우연히 마주치다 | huntsman 사냥꾼 |
hasten 서두르다 | chase 추격 | depart 떠나다, 출발하다 | whereon 무엇 위에, 무엇에 대해, 누구에게(=on what),
그 위에, 그에 대해(=on which) | fervently 열렬히, 강렬히 | deed 행동 | traitor 배반자

79

The Fox and the Crow
여우와 까마귀

A CROW / having stolen a bit of meat, / perched in a tree
까마귀 한 마리가   고기 덩어리를 훔쳐낸,   나무 위에 앉아서

/ and held it in her beak. A Fox, / seeing this, / longed
고기를 부리로 물고 있었다.   여우 한 마리는, 이를 보고,

to possess the meat himself, / and by a wily stratagem
그 고기 덩어리가 간절히 갖고 싶어서,   꾀를 부려 성공했다.

succeeded.

"How handsome is the Crow," / he exclaimed, / in
"까마귀 님은 정말 아름다우세요,"   여우가 소리쳤다.

the beauty of her shape / and in the fairness of her
"몸매도 아름답고   얼굴도 참 고우세요!

complexion! Oh, if her voice were only equal to her
아, 목소리도 미모만큼 아름답다면,

beauty, / she would deservedly be considered / the Queen
마땅히 되실 텐데

of Birds!"
새들의 여왕이!"

This he said deceitfully; / but the Crow, / anxious to
여우는 거짓으로 말했지만;   까마귀는,   입증하고 싶은 마음이

refute / the reflection cast upon her voice, / set up a loud
간절해서   자신에 목소리에 대한 비판을,   큰 소리로 까악 울었고,

caw / and dropped the flesh.
고기를 떨어뜨리고 말았다.

The Fox quickly picked it up, / and thus addressed the
여우가 재빨리 그것을 주워서는,   까마귀에게 말했다.

Cro / "My good Crow, / your voice is right enough, / but
"까마귀 님,   목소리는 정말 아름답네요,

your wit is wanting."
하지만 지능은 부족하군요."

long to 간절히 바란다 | possess 소유하다 | stratagem 책략, 술수 | fairness 금발, 흰 피부, 아름다운 피부
| deservedly 마땅히 | deceitfully 속여서 | anxious to ~하고 싶은 생각이 간절하다 | refute 논박하다,
입증하다 | wanting 부족한 | hedgehog 고슴도치 | rapid 빠른 | current 흐름 | ravine 산골짜기 | bruised
멍든, 상처입은 | swarm 떼 | blood-sucking 흡혈 | anguish 괴로움, 비통 | torment 고통을 안겨 주다,
괴롭히다 | by no means 결코 ~이 아닌(=never) | molest 폭행하다 | satiated 충분히 만족한, 물린

The Fox and the Hedgehog
여우와 고습도치

A FOX / swimming across a rapid river / was carried by
여우 한 마리가 급류의 강을 헤엄쳐 건너던   물살에 떠내려가 버렸고

the force of the current / into a very deep ravine, / where
                          깊은 산골짜기로,   그곳에 누

he lay / for a long time / very much bruised, sick, / and
워 있었다   오랫동안   크게 상처 입고, 고통스러워하며,

unable to move. A swarm of hungry blood-sucking flies
움직이지도 못한 채.   배고픈 흡혈 파리떼가

/ settled upon him. A Hedgehog, / passing by, / saw his
  여우 위에 앉았다.   고슴도치가,   곁을 지나가다가,   여우의 괴로움

anguish / and inquired / if he should drive away the flies
을 보고   물었다   파리를 쫓아주길 원하는지

/ that were tormenting him.
  여우에게 고통을 안겨 주고 있는.

"By no means," / replied the Fox; / "pray do not molest
"전혀,"   여우가 대답했다: "그것들을 때리지 마."

them."

"How is this?" / said the Hedgehog; / "do you not want to
"어떻게 하라고?"   고슴도치가 말했다: "파리를 없애고 싶지 않아?"

be rid of them?"

"No," / returned the Fox, / "for these flies / which you
"아니,"   여우가 대답했다,   "왜냐하면 이 파리들은   네가 보고 있는

see / are full of blood, / and sting me but little, / and if
      피를 실컷 빨아서,   별로 아프지 않아,

you rid me of these / which are already satiated, / others
그런데 네가 이 파리들을 쫓으면   이미 충분히 피를 빤,

more hungry will come / in their place, / and will drink
다른 배고픈 파리들이 와서   그것들을 대신할테고,   빨아먹고 말 거야

up / all the blood I have left."
     내게 남은 피를 전부."

The Fox and the Monkey
여우와 원숭이

A FOX and a Monkey were traveling together / on the
여우와 원숭이가 함께 여행하고 있었다

same road. As they journeyed, / they passed through a
같은 여정을.　여행을 하면서,　그들은 어느 무덤을 지나게 되었다

cemetery / full of monuments.
기념물이 가득 세워진.

"All these monuments / which you see," / said the Monkey,
"이 기념물들은　네가 보고 있는,'　원숭이가 말했다,

/ "are erected / in honor of my ancestors, / who were in
"세워진 거야　우리 조상들을 추모하여,

their day / freedmen and citizens of great renown."
당시 그들은　매우 유명한 노예와 시민이었거든."

The Fox replied, / "You have chosen a most appropriate
여우가 대답했다,　"가장 그럴듯한 주제를 골랐구나

subject / for your falsehoods, / as I am sure / none of your
거짓말로,　확신하건대　네 조상들 중 누구도

ancestors / will be able to contradict you."
네 말에 반박할 수 없을 테니."

A false tale often betrays itself.
거짓말은 종종 무심코 거짓임을 드러내는 법이다.

Key Expression

in one's day : 한창 때는

in one's day는 '한창 때는, 젊을 때는'이란 뜻을 가진 숙어입니다. one's day 에는 '잘나가는 때, 행복한 때, 최고의 순간'이라는 의미가 담겨 있어요. 우리말 속 담의 '쥐구멍에도 볕들 날 있다'에 해당하는 속담 'Every dog has his own day'도 여기에서 나온 것이죠. one's day를 활용한 표현을 더 알아볼까요.

▶ in somebody's day : ~가 한창 때, 젊을 때
▶ of somebody's day : ~가 살아 있던 시대에
▶ make somebody's day : ~의 하루를 행복하게 해 주다

ex) All these monuments which you see are erected in honor of my ancestors,
    who were in their day freedmen and citizens of great renown.
    네가 보고 있는 이 기념물들은 우리 조상들을 추모하여 세워진 거야, 그들은 한
    창 때 매우 유명한 노예와 시민이었거든.

cemetery 묘지 | monument 기념물 | erect 세우다 | in honor of ~에게 경의를 표하여, ~을 기념하여 | ancestor
조상 | renown 명성 | appropriate 적당한 | contradict 반박하다 | betray 드러내다 | nearly 거의 ~할 뻔하다 |
alarmed 두려워하는 | commence 시작하다 | prejudice 편견 | cluster 송이 | ripe 익은 | trellised 격자 모양의
| resort to~ (좋지 못한 것에) 기대다, 의지하다 | weary 지치게 하다 | disappointment 실망 | sour (맛이) 신

The Fox and the Lion
여우와 사자

WHEN A FOX / who had never yet seen a Lion, / fell in
여우 한 마리가   아직 사자를 본 적 없는,   사자 곁에

with him / by chance / for the first time / in the forest, /
떨어지자   우연히   생전 처음으로   숲속에서,

he was so frightened / that he nearly died with fear. On
여우는 매우 놀라   공포로 죽을 것 같았다.

meeting him / for the second time, / he was still much
사자와 마주쳤을 때   두 번째로,   여우는 깜짝 놀랐지만

alarmed, / but not to the same extent as at first.
처음만큼은 아니었다.

On seeing him the third time, / he so increased in boldness
세 번째 마주치자,   여우는 대담해져서

/ that he went up to him / and commenced a familiar
사자에게 다가가   친근하게 말을 걸었다.

conversation with him.

Acquaintance softens prejudices.
얼굴을 익히고 나면 편견은 없어지는 법이다.

The Fox and the Grapes
여우와 포도

A FAMISHED FOX saw / some clusters of ripe black
배고픈 여우 한 마리가 보았다   잘 익은 검은 포도송이를

grapes / hanging from a trellised vine. She resorted to all
격자로 뻗은 포도넝쿨에 매달려 있는.   여우는 모든 꾀를 냈지만

her tricks / to get at them, / but wearied herself / in vain, /
포도를 따기 위해,   지쳐 버렸다   헛되이,

for she could not reach them.
손이 닿지 않았기 때문에.

At last / she turned away, / hiding her disappointment / and
마침내   여우는 발길을 돌렸다,   실망을 감추고

saying: / "The Grapes are sour, / and not ripe / as I thought."
말하면서: "저것은 신 포도야,   그리고 익지도 않았어   내 생각에는."

The Fox and the Goat
여우와 염소

A FOX / one day / fell into a deep well / and could find no
여우 한 마리가 어느 날   깊은 우물에 빠져서   빠져 나올 수 없었다.

means of escape. A Goat, / overcome with thirst, / came
염소 한 마리가, 갈증을 풀려고,

to the same well, / and seeing the Fox, / inquired / if the
같은 우물에 와서,   여우를 보고,   물었다

water was good. Concealing his sad plight / under a merry
물이 맛있냐고.   곤경을 감추고   겉으로는 즐거운 척하며,

guise, / the Fox indulged / in a lavish praise of the water, /
여우는 떠들어댔다   물에 대한 온갖 찬사의 말을,

saying it was excellent beyond measure, / and encouraging
대단히 훌륭한 우물이라고 말하며,

him to descend.
염소에게 내려오라고 부추겼다.

The Goat, / mindful only of his thirst, / thoughtlessly
염소는,   목이 마른 것에 정신이 팔려서,   깊이 생각하지 않고 뛰어 내렸다.

jumped down, / but just as he drank, / the Fox informed
그러나 물을 마시자 마자,

him of the difficulty / they were both in / and suggested a
여우는 어려움에 대해 알려 주고   그들이 처해 있는   계획을 제안했다

scheme / for their common escape. "If," / said he, / "you
함께 빠져나가기 위한.   "만약," 여우가 말했다,

will place your forefeet / upon the wall / and bend your
"네가 앞발을 대고   벽에   머리를 숙여 준다면,

head, / I will run up your back / and escape, / and will help
내가 네 등 위로 뛰어올라   빠져나가서,   네가 나오도록 도와줄게

you out / afterwards."
그 후에."

The Goat readily assented / and the Fox leaped / upon his
염소는 선뜻 찬성했고   여우는 뛰어올랐다   염소의 등 위로.

back. Steadying himself with the Goat's horns, / he safely
염소의 뿔로 균형을 잡으면서,

reached the mouth of the well / and made off / as fast as he
여우는 안전하게 우물 입구에 도착해   달아났다   최대한 빨리.

could.

When the Goat upbraided him / for breaking his
염소가 여우를 나무라자   약속을 어긴 것에 대해,

promise, / he turned around / and cried out, / "You
여우는 돌아서서   소리쳤다,

foolish old fellow! If you had as many brains in your
"바보같은 친구여!   자네 머리 속에 지능이 있었다면

head / as you have hairs in your beard, / you would never
턱수염의 털 수만큼,   내려가지도 않았을 것이고

have gone down / before you had inspected the way up,
                빠져나갈 곳을 알아보기 전에,

/ nor have exposed yourself to dangers / from which you
자신을 그런 위험에 빠뜨리지도 않았을 거야   빠져나갈 구멍도 없는."

had no means of escape."

Look before you leap.
뛰어 오르기 전에 먼저 살펴야 한다.

Key Expression

속담 look before you leap

look before you leap은 '뛰기 전에 잘 살펴보라'는 뜻으로 '잘 생각해 본 후
에 행동하라'는 의미를 담고 있습니다.
우리말로 치면 '돌다리도 두드려 보고 건너라'에 해당하는 속담입니다.
우리 속담에 해당하는 다른 표현들에 대해 알아볼까요.

ex) Once bitten, twice shy.
　　자라 보고 놀란 가슴 솥뚜껑 보고 놀란다.
　　What's learned in the cradle is carried to the grave.
　　세 살 버릇 여든까지 간다.
　　Every Jack has his Jill.
　　짚신도 짝이 있다.
　　Speak of the devil.
　　호랑이도 제 말하면 온다.

well 우물 I escape 탈출하다 I conceal 감추다, 숨기다 I plight 곤경 I guise 겉모습 I indulge 마음껏 하다,
탐닉하다 I lavish 호화로운, 풍성한 I praise 칭찬, 찬사 I beyond measure 몹시, 대단히 I encourage 격려하다,
부추기다 I mindful 염두에 둔, 의식하는 I thoughtlessly 생각이 모자라서, 깊이 생각하지 않고 I scheme 계획,
책략 I common 공동의 I forefeet 앞발 I readily 선뜻, 기꺼이 I assent 찬성하다 I leap 뛰다, 뛰어오르다
I steady 균형을 잡다 I upbraid 질책하다, 호되게 나무라다 I brain 뇌 I beard 턱수염 I inspect 조사하다 I
expose 드러내다

The Fowler and the Viper
새 사냥꾼과 독사

A FOWLER, / taking his bird-lime and his twigs, / went
새 사냥꾼이,　　　　　새 잡는 끈끈이와 나뭇가지를 들고,

out to catch birds. Seeing a thrush / sitting upon a tree, / he
새 사냥을 나섰다.　　　개똥지빠귀를 발견하고　　나무 위에 앉아 있는,

wished to take it, / and fitting his twigs to a proper length,
사냥꾼은 그것을 잡고 싶어서,　나뭇가지를 적당한 길이로 조절한 후,

/ watched intently, / having his whole thoughts directed
뚫어지게 쳐다보았다,　　　온 정신을 쏟은 채

/ towards the sky. While thus looking upwards, / he
하늘에.　　　　　그렇게 위쪽을 바라보다가,

unknowingly trod upon a Viper / asleep just before his feet.
그는 모르고 독사를 밟아버렸다　　　발 바로 앞에서 잠자고 있던.

The Viper, / turning about, / stung him, / and falling into a
독사가,　　　뒤돌아보고,　　사냥꾼을 물자,　　기절해 쓰러지면서,

swoon, / the man said to himself, / "Woe is me! That while
기절해 쓰러지면서,　사냥꾼은 혼잣말을 했다,　　"내가 어리석었구나!

I purposed to hunt another, / I am myself fallen unawares
사냥에 정신이 팔린 사이,　　　내 자신이 죽음의 덫에 빠진 것을 몰랐다니."

into the snares of death."

The Two Frogs (1)
두 마리의 개구리

TWO FROGS dwelt / in the same pool. When the pool
개구리 두 마리가 살고 있었다　　같은 연못에.　　　　물이 말라버리자

dried up / under the summer's heat, / they left it / and set
여름의 열기로,　　　　　　그들은 연못을 떠나

out together / for another home.
함께 길을 나섰다　　다른 살 곳을 찾아서.

fowler 새 사냥꾼 | viper 독사 | bird-lime 새 잡는 끈끈이 | twig 잔가지 | thrush 개똥지빠귀 | proper
적절한 | intently 골똘하게, 여념없이, 오로지 | direct 겨냥하다, 향하다 | unknowingly 모르고 | tread 발을
디디다, 밟다 | turn about 뒤돌아보다 | swoon 기절하다 | snare 덫 | dwell 살다 | chance to 우연히 ~하다
| amply 충분히 | supply 공급하다 | abide 머무름, 거처 | furnish 공급하다 | caution 조심 | depth 깊이 |
consequence 결과

As they went along / they chanced to pass a deep well,
함께 길을 가다가   개구리들은 깊은 우물을 지나게 되었다.

/ amply supplied with water, / and when they saw it, /
물이 가득한,   그것을 보고,

one of the Frogs said to the other, / "Let us descend / and
한 개구리가 다른 개구리에게 말했다.   "내려가서

make our abode / in this well: / it will furnish us / with
살도록 하자   이 우물에: 우물이 마련해 줄 거야

shelter and food."
쉴 곳과 음식을."

The other replied / with greater caution, / "But suppose /
다른 개구리가 대답했다   매우 조심하며,   "하지만 상상해 봐

the water should fail us. How can we get out again / from
이 우물이 적당하지 않다는 것을,   어떻게 다시 빠져 나오지

so great a depth?"
저렇게 깊은 우물 속에서?"

Do nothing / without a regard to the consequences.
행동하면 안 된다   결과를 생각하지 않고.

Key Expression

공급동사의 전치사 with

furnish A with B 처럼 '공급하다, 제공하다'의 뜻을 가진 동사들은 4형식의
수여동사로 착각하기 쉽지만, 실제 3형식으로 사용되는 동사이며 전치사 with
를 함께 씁니다.

▶ furnish A with B = furnish B for/to A : A에게 B를 제공하다
▶ provide A with B = provide B for A : A에게 B를 제공하다
▶ supply A with B = supply B for/to A : A에게 B를 공급하다
▶ present A with B = present B to A : A에게 B를 선물하다
▶ entrust A with B = entrust B to A : A에게 B를 맡기다

ex) As they went along they chanced to pass a deep well, amply supplied with
water.
그들은 함께 길을 가다가 물이 가득히 차 있는 깊은 우물을 지나게 되었다.
It will furnish us with shelter and food.
우물이 쉴 곳과 음식을 마련해 줄 거야.

The Two Frogs (2)
두 마리의 개구리

TWO FROGS were neighbors. One inhabited a deep
개구리 두 마리가 이웃에 살고 있었다.   한 마리는 깊은 연못에 살았고,

pond, / far removed from public view; / the other lived
사람들 눈에 띄지 않는 먼 곳에;   다른 개구리는 살았다

/ in a gully / containing little water, / and traversed by a
도랑에   물이 거의 없고,   시골길을 가로질러 난.

country road.

The Frog / that lived in the pond / warned his friend / to
개구리는   연못에 사는   친구에게 경고하며

change his residence / and entreated him / to come and
이사를 가야 한다고   청했다   와서 자신과 함께

live with him, / saying / that he would enjoy / greater
살자고,   말하면서   즐기게 될 것이라고   위험으로부터

safety from danger / and more abundant food. The other
벗어난 안전한 삶과   먹을 것도 훨씬 많다고.   다른 개구리는

refused, / saying / that he felt it so very hard / to leave a
거절했다,   말하면서   힘들 것 같다고   그곳을 떠나는 것이

place / to which he had become accustomed.
매우 익숙해져 버린.

A few days afterwards / a heavy wagon passed through
며칠 후에   커다란 마차가 도랑을 지나가면서

the gully / and crushed him to death / under its wheels.
개구리를 치어 죽게 했다   바퀴로.

A willful man will have his way to his own hurt.
고집센 사람은 자신을 다치게 하는 길을 선택하게 될 것이다.

inhabit 살다 | gully 도랑 | traverse 가로지르다 | residence 거주지 | abundant 풍부한 | wagon 4륜
우마차 | crush 으스러뜨리다 | wheel 바퀴 | willful 제 마음대로의, 고집 센 | established 인정받는, 확립된 |
ruler 통치자, 지배자 | simplicity 순수함 | cast 던지다 | splash 첨벙 하는 소리 | occasion ~을 야기하다 |
motionless 움직이지 않는 | dismiss 떨쳐 버리다 | squat 쪼그리고 있다 | contempt 경멸, 무시 | ill-treated
학대당하는, 부당한 대우를 받는 | appointment 임명, 지명 | inert 힘이 없는 | deputation 대표단, 사절단 |
sovereign 군주, 국왕 | eel 장어 | govern 통치하다, 다스리다 | complaint 불평, 불만 | heron 왜가리 | prey
먹이로 삼다 | croak 개골개골하다

The Frogs Asking for a King
왕을 달라고 부탁한 개구리들

THE FROGS, / grieved at having no established Ruler, / sent
개구리들은,   정해진 통치자가 없는 것에 슬퍼하여,

ambassadors to Jupiter / entreating for a King. Perceiving
제우스에게 사절을 보내   왕을 보내 달라고 간청했다.

their simplicity, / he cast down a huge log / into the lake. The
그들의 단순함을 알아채고, 제우스는 커다란 통나무를 던져 주었다   호수에.

Frogs were terrified / at the splash / occasioned by its fall / and
개구리들은 깜짝 놀라서   첨벙 하는 소리에   통나무가 떨어지면서 낸

hid themselves / in the depths of the pool.
몸을 숨겼다   호수 깊은 곳에.

But as soon as they realized / that the huge log was
하지만 깨닫자마자   그 커다란 소나무가 움직이지 않는다는 것을,

motionless, / they swam again to the top of the water, /
        개구리들은 다시 물 위로 헤엄쳐와서,

dismissed their fears, / climbed up, / and began squatting on it
공포를 떨쳐버리고,   나무 위로 올라가,   그 위에 쪼그리고 앉기 시작했다

/ in contempt.
무시하면서.

After some time / they began to think themselves ill-treated
얼마 후   개구리들은 자신들이 부당한 대우를 받았다고 생각했고

/ in the appointment of so inert a Ruler, / and sent a second
그렇게 힘없는 군주를 보내 준 것에 대해,   제우스에게 다시 한 번 사절을

deputation to Jupiter / to pray / that he would set over them
보내어   간청했다   다른 왕을 보내 달라고.

another sovereign. He then gave them an Eel / to govern them.
그러자 신은 장어를 보내   개구리를 다스리게 했다.

When the Frogs discovered his easy good nature, / they
개구리들은 장어의 느긋하고 착한 성품을 보고,

sent yet a third time to Jupiter / to beg him / to choose for
제우스에게 세 번째로 사절을 보내   간청했다   또 다른 왕을 골라 달라고.

them still another King. Jupiter, / displeased with all their
        제우스는,   개구리들의 불평불만에 화가 나서,

complaints, / sent a Heron, / who preyed upon the Frogs / day
왜가리를 보냈고,   왜가리는 개구리들을 먹이로 삼아

by day / till there were none left to croak / upon the lake.
매일 매일   마침내 개굴거리는 생물이 남지 않게 되었다   호수에는.

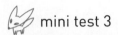

A. 다음 문장을 해석해 보세요.

(1) Your children are in great danger; / for as soon as you go out / with your litter / to find food, / the Eagle is prepared to pounce / upon one of your little pigs.
→

(2) Not long after they had agreed upon this plan, / the Eagle, / being in want of provision / for her young ones, / swooped down / while the Fox was out, / seized upon one of the little cubs, / and feasted herself and her brood.
→

(3) That I might attain your royal hand, / there is nothing that I would not have promised, / however much I knew / that I must fail in the performance.
→

(4) On meeting him / for the second time, / he was still much alarmed, / but not to the same extent as / at first.
→

B. 다음 주어진 문장이 되도록 빈칸에 써 넣으세요.

(1) 내가 확실히 아는 바로는 그것은 갈까마귀란다.

_____ he is a Daw.

(2) 너희들 사이에 분열이 일어난다면, 너희들은 이 나뭇가지처럼 쉽게 부러져 버릴 것이다.

If you are divided among yourselves, _____

_____

(3) 만약 당신의 행동이 말과 같았다면 진심으로 고맙다는 인사를 했어야겠죠.

I should have thanked you fervently _____

_____ .

A. (1) 당신 새끼들이 위험에 처해 있어요: 왜냐하면 당신이 새끼들을 데리고 먹이를 찾으러 굴을 나서자마자, 독수리가 덮치려고 하니까요. (2) 그들이 이 계획에 합의한지 얼마 지나지 않아, 독수리는 새끼들에게 줄 먹이가 부족해져서, 여우가 밖에 나간 사이 급강하하여 새끼 한 마리를 잡아서 새끼들과 함께 먹었다.

(4) 돌다리도 두드려 보고 건너라.

→

C. 다음 주어진 문구가 알맞은 문장이 되도록 순서를 맞춰 보세요.

(1) 고양이는 하루 종일 망을 봤다.
(through / lookout / the day / kept / a / She / all)
→

(2) 끼리끼리 몰려다니는 법이다.
(a / together / flock / of / Birds / feather)
→

(3) 내 자신이 죽음의 덫에 빠진 것을 몰랐다.
(myself / death / unawares / the snares / fallen / of / I am / into)
→

(4) 그것이 우리에게 쉴 곳과 음식을 마련해 줄 거야.
(shelter / furnish / it / and / us / food / will / with)
→

D. 다음 단어에 대한 맞는 설명과 연결해 보세요.

(1) swoop ▶ ◀ ① spread a layer of the substance over the surface

(2) gobble ▶ ◀ ② suddenly move downwards through the air

(3) smear ▶ ◀ ③ great mental suffering or physical pain

(4) anguish ▶ ◀ ④ eat quickly and greedily

Answer

4

The Gamecocks and the Partridge
싸움닭과 자고새

A MAN had two Gamecocks / in his poultry-yard. One
한 남자가 싸움 닭 두 마리를 기르고 있었다   사육장에서.

day / by chance / he found a tame Partridge / for sale. He
어느 날 우연히   그는 길들여진 자고새를 발견했다   팔고 있는.

purchased it / and brought it home / to be reared / with
그는 그 새를 사서   집으로 데려와   길렀다

his Gamecocks.
싸움닭과 함께.

When the Partridge was put into the poultry-yard, / they
자고새를 사육장에 넣자,   싸움닭들

struck at it / and followed it about, / so that the Partridge
은 새를 공격하며 졸졸 따라다녔다.   그러자 자고새는 몹시 귀찮아하며

became grievously troubled / and supposed / that he was
                                                생각했다

thus evilly treated / because he was a stranger.
자신이 괴롭힘을 당하는 거라고 낯선 존재라서.

Not long afterwards / he saw / the Cocks fighting together
얼마 후   자고새는 봤다 수탉들이 서로 싸우면서

/ and not separating / before one had well beaten the
떨어지지 않는 것을   한쪽이 승리할 때까지.

other. He then said to himself, / "I shall no longer distress
그러자 자고새는 생각했다,   "더 이상은 괴로워하지 않겠어

myself / at being struck at / by these Gamecocks, / when I
공격 받는다고   이 수탉들에게,   알았으니까

see / that they cannot even refrain from quarreling / with
수탉들은 싸움을 그만둘 수 없다는 것을

each other."
서로."

---

gamecock 싸움닭 | partridge 자고새(꿩과의 새) | poultry-yard 사육장 | tame 길들여진 | rear 기르다,
사육하다 | follow about 졸졸 따라다니다 | grievously 몹시, 심하게 | trouble 괴롭히다, 귀찮게 하다 | evilly
사악하게, 아주 불쾌하게 | treat 대하다, 여기다 | beat 이기다 | distress 괴롭히다 | refrain 삼가다

The Gnat and the Lion
각다귀와 사자

A GNAT came and said to a Lion, / "I do not in the least
각다귀 한 마리가 사자에게 다가가 말했다.　　　　　　　"나는 네가 조금도 무섭지 않고,

fear you, / nor are you stronger than I am. For in what
넌 나보다 힘이 세지도 않잖아.

does your strength consist? You can scratch with your
네가 뭐가 힘이 세다는 거지?　　　　　　넌 발톱으로 할퀴고

claws / and bite with your teeth / an a woman in her
이빨로 물 수는 있겠지　　　　　　암컷과 싸울 때.

quarrels. I repeat / that I am altogether more powerful /
다시 말하지만　　　내가 훨씬 힘이 세거든

than you; / and if you doubt it, / let us fight / and see who
너보다;　　　못 믿겠다면　　　　　　나랑 싸워서

will conquer."
누가 이기는지 보자."

The Gnat, / having sounded his horn, / fastened himself
각다귀는,　　　더듬이로 소리를 내며,　　　　사자 위에 바싹 붙어서

upon the Lion / and stung him / on the nostrils / and the
쏘았다　　　　　　콧구멍과

parts of the face devoid of hair. While trying to crush
얼굴의 털이 없는 부분을.　　　　　　하지만 각다귀를 잡으려다,

him, / the Lion tore himself with his claws, / until he
사자는 발톱으로 자신을 할퀴어 버렸고,

punished himself severely. The Gnat thus prevailed over
마침내 심한 상처를 입혀 버렸다.　　　　이렇게 각다귀는 사자에게 이겼고,

the Lion, / and, / buzzing about in a song of triumph, /
그리고는, 승리의 노래를 윙윙거리며,

flew away.
날아가 버렸다.

gnat 각다귀(모기와 비슷하게 생긴 작은 곤충) | consist 있다 | scratch 긁다, 할퀴다 | doubt 의심하다 | conquer
이기다 | fasten 매다 고정시키다 잠그다 | nostril 콧구멍 | devoid of ~이 전혀 없는 | punish 처벌하다, 벌주다 |
severely 심하게 | prevail 이기다 | buzzing 윙윙거리는 | triumph 승리

But shortly afterwards / he became entangled in the
그러나 잠시 후   각다귀는 거미줄에 걸려

meshes of a cobweb / and was eaten by a spider. He
                    거미에게 먹혀 버렸다.

greatly lamented his fate, / saying, / "Woe is me! That
각다귀는 자신의 운명을 한탄하며,   말했다,   "내가 어리석었구나!

I, / who can wage war successfully / with the hugest
내가, 성공적으로 싸워 이길 수 있는   가장 큰 맹수와,

beasts, / should perish myself / from this spider, / the
        죽음을 당하게 되다니   거미로 인해,

most inconsiderable of insects!"
가장 하찮은 곤충인!"

The Gnat and the Bull
각다귀와 황소

A GNAT settled on the horn of a Bull, / and sat there /
각다귀 한 마리가 황소 뿔에 내려앉아,   그곳에 앉아 있었다

a long time. Just as he was about to fly off, / he made a
오랫동안.   막 날아가려고 하다가,   각다귀는 윙윙 소리

buzzing noise, / and inquired of the Bull / if he would
를 내며,   황소에게 물었다

like him to go.
자신이 가기를 바라느냐고.

The Bull replied, / "I did not know you had come, / and I
황소가 대답했다,   "내가 온 것도 몰랐어,   그러니

shall not miss you / when you go away."
널 그리워 하지도 않을 거야   네가 가 버린다 해도."

Some men are of more consequence / in their own eyes /
어떤 사람들은 더 중요시한다   자신의 눈으로 보는 것을

than in the eyes of their neighbors.
주위 사람들의 눈에 보이는 것보다.

cobweb 거미줄 | spider 거미 | inconsiderable 하찮은 | bull 황소 | consequence 중요함

The Goat and the Goatherd
염소와 염소지기

A GOATHERD had sought to bring back / a stray goat
한 염소지기가 돌려보내려 했다   길 잃은 염소를

/ to his flock . He whistled / and sounded his horn / in
무리로.   그는 휘파람을 불고   뿔피리를 불었지만   소용

vain; / the straggler paid no attention / to the summons.
없었다;   낙오된 염소는 주의를 기울이지 않았다   부르는 소리에.

At last / the Goatherd threw a stone, / and breaking its
마침내   염소지기는 돌을 던져   염소 뿔을 부러뜨려 버렸고,

horn, / begged the Goat / not to tell his master. The Goat
그러자 염소에게 애원했다   주인에게 말하지 말라고.   염소는 대답했다.

replied, / "Why, / you silly fellow, / the horn will speak /
"저런,   어리석기는,   뿔이 말해줄 텐데

though I be silent."
내가 가만히 있어도."

Do not attempt to hide / things which cannot be hid.
숨기려 하지 마라   숨길 수 없는 일을.

Key Expression

that's (the reason) why ~ : 그것이 바로 ~한 이유이다

'That's the reason why ~'는 관계부사 구문으로 '그것이 바로 ~한 이유이다'
라는 의미를 나타냅니다. 하지만 '그래서 ~하는 것이다'와 같이 앞 문장의 결과를
나타내는 의미로 해석하는 것이 자연스러워요. 이때 관계부사 why의 선행사인
the reason은 생략이 가능합니다.
또한 이 구문은 'That's because'와 비교해서 알아두어야 합니다.

▶(원인), That's why ~ (결과)
▶(결과), That's because~ (원인)

ex) That is the very reason why we are so cautious.
그게 바로 우리가 그토록 조심하는 이유에요.
(=그래서 우리가 그토록 조심하는 거에요.)

goatherd 염소지기 |stray 옆길로 새다 |flock (양·염소·새의) 떼 |whistle 휘파람을 불다 |straggler 낙오자
|pasture 초원 |eventide 저녁 |mingle 섞다 |herd (짐승의) 떼 |be obliged to 어쩔 수 없이 ~하다 |fold
양의 우리 |entice 유혹하다, 유혹하다 |thaw 해빙기 |scamper 날쌔게 움직이다 |ingratitude 은혜를 모름,
배은망덕 |cautious 조심스러운, 신중한

The Goatherd and the Wild Goats
염소지기와 야생 염소들

A GOATHERD, / driving his flock / from their pasture / at
한 염소지기가,   염소 떼를 몰고 돌아오다가   초원에서

eventide, / found some Wild Goats / mingled among them,
저녁에,   야생 염소 몇 마리를 발견하고   무리에 섞여 있던,

/ and shut them up together with his own / for the night.
자신의 염소 떼와 함께 가뒀다   그 날 밤 동안.

The next day / it snowed very hard, / so that he could not
다음 날   눈이 많이 내렸고,   그래서 염소지기는 염소 떼를 데려

take the herd / to their usual feeding places, / but was
가지 못했고   평소 풀을 뜯던 곳으로,

obliged to keep them / in the fold. He gave his own goats
가둬 놓을 수밖에 없었다   우리 속에.   그는 자신의 염소에게 주었고

/ just sufficient food / to keep them alive, / but fed the
겨우 충분한 먹이를   살아있기에,   반면 낯선 염소들에게는

strangers / more abundantly / in the hope of enticing them
먹였다   더 많은 먹이를   유인하려는 생각에

/ to stay with him / and of making them his own.
계속 남아있도록   그래서 자신의 것으로 삼으려고.

When the thaw set in, / he led them all out to feed, / and
날씨가 풀려서,   염소지기가 염소 떼를 먹이러 나가자,

the Wild Goats scampered away / as fast as they could /
야생 염소들은 날쌔게 달아나 버렸다   최대한 빨리

to the mountains. The Goatherd scolded them / for their
산으로.   염소지기는 염소를 꾸짖었다

ingratitude / in leaving him, / when during the storm / he
은혜도 모르고   자신을 떠나 버린 것에,   눈보라 속에서

had taken more care of them / than of his own herd.
더 잘 돌봐주었음에도   자신의 염소 떼보다.

One of them, / turning about, / said to him: / "That is the
염소 중 한 마리가,   돌아보며,   그에게 말했다:

very reason / why we are so cautious; / for if you yesterday
"바로 그래서죠   우리가 매우 조심하는 건: 왜냐하면 당신이 어제

/ treated us better / than the Goats you have had so long, /
우리를 더 잘 다뤘다면   오랫동안 길러왔던 염소보다,

it is plain also that / if others came after us, / you would in
그것은 분명히   우리 다음에 다른 염소가 왔을 때,

the same manner / prefer them to ourselves."
똑같은 방식으로   우리보다 그 염소들을 더 좋아할 테니까요."

Old friends cannot with impunity be sacrificed / for new
오랜 친구를 희생해서는 안 되는 법이다

ones.
새로운 친구를 위해.

The Goods and the Ills
선과 악

ALL the Goods were / once / driven out / by the Ills
모든 선(善)이   옛날에   내쫓겼다   악(惡)에 의해

/ from that common share / which they each had / in
공동의 몫으로부터   각자 차지하고 있던

the affairs of mankind; / for the Ills / by reason of their
인류의 역사 속에서;   왜냐하면 악은   그 수가 많다는 이유로

numbers / had prevailed to possess the earth.
           이 세계를 차지했기 때문이다.

The Goods wafted themselves to heaven / and asked for a
선은 하늘로 올라가

righteous vengeance / on their persecutors. They entreated
정당한 복수를 요구했다   박해자들에게.   그들은 제우스에게

Jupiter / that they might no longer / be associated with
청했다   자신들이 더 이상   악과 어울리지 않도록,

the Ills, / as they had nothing in common / and could not
그들은 공통점이 전혀 없고   같이 살 수도 없는데다,

live together, / but were engaged in unceasing warfare; /
끊임없는 전쟁을 하고 있기 때문에;

and that an indissoluble law might be laid down / for their
그러니 영원한 법이 제정되도록 해 달라고

future protection.
앞으로 자신들을 보호하기 위한.

Jupiter granted their request / and decreed / that
제우스는 그들의 요청을 받아들여   법령을 발표했다

henceforth / the Ills should visit the earth / in company
앞으로   악은 이 세상에 가야 한다고

with each other, / but that the Goods should / one by one
서로 함께,   하지만 선은   하나씩

/ enter the habitations of men.
   인간들의 마을에 들어가야 한다고.

Hence / it arises that Ills abound, / for they come not one
그리하여   악은 그 수가 많아지게 되었다.   왜냐하면 악은 하나씩 오지 않고,

by one, / but in troops, / and by no means singly: / while
         무리지어 와서,   결코 하나만 있지 않았기 때문에;

the Goods proceed from Jupiter, / and are given, / not
반면 선은 제우스로부터 나와,   받게 되었고,   모두

alike to all, / but singly, / and separately; / and one by
동등하지 않고,   단독으로,   따로따로;   그리하여 하나씩

one / to those who are able to discern them.
       선을 알아볼 수 있는 사람들에게 갔기에.

Key Expression 🔑

by no means 결코 ~이 아닌

by no means는 '결코 ~이 아닌', 즉 never와 같은 의미를 가진 숙어입니다.
not ~ by any means와 같이 풀어서 사용하기도 합니다.
비슷한 형태로 '결코 ~이 아닌'의 뜻을 가진 숙어로 in no sense, in no wise,
in no way 등도 있습니다.

ex) Hence it arises that Ills abound, for they come not one by one, but in troops,
and by no means singly.
그리하여 악은 그 수가 많아지게 되었다. 왜냐하면 악은 하나씩 오지 않고, 무리
지어 와서, 결코 하나만이 아니었기 때문이다.

---

manner 방식 | impunity 처벌을 받지 않음 | ill 악, 불행 | drive out 몰아내다 | affair 사건, 일 | mankind 인류
| waft 퍼지다 | righteous 당연한, 정당한 | vengeance 복수 | persecutors 박해자 | be associated with ~
와 관계 있다 | engage 사로잡다, 고용하다 | unceasing 끊임없는 | warfare 전투 | indissoluble 서로 떼어놓을
수 없는, 영원히 깨지지 않는 | protection 보호 | decreed 법령, 칙령 | in company with ~와 함께, 동시에 |
habitation 거주, 주거 | hence 이런 이유로 | arise 생기다, 발생하다 | abound 아주 많다, 풍부하다 | troop 군대,
무리 | singly 혼자, 하나씩 | alike 비슷한 | discern 알아차리다, 파악하다

The Grasshopper and the Owl
베짱이와 올빼미

AN OWL, / accustomed / to feed at night / and to sleep
올빼미 한 마리가,   익숙해진   밤에 먹이를 먹고

during the day, / was greatly disturbed / by the noise
낮에 잠을 자는데,   방해를 받았다

of a Grasshopper / and earnestly besought her / to stop
베짱이 소리에   그래서 간절하게 애원했다

chirping.
그만 좀 울라고.

The Grasshopper refused to desist, / and chirped louder
베짱이는 그만두기를 거절하며,   점점 더 크게 울었고

and louder / the more the Owl entreated. When she saw
            올빼미는 더 간절히 애원했다.   알게 되자

/ that she could get no redress / and that her words were
아무 보상도 얻지 못하고   자신의 말이 무시당했음을,

despised, / the Owl attacked the chatterer / by a stratagem.
            올빼미는 수다쟁이를 공격했다   꾀를 내서.

"Since I cannot sleep," / she said, / "on account of your
"잠을 잘 수 없어서,"   올빼미가 말했다,   "네 노래 소리 때문에,

song / which, believe me, / is sweet as the lyre of Apollo,
정말로,   아폴로의 리라 소리처럼 아름다운.

/ I shall indulge myself in drinking some nectar / which
넥타를 실컷 마셔야겠구나

Pallas lately gave me. / if you do not dislike it, / come to
최근에 팔라스께서 주신.   너도 마시고 싶으면,   내게 와서

me / and we will drink it together."
    같이 마셔보자."

The Grasshopper, / who was thirsty, / and pleased / with
베짱이는,   목이 말랐고,   기뻐서

the praise of her voice, / eagerly flew up. The Owl came
자신의 목소리를 칭찬받자,   흔쾌히 날아올랐다.

forth from her hollow, / seized her, / and put her to death.
그러자 올빼미가 굴에서 나와,   베짱이를 잡아,   죽여 버렸다.

The Hares and the Foxes
토끼와 여우

THE HARES waged war / with the Eagles, / and called
토끼들이 전쟁을 벌이다가　　　독수리들과,

upon the Foxes / to help them. They replied, / "We would
여우를 불러　　　도와달라고 했다.　여우들이 대답했다,

willingly have helped you, / if we had not known / who
"기꺼이 너희들을 도왔을텐데,　　　만약 우리가 몰랐다면

you were, / and with whom you were fighting."
너희가 누구인지,　그리고 누구랑 싸우는지."

Count the cost / before you commit yourselves.
비용을 계산해 보라　　행동하기 전에.

The Hare and the Hound
토끼와 사냥개

A HOUND started a Hare / from his lair, / but after a
사냥개가 쫓기 시작했다　　　굴 속에서 나온 토끼를,　하지만 오래 달린 후,

long run, / gave up the chase. A goat-herd seeing him
주격을 포기했다.　　염소떼가 이를 보고,

stop, / mocked him, / saying / "The little one is the best
　　사냥개를 조롱하며,　말했다　"저 작은 토끼가 더 잘 달리는구나

runner / of the two." The Hound replied, / "You do not
달리기　둘 중에."　　사냥개가 대답했다,

see the difference between us: / I was only running / for
"우리 둘의 차이점을 모르는군요:　　난 달리고 있었을 뿐이지만　저녁

a dinner, / but he for his life."
거리를 위해,　하지만 토끼는 살기 위해서였지요."

---

owl 올빼미, 부엉이 | disturb 방해하다 | chirp 짹짹거리다, 찍찍거리다 | desist 그만두다 | redress 보상 |
despise 경멸하다 | chatterer 수다쟁이 | lyre 리라(고대 현악기) | Apollo 아폴로(고대 그리스·로마 신화의
태양신으로 시·음악·예언 등을 주관하는 신) | nectar 과일즙, 신들이 마시는 음료로 불리는 넥타 | Pallas 팔라스
(아테나 여신을 일컫는 말) | wage 전쟁을 벌이다 | willingly 기꺼이 | cost 비용 | lair (야생 동물의) 집, 굴 |
goat-herd 염소떼 | mock 놀리다, 조롱하다

101

The Hares and the Frogs
토끼와 개구리

THE HARES, / oppressed by their own exceeding
토끼들이,　　지나치게 겁이 많은 나머지

timidity / and weary of the perpetual alarm / to which
　　　　끊임없이 경계하는데 지쳐서

they were exposed, / with one accord determined / to
자신들이 노출되는 것에,　　의견을 모아 결정했다

put an end to themselves and their troubles / by jumping
자신들의 목숨과 고생을 끝내기로

from a lofty precipice / into a deep lake below.
높은 벼랑에서 뛰어내려　　깊은 호수 밑으로 들어가서.

As they scampered off / in large numbers / to carry out
토끼들이 달려가고 있을 때　　무리를 지어　　자신들의 결심을 실행

their resolve, / the Frogs lying on the banks of the lake /
에 옮기기 위해,　　호숫가에 누워 있던 개구리들이

heard the noise of their feet / and rushed helter-skelter /
토끼들의 발자국 소리를 듣고　　미끄럼틀로 돌진하여

to the deep water / for safety.
깊은 물 속으로 들어갔다　　안전을 위해.

On seeing the rapid disappearance of the Frogs, / one
개구리들이 빠르게 사라지는 것을 보고,

of the Hares cried out / to his companions: / "Stay, / my
토끼 한 마리가 소리쳤다　　동료들에게,　　"멈춰,

friends, / do not do as you intended; / for you now see /
친구들아,　　계획은 그만두자:　　왜냐하면 너희들도 지금 봤잖아

that there are creatures / who are still more timid than
그곳에는 이미 동물들이 있어　　우리보다 겁이 훨씬 많은."

ourselves."

---

oppress 억압하다 | exceeding 엄청난, 굉장한 | timidity 겁 많음 | perpetual 끊임없이 계속되는, 빈번한 |
accord 부여하다, 일치하다 | precipice 벼랑 | scamper 날째게 움직이다 | resolve 결심 | rush 돌진하다 |
helter-skelter 나선형 미끄럼틀 | disappearance 사라짐, 소멸 | tortoise 거북 | ridicule 비웃다, 조롱하다 |
pace 속도 | assertion 주장 | appointed 정해진, 약속된 | steady 꾸준한 | wayside 길가 | asleep 잠이 든 |
doze 깜빡 잠이 들다, 졸다 | fatigue 피로

The Hare and the Tortoise
토끼와 거북이

A HARE / one day / ridiculed / the short feet and
토끼 한 마리가   어느 날   비웃었다   짧은 다리와 느린 걸음을

slow pace / of the Tortoise, / who replied, / laughing: /
           거북이의,   그러자 거북이가 대답했다, 웃으며:

"Though you be swift as the wind, / I will beat you / in
"네가 바람처럼 빠르다고 해도,   내가 널 이길 거야

a race." The Hare, / believing her assertion to be simply
경주에서는." 토끼는,   거북이의 주장이 말도 안 된다고 생각하여,

impossible, / assented to the proposal; / and they agreed /
              제안을 받아들였다;   그리고 그들은 동의했다

that the Fox should choose the course / and fix the goal.
여우가 경주 코스를 고르고   결승점을 정하도록.

On the day appointed for the race / the two started
경기가 열리기로 한 날   두 동물은 함께 출발했다.

together. The Tortoise never for a moment stopped, / but
           거북이는 잠시도 쉬지 않고,

went on / with a slow but steady pace / straight to the end
계속 갔다   느리지만 꾸준하게   곧장 결승점을 향해.

of the course.

The Hare, / lying down by the wayside, / fell fast asleep.
토끼는,   길가에 누워 있다가,   잠들어 버렸다.

At last / waking up, / and moving as fast as he could,
마침내   잠에서 깨어나,   최대한 빨리 움직였으나,

/ he saw / the Tortoise had reached the goal, / and was
   토끼는 보고 말았다 거북이가 결승점에 도착하여,

comfortably dozing / after her fatigue.
완전히 잠들어 버린 것을   피곤에 지쳐.

Slow but steady wins the race.
느리지만 꾸준한 사람이 경주에서 이기는 법이다.

The Herdsman and the Lost Bull
목동과 길 잃은 황소

A HERDSMAN / tending his flock / in a forest / lost
한 목동이,   소떼를 돌보고 있던   숲 속에서   수송아지를

a Bull-calf / from the fold. After a long and fruitless
잃어버렸다   무리에서.   오랫동안 성과 없는 수색 끝에,

search, / he made a vow that, / if he could only discover /
양치기는 맹세했다,   만약 찾기만 하면

the thief who had stolen the Calf, / he would offer a lamb
송아지를 훔쳐간 도둑을,   양을 제물로 바치겠다고

in sacrifice / to Hermes, Pan, / and the Guardian Deities
헤르메스와 판에게,   그리고 숲 속의 수호신들에게.

of the forest. Not long afterwards, / as he ascended a
잠시 후,   목동은 작은 언덕을 올라갔다가,

small hillock, / he saw / at its foot / a Lion feeding on the
보았다   언덕 밑에서   사자가 송아지를 잡아먹고 있는

Calf.
것을.

Terrified at the sight, / he lifted his eyes and his hands
그 광경에 겁이 나서,   목동은 두 눈과 손을 하늘로 치켜 들고,

to heaven, / and said: / "Just now / I vowed to offer a
외쳤다: "방금 전   양을 바치겠다고 맹세했습니다

lamb / to the Guardian Deities of the forest / if I could
숲의 수호신들께   알 수만 있다면

only find out / who had robbed me; / but now that I have
누가 훔쳐갔는지;   하지만 도둑을 찾았으니,

discovered the thief, / I would willingly add a full-grown
기꺼이 황소 한 마리도 바치겠습니다

Bull / to the Calf I have lost, / if I may only secure my
잃어버린 송아지와,   빠져나갈 수 있게만 해 주신다면

own escape / from him / in safety."
도둑으로부터   안전하게."

herdsman 목동, 양치기 | tend 돌보다 | bull-calf 수송아지 | fruitless 성과 없는 | vow 맹세, 서약 | Hermes
헤르메스(그리스 신화에서 신들의 사자(使者)이자 과학·웅변·상업 등의 신, 로마 신화의 머큐리에 해당) | Pan 판
(그리스 신화에서 목동의 신으로 헤르메스의 아들) | Guardian 수호자 | Deities 신 | hillock 작은 언덕 |
terrified 무서워하는, 겁이 난 | now that ~이므로, ~이기 때문에 | hawk 매 | pigeon 비둘기 | appearance
출현, 등장 | cote 가축 우리 | havoc 대파괴, 큰 혼란 | slew 휙 돌다 | remedy 해결책, 치료 | disease 질병

The Hawk, the Kite, and the Pigeons
매, 솔개, 그리고 비둘기

THE PIGEONS, / terrified by the appearance of a Kite,
비둘기들은,   솔개가 나타나자 놀라서,

/ called upon the Hawk / to defend them. He at once
매에게 부탁했다   보호해 달라고.   매는 즉시 승낙했다.

consented. When they had admitted him / into the cote, /
비둘기들이 매를 받아들였을 때   우리 안에,

they found / that he made more havoc / and slew a larger
알게 되었다   매는 훨씬 심각한 피해를 일으키며   더 많은 비둘기들을 채어 가

number of them / in one day / than the Kite could pounce
버린 것을   하루만에   솔개가 공격할 수 있는 것보다

upon / in a whole year.
         1년 동안.

Avoid a remedy that is worse than the disease.
병보다 더 심각한 치료약은 피해야 한다.

The Hen and the Golden Eggs
암탉과 금달걀

A COTTAGER and his wife had a Hen / that laid a
시골에 사는 한 부부에게 암탉 한 마리가 있었다

golden egg / every day. They supposed / that the Hen
금달걀을 낳는 매일. 부부는 상상했고 암탉은 틀림없이 엄청난

must contain a great lump of gold / in its inside, / and /
금 덩어리를 가지고 있을 거라고 몸 속에, 그래서

in order to get the gold / they killed it. Having done so, /
그 금을 가지기 위해 암탉을 죽여 버렸다. 암탉이 죽은 후,

they found to their surprise / that the Hen differed in no
부부는 깜짝 놀랐다 그 암탉은 다른 점이 전혀 없었기 때문에

respect / from their other hens.
다른 암탉들과.

The foolish pair, / thus hoping to become rich / all at
멍청한 부부는, 이렇게 부자가 되려다가

once, / deprived themselves / of the gain of which they
단번에, 빼앗겨 버렸다 확실히 얻을 수 있는 것을

were assured / day by day.
매일 매일.

Hercules and the Wagoner
헤라클레스와 마부

A CARTER was driving a wagon / along a country
마부가 마차를 몰고 있었다 시골길을 따라,

lane, / when the wheels sank down deep / into a rut.
그때 바퀴가 깊게 빠져 버렸다 바퀴 자국에.

The rustic driver, / stupefied and aghast, / stood looking
시골 마부는, 깜짝 놀라고 겁에 질려, 마차를 바라보며 선 채,

at the wagon, / and did nothing / but utter loud cries to
아무것도 하지 못하고 큰 소리로 헤라클레스를 부를 뿐이었다

Hercules / to come and help him.
와서 도와 달라고.

hen 암탉 ǀcottgear 시골 오두막에 사는 사람 ǀlump 덩어리 ǀdiffer 다르다 ǀdeprive 빼앗다 ǀassure
장담하다 ǀHercules 헤라클레스 (그리스 신화에서 제우스신의 아들로 힘센 영웅) ǀwagoner 마부 ǀcarter
짐마차꾼, 마부 ǀlane 길 ǀsink 가라앉다, 빠지다 ǀrut 바퀴 자국 ǀrustic 시골의 ǀstupefy 깜짝 놀라게 하다,
멍하게 만들다 ǀaghast 경악한, 겁에 질린 ǀutter 발언하다, 말하다

Hercules, / it is said, / appeared / and thus addressed him:
헤라클레스가, 말한 대로, 나타나서 마부에게 이렇게 말했다:

/ "Put your shoulders to the wheels, / my man. Goad on
"어깨로 바퀴를 받치게나, 이보게.

your bullocks, / and never more pray to me for help, / until
송아지를 몰아대게, 내게 도움을 청하지 말게나,

you have done your best / to help yourself, / or depend
최선을 다했을 때까지는 스스로, 그렇지 않으면 의지하게

upon it / you will henceforth pray in vain."
될 것이네 이후에도 죽 헛된 기도에."

Self-help is the best help.
스스로 돕는 것이 최선인 법이다.

The Horse and the Stag
말과 수사슴

AT ONE TIME / the Horse had the plain / entirely to
옛날에는 말이 평원을 소유하고 있었다 전부 혼자서.

himself. Then a Stag intruded into his domain / and shared
그러다가 수사슴이 말의 구역에 침입하여

his pasture.
초원을 공유했다.

The Horse, / desiring to revenge himself / on the stranger, /
말은, 복수를 꿈꾸며 침입자에게,

asked a man / if he were willing to help him / in punishing
한 남자에게 물었다 자신을 도와줄 수 있는지 수사슴을 혼내는데,

the Stag. The man replied that / if the Horse would receive
남자는 대답했다 만약 말이 받아들이고

/ a bit in his mouth / and agree to carry him, / he would
입에 재갈을 물리는 것을 데려가는데 동의한다면,

contrive effective weapons / against the Stag. The Horse
효과적인 무기를 주겠다고 수사슴에 대항할.

consented / and allowed the man to mount him.
말은 동의했고 남자가 재갈을 물리도록 허락했다.

---

goad 못살게 굴다, 들들 볶다 | bullock 거세한 수송아지 | stag 수사슴 | at one time 동시에, 일찍이 | plain
평원 | intrude 침범하다 | bit 재갈 | effective 효과적인 | weapon 무기 | mount 올라가다

From that hour / he found / that instead of obtaining
그때부터   말은 알았다   복수하는 대신

revenge / on the Stag, / he had enslaved himself / to the
          수사슴에게,   노예가 되었다

service of man.
사람에게 봉사하기 위한.

The Huntsman and the Fisherman
사냥꾼과 낚시꾼

A HUNTSMAN, / returning with his dogs / from the field,
한 사냥꾼이,   개를 끌고 돌아오는 길에   들판으로부터,

/ fell in by chance / with a Fisherman / who was bringing
우연히 마주쳤다   낚시꾼과   집으로 가져오던

home / a basket well laden with fish. The Huntsman
물고기로 가득 찬 바구니를.   사냥꾼은 물고기가 탐이 났고,

wished to have the fish, / and their owner experienced an
                        물고기 주인은 마찬가지로 원했다

equal longing / for the contents of the game-bag.
              사냥 가방 안에 든 것을.

They quickly agreed to exchange / the produce of their
그들은 즉시 바꾸기로 합의했다   자신들의 그날 수확물을.

day's sport. Each was so well pleased / with his bargain
두 사람은 각자 매우 기뻐했고   자신들의 거래에

/ that they made for some time / the same exchange / day
그래서 얼마동안   같은 식의 거래를 했다

after day.
매일 매일.

Finally / a neighbor said to them, / "If you go on in
이윽고   한 이웃이 그들에게 말했다,   "이런 식으로 계속한다면,

this way, / you will soon destroy / by frequent use / the
          당신들은 곧 망치게 될 거요   자주 해서

pleasure of your exchange, / and each will again wish to
거래의 기쁨을,   그리고 각자가 다시금 원하게 될 것이요

retain / the fruits of his own sport."
       자신의 수확물을."

Abstain and enjoy.
즐기는 데에는 절제가 필요하다.

The Hunter and the Woodman
사냥꾼과 나무꾼

A HUNTER, / not very bold, / was searching for the
한 사냥꾼이, 그다지 용기가 없는, 사자의 흔적을 찾고 있었다.

tracks of a Lion. He asked / a man felling oaks / in the
그는 물었다 떡갈나무를 베고 있는 사람에게

forest / if he had seen any marks of his footsteps / or
숲 속에서 사자의 발자국을 본 적이 있는지

knew where his lair was. "I will," / said the man, / "at
혹은 사자 굴의 위치를 아는지. "내가," 그 사람이 말했다,

once / show you the Lion himself."
"즉시 당신에게 사자를 보여 주겠소."

The Hunter, / turning very pale / and chattering with his
사냥꾼은, 매우 창백해지고 이빨을 덜덜 떨면서

teeth / from fear, / replied, / "No, / thank you. I did not
공포로, 대답했다, "아니, 괜찮아요. 그것을 부탁한 게

ask that; / it is his track only / I am in search of, / not the
아니오; 사자의 흔적 뿐이라오 내가 찾고 있는 것은,

Lion himself."
사자 자체가 아니라."

The hero is brave / in deeds as well as words.
영웅은 용감하다 말뿐만 아니라 행동에서도.

Key Expression

A as well as B : B 뿐만 아니라 A도

A as well as B는 'B 뿐만 아니라 A도'라는 의미의 구문입니다. 뒤부터 해석
하여 뒤에 동사가 따라올 경우 동사의 수는 A에 일치시켜야 한다는 점에 유의
하세요.
비슷한 의미의 구문으로 not only A but also B가 있는데 이는 'A 뿐만 아니
라 B도'의 뜻이므로 A와 B의 위치가 반대가 됩니다.

ex) The hero is brave in deeds as well as words.
영웅은 말뿐만 아니라 행동에서도 용감하다.

---

enslave 노예로 만들다 | huntsman 사냥꾼 | fisherman 낚시꾼 | laden 잔뜩 실은 | experience 겪다,
경험하다 | longing 갈망 | exchange 교환하다 | produce 생산품, 수확물 | bargain 흥정, 거래 | frequent
잦은, 빈번한 | retain 유지하다 | fruit 산물 | abstain 삼가다 | track 자취 | fell 넘어뜨리다 | footstep 발자국 |
lair (들짐승의) 굴, 은신처 | pale 창백한

The Jackdaw and the Doves
갈까마귀와 비둘기

A JACKDAW, / seeing some Doves / in a cote
갈까마귀 한 마리가,   비둘기들을 보고

abundantly provided with food, / painted himself white
음식으로 가득 찬 둥지 속에 있는,   자신의 몸을 하얗게 칠하고

/ and joined them / in order to share their plentiful
비둘기 속으로 들어갔다   풍부한 먹이를 나눠 먹기 위해.

maintenance.

The Doves, / as long as he was silent, / supposed him to
비둘기들은,   갈까마귀가 입을 다물고 있는 동안에는,   자신들의 일행이라 여겨

be one of themselves / and admitted him to their cote.
둥지로 받아들였다.

But when one day / he forgot himself / and began to
하지만 어느 날   갈까마귀가 무심코   울음 소리를 내기 시작하자,

chatter, / they discovered his true character / and drove
비둘기들은 그 정체를 알아차리고   쫓아냈다,

him forth, / pecking him with their beaks. Failing to
부리로 쪼면서.   먹이를 얻는데 실패하자

obtain food / among the Doves, / he returned to the
비둘기 사이에서,   갈까마귀는 자신의 무리로 돌아갔다.

Jackdaws.

They too, / not recognizing him / on account of his color,
까마귀들 또한,   갈까마귀를 알아보지 못했고   색깔 때문에,

/ expelled him from living with them. So desiring two
자신들과 함께 살지 못하도록 쫓아 버렸다.   그렇게 두 가지 목적을 바라

ends, / he obtained neither.
다가   갈까마귀는 아무것도 얻지 못하고 말았다.

dove 비둘기 | painted 색칠한, 꾸며진 | plentiful 풍부한 | maintenance 유지 | peck 쪼다 | recognize 알아보다 | expel 쫓아내다, 추방하다

The Jackdaw and the Fox
갈까마귀와 여우

A HALF-FAMISHED JACKDAW seated himself / on a
반쯤 굶주린 갈까마귀가 앉아 있었다

fig-tree, / which had produced some fruit / entirely out
무화과 나무에, 그 나무는 열매를 맺은 적이 있었고   철이 지나서도,

of season, / and waited / in the hope / that the figs would
그래서 기다렸다   희망으로   열매가 익을 거라는.

ripen.

A Fox / seeing him sitting so long / and learning the
여우는   갈까마귀가 오랫동안 앉아 있는 것을 보다가

reason of his doing so, / said to him, / "You are indeed,
그렇게 하고 있는 이유를 알아차리고,   말했다,   "넌 정말로,

/ sir, / sadly deceiving yourself; / you are indulging a
이봐,   바보같기는;   희망에 빠져 버렸구나

hope / strong enough to cheat you, / but which will never
네 자신을 속일 정도로 강렬한,

reward you with enjoyment."
하지만 기쁨의 보상을 절대 받지 못할 거야."

Jupiter, Neptune, Minerva, and Momus
제우스, 포세이돈, 아테나, 그리고 모무스

ACCORDING to an ancient legend, / the first man was
고대 전설에 따르면,   최초의 인간은 제우스가

made by Jupiter, / the first bull by Neptune, / and the first
만들었고,   최초의 황소는 포세이돈이,

house by Minerva.
그리고 최초의 집은 아테나가 만들었다.

On the completion of their labors, / a dispute arose / as to
신들의 작업이 끝나자,   논쟁이 벌어졌다

which had made the most perfect work. They agreed to /
무엇이 가장 완벽한 작품인지에 대해.   그들은 합의했다

appoint Momus as judge, / and to abide by his decision.
모무스를 심판으로 삼아,   그의 결정을 따르기로.

Momus, / however, / being very envious of the handicraft
모무스는, 하지만, 각각의 작품을 매우 시기하며,

of each, / found fault with all.
모두에 대해 트집을 잡았다.

He first blamed the work of Neptune / because he had not
모무스는 먼저 포세이돈의 작품을 비난했다 황소의 뿔을 만들지 않았다고

made the horns of the bull / below his eyes, / so he might
눈 아래, 더 잘 볼 수 있도록

better see / where to strike. He then condemned the work
어디를 들이받아야 하는지. 그리고 나서 제우스의 작품을 비판했다,

of Jupiter, / because he had not placed the heart of man
사람의 심장을 놓지 않았다고

/ on the outside, / that everyone might read the thoughts
몸 바깥 쪽에, 모든 사람이 사악한 생각을 읽고

of the evil / disposed and take precautions / against the
미리 조심할 수 있도록

intended mischief.
고의적인 나쁜 짓에 대해.

And, / lastly, / he inveighed against Minerva / because
그리고, 마지막으로, 아테나에게 독설을 퍼부었다

she had not contrived iron wheels / in the foundation of
쇠로 된 바퀴를 사용하지 않았다고 집의 기초를 지을 때,

her house, / so its inhabitants might more easily remove
그 안에 사는 사람들이 더 쉽게 이동할 수 있도록

/ if a neighbor proved unpleasant. Jupiter, / indignant at
이웃이 마음에 들지 않을 경우. 제우스는,

such inveterate faultfinding, / drove him from his office of
이러한 상습적인 헐뜯기에 분노하여, 모무스를 심판의 자리에서 끌어내리고

judge, / and expelled him / from the mansions of Olympus.
추방했다 올림푸스 신전에서.

fig-tree 무화과나무 | ripen 익다 | deceive 속이다 | cheat 속이다 | Neptune 넵튠 (로마 신화에서 바다의
신으로 그리스 신화의 포세이돈에 해당) | Minerva 미네르바 (로마 신화에서 지혜와 용맹의 여신으로 그리스 신화의
아테나 여신에 해당) | Momus 모무스 (그리스 신화의 조롱·비난의 신) | according to ~에 따르면 | legend 전설
| completion 완성 | appoint 임명하다 | abide by 지키다 | envious 부러워하는 | handicraft 수공예품 |
fault 잘못 | condemn 비난하다 | dispose 배치하다 | take precautions against ~에 조심하다, ~의 대비책을
강구하다 | mischief 나쁜 짓 | inveigh 통렬히 비난하다, 독설을 퍼붓다 | iron 철, 쇠 | foundation 토대, 기초 |
inhabitant 주민, 거주자 | prove 증명하다 | indignant 분개한 | inveterate 상습적인 | faultfinding 흠잡기를
일삼는 | office 직무 | mansion 대저택

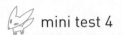
A. 다음 문장을 해석해 보세요.

(1) I shall no longer distress myself / at being struck at / by these Gamecocks, / when I see / that they cannot even refrain from quarreling / with each other.
→

(2) He gave his own goats / just sufficient food / to keep them alive, / but fed the strangers / more abundantly / in the hope of enticing them / to stay with him / and of making them his own.
→

(3) Now that I have discovered the thief, / I would willingly add a full-grown Bull / to the Calf I have lost, / if I may only secure my own escape / from him / in safety.
→

(4) He first blamed the work of Neptune / because he had not made the horns of the bull / below his eyes, / so he might better see / where to strike.
→

B. 다음 주어진 문장이 되도록 빈칸에 써 넣으세요.

(1) 그것이 바로 우리가 그토록 조심하는 이유예요.

That is the very reason _____.

(2) 네가 바람처럼 빠르다고 해도, 경주에서는 내가 널 이길 거야.

_____, I will beat you in a race.

(3) 스스로 돕는 것이 최선이다.

→

(4) 내가 찾고 있는 것은 사자가 아니라, 사자의 흔적 뿐이에요.

_____, not the Lion himself.

A. (1) 더 이상은 이 수탉들에게 공격받는다고 괴로워하지 않겠어, 수탉들은 서로 싸움을 그만둘 수 없다는 것을 알았으니까, (2) 그는 자신의 염소에게 겨우 살아있기에 충분한 먹이를 주었지만, 반면 낯선 염소들에게는 계속 남아있도록 유인하여 자신의 것으로 삼으려는 생각에 더 많은 먹이를 먹였다. (3) 도둑을 찾았으

C. 다음 주어진 문구가 알맞은 문장이 되도록 순서를 맞춰 보세요.

(1) 나는 네가 조금도 무섭지 않고, 넌 나보다 힘이 세지도 않아.
   (than / are / nor / you / I / stronger / am)

   I do not in the least fear you,
   _____ .

(2) 어떤 사람들은 <u>자신의 눈으로 보는 것보다</u> 주위 사람들의 눈에 보이는 것을 <u>더
   중요시한다</u>.
   (own / in / consequence / their / more / of / eyes)

   Some men are _____
   _____ than in the eyes of their neighbors.

(3) 까마귀들 또한, 색깔 때문에 갈까마귀를 알아보지 못했고, 쫓아 버렸다.
   (of / him / his color / account / recognizing / on / not)

   They too, _____ ,
   expelled him from living with them.

(4) 신들의 작업이 끝나자, <u>무엇이 가장 완벽한 작품인지에 대해</u> 논쟁이 벌어졌다.
   (work / to / which / had / the / as / made / most / perfect)

   On the completion of their labors, a dispute arose _____
   _____ .

D. 의미가 비슷한 것끼리 서로 연결해 보세요.

(1) refrain   ▶   ◀ ① without
(2) devoid of   ▶   ◀ ② inveigh
(3) vengeance   ▶   ◀ ③ abstain
(4) condemn   ▶   ◀ ④ revenge

Answer

니, 잃어버린 송아지와 도둑으로부터 안전하게 빠져나갈 수 있게만 해 주신다면 기꺼이 황소 한 마리도
바치겠다. (4) 모무스는 먼저 어디를 공격할지 더 잘 볼 수 있도록 황소의 뿔을 눈 아래 만들지 않았다며
포세이돈의 작품을 비난했다. | B. (1) why we are so cautious (2) Though you be swift as the wind
(3) Self-help is the best help. (4) It is his track only I am in search of | C. (1) nor are you stronger
than I am (2) of more consequence in their own eyes (3) not recognizing him on account of his
color (4) as to which had made the most perfect work | D. (1) ③ (2) ① (3) ④ (4) ②

115

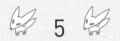

5

The Kid and the Wolf
아이와 늑대

A KID / standing on the roof of a house, / out of harm's
아이가   지붕 위에 서 있던,   위험을 피해,

way, / saw a Wolf passing by / and immediately / began
       늑대가 지나가는 것을 보고   즉시

to taunt and revile him. The Wolf, / looking up, / said, /
비웃으며 욕하기 시작했다.   늑대는,   위를 쳐다보고,   말했다,

"Sirrah! I hear thee: / yet / it is not thou / who mockest me,
"이봐!   네 목소리가 들려: 하지만 네가 아니라   날 조롱한 것은,

/ but the roof / on which thou art standing."
     지붕이란다   네가 서 있는."

Time and place often give the advantage / to the weak /
시간과 장소가 종종 이점이 되곤 한다   약한 생물에게

over the strong.
강한 생물보다.

The King's Son and the Painted Lion
왕의 아들과 색칠한 사자

A KING, / whose only son was fond of martial exercises, /
어느 왕이,   무술 연습을 좋아하는 외아들이 있는,

had a dream / in which he was warned / that his son would
꿈을 꾸었는데   꿈 속에서 경고를 들었다   아들이 살해될 것이라고

be killed / by a lion. Afraid the dream should prove true,
           사자에게.   꿈이 실현될까봐 두려워서,

/ he built / for his son / a pleasant palace / and adorned
     왕은 만들었고 아들을 위해   즐거운 궁전을   벽을 장식했는데

its walls / for his amusement / with all kinds of life-sized
즐거움을 위해   다양한 종류의 실제 크기의 동물들로,

animals, / among which was the picture of a lion.
그 중에는 사자 그림도 있었다.

When the young Prince saw this, / his grief at being
왕자가 이것을 보자,   이렇게 갇힌 것에 대한 슬픔이

thus confined / burst out afresh, / and, / standing near
다시금 북받쳐 올라왔고,   그래서,   사자 가까이 서서,

the lion, / he said: / "O you most detestable of animals!
말했다: "오 정말 혐오스러운 동물이구나!

Through a lying dream of my father's, / which he saw in
아버지의 거짓말같은 꿈으로 인해,   꿈에서 널 봤기 때문에,

his sleep, / I am shut up / on your account / in this palace
난 갇혀 있는 거야   너 때문에   이 성 안에

/ as if I had been a girl: / what shall I now do to you?"
여자 아이처럼: 이제 난 네게 뭘 해야 할까?"

With these words / he stretched out his hands / toward
이 말을 하면서   그는 손을 뻗었다

a thorn-tree, / meaning to cut a stick from its branches
가시나무 쪽으로,   나뭇가지를 꺾으려는 생각에

/ so that he might beat the lion. / but one of the tree's
사자를 때리려고,

prickles pierced his finger / and caused great pain and
하지만 나무의 가시가 그의 손가락을 찔러서   큰 아픔과 함께 염증이 생겼다,

inflammation, / so that the young Prince fell down / in a
그래서 왕자는 쓰러졌다

fainting fit. A violent fever suddenly set in, / from which
정신이 혼미해져.   갑자기 심한 열병이 생겼고,   죽고 말았다

he died / not many days later.
며칠 지나지 않아.

We had better bear our troubles bravely / than try to
문제는 용감하게 극복하는 것이 낫다

escape them.
피하려고 하기 보다.

out of harm's way 피해를 입지 않도록, 안전한 곳으로 | taunt 놀리다, 비웃다 | revile 매도하다, 욕하다 | sirrah
야, 이봐, 이놈아 (손아랫사람이나 아이들을 부르는 말) | thee 목적격 you의 고어형 | mock 놀리다, 흉내내다(est
는 고어 2인칭 thou와 함께 쓰이는 동사(2인칭·단수·현재 및 과거)의 어미) | be fond of ~을 좋아하다 | martial
싸움의, 전쟁의 | adorn 꾸미다, 장식하다 | confine 국한시키다, 가두다 | afresh 새로, 다시 | detestable
혐오스러운 | thorn-tree 가시나무 | prickle 가시, 바늘 | pierce 찌르다 | inflammation 염증

The Kingdom of the Lion
사자의 왕국

THE BEASTS of the field and forest / had a Lion as their
들판과 숲의 짐승들이 　　　　　　　　　사자를 왕으로 섬기고 있었다.

king. He was neither wrathful, cruel, / nor tyrannical, /
사자는 화내거나 잔인하지 않았고, 　　　　폭군도 아니었으며,

but just and gentle / as a king could be.
공정하고 관대하기만 했다 　어떤 왕도 못지 않게.

During his reign / he made a royal proclamation / for
통치 기간 중에 　　사자는 포고령을 내렸다

a general assembly / of all the birds and beasts, / and
대회의를 소집하는 　　　모든 조류와 동물들의,

drew up conditions / for a universal league, / in which
그리고 조건을 작성했다 　전체 동맹을 위한,

the Wolf and the Lamb, / the Panther and the Kid, / the
늑대와 양, 　　　　　　　表범과 새끼 염소,

Tiger and the Stag, / the Dog and the Hare, / should live
호랑이와 수사슴, 　　　개와 산토끼가, 　　　　　함께 살아야 한다고

together / in perfect peace and amity.
완전한 평화와 우정 속에서.

The Hare said, / "Oh, / how I have longed to see / this
산토끼가 말했다, 　　"오, 　　얼마나 보기를 원했던가 　　이런 날을,

day, / in which the weak shall take their place / with
약자들이 자리를 차지하게 될

impunity / by the side of the strong." And after the Hare
무사히 　　강자들 옆에서." 　　　　그리고 산토끼는 이렇게 말한 후,

said this, / he ran for his life.
목숨을 부지하게 위해 도망쳤다.

---

wrathful 격노한, 분노한 | tyrannical 폭군적인 | just 공정한 | gentle 너그러운, 관대한 | reign 통치 (기간) |
proclamation 포고령, 선언 | draw up 작성하다 | league 동맹 | panther 표범 | kid 새끼 염소 | amity 우호,
우정 | with impunity 무사히, 해를 입지 않고 | privilege 특권 | neigh 말의 울음 소리 | enchanted 매료된 |
mourn 슬퍼하다, 애도하다 | invoke 기원하다, (신에게) 호소하다 | prolong 연장시키다 | outrage 화나게 하다
filch 훔치다 | altar 제단 | sacrifice 제물 | prosperity 번영, 번창 | adversity 역경

The Kites and the Swans
솔개와 백조

TEE KITES of olden times, / as well as the Swans, / had
옛날 옛적 솔개는,   백조와 마찬가지로,

the privilege of song. But having heard the neigh of the
노래하는 특권을 갖고 있었다.   하지만 말의 울음 소리를 듣고,

horse, / they were so enchanted / with the sound, / that
           무척 매료되어   그 소리에,

they tried to imitate it; / and, / in trying to neigh, / they
흉내 내려고 했다;   그리고,   그 소리를 내려고 애쓰다가,   잊어버리

forgot / how to sing.
고 말았다   노래하는 법을.

The desire for imaginary benefits / often involves / the
상상 속의 이익을 바라는 일은   종종 포함하곤 한다

loss of present blessings.
현재의 축복의 상실을.

The Sick Kite
병든 솔개

A KITE, / sick unto death, / said to his mother: / "O
솔개 한 마리가,   병으로 죽어가던,   엄마에게 말했다:

Mother! Do not mourn, / but at once / invoke the gods /
"오 어머니!   슬퍼하지 마시고,   당장   신에게 기원해 주세요

that my life may be prolonged." She replied, / "Alas! My
제 삶이 연장될 수 있도록."   어미 솔개가 대답했다, "저런!

son, / which of the gods / do you think / will pity you?
아들아,   어떤 신이   네 생각에는   널 동정하겠느냐?

Is there one / whom you have not outraged / by filching
있을까   네가 화나게 하지 않은 신이

from their very altars / a part of the sacrifice / offered up
신들의 제단에서 훔쳐 버려서   제물을

to them?"
그들에게 바쳐진?"

We must make friends / in prosperity / if we would have
친구가 되어야 한다   부유할 때   도움을 바란다면

their help / in adversity.
           역경의 시기에.   119

The Laborer and the Snake
노동자와 뱀

A SNAKE, / having made his hole / close to the porch
뱀 한 마리가,   굴을 판   오두막 현관 가까이에,

of a cottage, / inflicted a mortal bite / on the Cottager's
오두막 주인의 어린 아들을.   물어 죽여 버렸다

infant son. Grieving over his loss, / the Father resolved
아들을 잃고 슬퍼하며,

to kill the Snake.
아버지는 뱀을 죽이기로 결심했다.

The next day, / when it came out of its hole / for food,
다음 날,   뱀이 굴에서 나오자   먹이를 찾으러,

/ he took up his axe, / but by swinging too hastily, /
그는 도끼를 집어들었지만,   너무 성급하게 휘두른 나머지,

missed its head / and cut off only the end of its tail.
뱀의 머리를 치지 못하고   꼬리만 자르고 말았다.

After some time / the Cottager, / afraid that the Snake
얼마 후,   오두막 주인은,   뱀이 자신도 물까 봐 두려워하며,

would bite him also, / endeavored to make peace, / and
화해하고자 노력하여,

placed some bread and salt / in the hole. The Snake, /
빵과 소금을 놓았다   굴 안에.   뱀은,

slightly hissing, / said: / "There can henceforth be no
작게 쉬익 소리를 내며,   말했다: "앞으로 평화는 있을 수 없죠

peace / between us; / for whenever I see you / I shall
우리 사이에는: 왜냐하면 난 당신을 볼 때마다

remember the loss of my tail, / and whenever you see me
꼬리를 잃은 일을 기억할 것이고,   당신은 날 볼 때마다

/ you will be thinking of the death of your son."
아들의 죽음을 떠올릴 테니까요."

No one truly forgets injuries / in the presence of him /
누구도 상처를 진짜로 잊지 못한다   당사자의 앞에서

who caused the injury.
상처를 입힌.

---

laborer 노동자 | porch 현관 | hastily 급히, 성급하게 | make peace 화해하다 | hiss 쉬익 하는 소리를 내다
henceforth 이후로 (쭉)

The Lark and Her Young Ones
종달새와 새끼들

A LARK had made her nest / in the early spring / on the
종달새 한 마리가 둥지를 지었다   이른 봄에

young green wheat. The brood had almost grown / to
푸른 밀밭에.   새끼들은 거의 자라서

their full strength / and attained the use of their wings /
어른 새로   날개를 사용할 줄도 알았고

and the full plumage of their feathers, / when the owner
깃털도 다 자라게 되었다,   그때 밀밭 주인은,

of the field, / looking over his ripe crop, / said, / "The
          다 익은 작물을 살펴보면서,   말했다,

time has come / when I must ask all my neighbors / to
"때가 되었구나   이웃들에게 부탁해야 할

help me with my harvest."
수확을 도와달라고."

One of the young Larks / heard his speech / and related
새끼 종달새 한 마리가   그의 말을 듣고   어미새에게 말했다,

it to his mother, / inquiring of her / to what place they
          물어보면서   어느 곳으로 옮겨야 하는지

should move / for safety.
          안전하려면.

Key Expression ❣

no longer ~ : 더 이상 ~아닌, ~하지 않는

no longer는 '더 이상 ~아닌, ~하지 않는'이라는 의미를 가진 표현으로 not ~
any longer로 풀어 쓸 수 있습니다.
no longer는 비슷한 의미를 가진 no more와 비교해서 알아두어야 합니다.
no more는 더 이상의 양, 혹은 동작을 다시 재개할 것인지의 여부에 초점을 맞
춘 반면, no longer의 경우는 상태를 지속할 것인지가 초점이 됩니다. 즉, 뒤따
르는 동사가 동작을 강조한 동사인가, 상태를 강조한 동사인가에 따라 쓰임이 달
라집니다.

ex) He no longer trusts his friends, but will reap the field himself.
     그는 더 이상 친구들을 믿지 않고, 직접 추수하려 한다.
    I will no more complain, nor wish myself dead.
     나는 더 이상 불평하지도, 죽기를 바라지도 않을 거야.

"There is no occasion to move / yet, / my son," / she
"옮길 때가 아니란다   아직은, 아들아,"   어미새가

replied; / "the man / who only sends to his friends / to
대답했다;   "저 사람은   그저 친구들에게 전하는

help him with his harvest / is not really in earnest."
수확을 도와달라고   정말 진심이 아니란다."

The owner of the field / came again / a few days later /
밀밭 주인은   다시 와서   며칠 후에

and saw the wheat shedding the grain / from excess of
밀이 낱알을 떨어뜨리는 것을 봤다   너무 익어서.

ripeness. He said, / "I will come myself tomorrow / with
                그가 말했다,   "내일 직접 와야지

my laborers, / and with as many reapers as I can hire, /
일꾼들을 데리고,   가능한 한 많은 수확 일꾼을 고용하여,

and will get in the harvest."
그리고 수확을 해야겠구나."

The Lark / on hearing these words / said to her brood, /
종달새는   이 말을 듣자   새끼들에게 말했다,

"It is time now / to be off, / my little ones, / for the man
"이제 시간이 되었구나   떠나야 할,   아가들아,   왜냐하면 그 사람이

is in earnest / this time; / he no longer trusts his friends, /
진지하니까   이번에는;   그는 더 이상 친구들을 믿지 않고,

but will reap the field himself."
직접 추수하려 하니."

Self-help is the best help.
스스로 돕는 것이 최선이다.

---

lark 종달새 | brood 한 배의 새끼 | plumage (집합적) 깃털 | harvest 수확 | relate 이야기 하다, 말하다 |
earnest 진지한, 진심 어린 | shed (피부, 껍질 등을) 떨어뜨리다 | grain 낱알, 알곡 | ripeness 익음 | reaper
수확하는 사람 | reap 수확하다, 거두다

The Lark Burying Her Father
아버지를 묻은 종달새

THE LARK / (according to an ancient legend) / was
종달새는　　　(고대 전설에 따르면)　　　　　　　　　　창조되었다고

created / before the earth itself, / and when her father
한다　　　　육지가 생기기도 전에,　　　　　그래서 아버지가 죽었을 때,

died, / as there was no earth, / she could find no place / of
죽자,　　육지가 없어서,　　　　　종달새는 장소를 찾을 수 없었다

burial for him. She let him lie uninterred / for five days, /
아버지를 묻을.　　종달새는 아버지를 묻지 않은 채 두었다　닷새 동안,

and on the sixth day, / not knowing what else to do, / she
그리고 6일째 되는 날,　　　　달리 어떻게 할지 몰라서,

buried him / in her own head.
아버지를 묻었다　자신의 머리 속에.

Hence she obtained her crest, / which is popularly said / to
그래서 종달새는 볏을 얻었고,　　　　그 볏은 널리 알려졌다

be her father's grave-hillock.
아버지의 무덤이라고.

Youth's first duty is reverence to parents.
젊은이의 첫번째 의무는 부모 공경이다.

The Sick Lion
병든 사자

A LION, / unable from old age and infirmities / to provide
사자 한 마리가,　늙고 병들어서　　　　　　　　스스로 먹이를

himself with food / by force, / resolved to do so / by
구할 수 없게 되자　힘으로,　　　하기로 결심했다

artifice. He returned to his den, / and lying down there,
계략을 써서. 사자는 굴로 돌아와,　　　　그곳에 누워,

/ pretended to be sick, / taking care / that his sickness
아픈 척 했다,　　　　처리하며　　　자신의 병이 널리 알려지도록.

should be publicly known.

The beasts expressed their sorrow, / and came / one by
짐승들은 슬픔을 표현하며,   왔다   한 마리씩

one / to his den, / where the Lion devoured them.
사자굴로,   그곳에서 사자는 짐승들을 잡아먹었다.

After many of the beasts had thus disappeared, / the
이렇게 많은 짐승들이 사라진 후,

Fox discovered the trick / and presenting himself to the
여우는 속임수를 발견하여   사자에게 모습을 드러내고는,

Lion, / stood on the outside of the cave, / at a respectful
굴 밖에 서서,   거리를 둔 채,

distance, / and asked him / how he was.
                사자에게 물었다   건강이 어떤지.

"I am very middling," / replied the Lion, / "but why do
"그저 그래,"   사자가 대답했다,

you stand without? Pray enter within / to talk with me."
"하지만 넌 왜 밖에 서 있느냐? 안으로 들어와서   나와 이야기를 나누자."

"No, / thank you," / said the Fox. "I notice / that there are
"아니요, 괜찮아요."   여우가 대답했다.   "발견했거든요

many prints of feet / entering your cave, / but I see no
많은 발자국이 있는 것을   굴로 들어가는,   하지만 흔적을 찾을 수

trace / of any returning."
없네요.   굴에서 나오는."

He is wise / who is warned / by the misfortunes of
현명한 사람이다   경계할 줄 아는 이가   다른 사람의 불행을 보고.

others.

burial 매장 | uninterred 매장되지 않은 | crest (새의) 볏, 관모 | popularly 널리, 일반에게 | reverence 존경,
공손 | infirmity 병약 | artifice 책략, 계략 | den (야생 동물이 사는) 굴 | respectful 경의를 표하는, 공손한 |
middling 보통의

The Lioness
암사자

A CONTROVERSY prevailed / among the beasts of the
논쟁이 벌어졌다   들판의 동물들 사이에서

field / as to which of the animals / deserved the most
         어느 동물이   인정받아야 하는지에 대해

credit / for producing the greatest number of whelps / at
        가장 많은 수의 새끼를 낳는 것으로   한 번

a birth. They rushed clamorously / into the presence of
낳을 때마다. 그들은 시끄럽게 떠들며 달려가서   암사자가 있는 곳으로

the Lioness / and demanded of her / the settlement of the
                    요구했다   이 논쟁을 해결해 달라고.

dispute.

"And you," / they said, / "how many sons have you /
"그런데 당신은,"   동물들이 말했다,   "얼마나 많은 새끼를 낳나요

at a birth?" The Lioness laughed at them, / and said:
한 번에?"   암사자는 그들을 비웃으며,   말했다:

/ "Why! I have only one; / but that one is altogether a
   "어머나!   나는 한 마리만 낳지: 하지만 그 한 마리는 정말 좋은 혈통의 사자야."

thoroughbred Lion."

The value is in the worth, / not in the number.
가치라는 것은 가치 그 자체에 있는 것이지,   수에 있는 것이 아니다.

The Lion and the Bull
사자와 황소

A LION, / greatly desiring to capture a Bull, / and yet
사자 한 마리가,   간절히 황소를 잡고 싶어 하지만,

afraid to attack him / on account of his great size, /
공격하기 두려워하는   황소의 거대한 크기 때문에,

resorted to a trick / to ensure his destruction.
계략을 사용했다   황소를 확실히 잡기 위한.

---

lioness 암사자 | clamorously 소란스럽게 | dispute 분쟁, 논쟁 | thoroughbred 혈통이 좋은, 좋은 가문의 |
ensure 보장하다, 확실히 하다 | destruction 파괴, 파멸

He approached the Bull / and said, / "I have slain a fine
사자는 황소에게 다가가서   말했다,   "내가 좋은 양 한 마리를 죽였네,

sheep, / my friend; / and if you will come home / and
친구여;   그러니 자네가 우리집에 와서

partake of him with me, / I shall be delighted / to have
나와 함께 먹는다면,   기쁘겠네

your company." The Lion said this / in the hope that, /
동행이 되어 준다면."   사자는 이렇게 말했다   바라면서,

as the Bull was in the act of reclining to eat, / he might
황소가 편히 식사하는 동안,

attack him to advantage, / and make his meal on him.
유리하게 공격할 수 있기를,   그래서 황소를 식사로 삼게 되기를.

The Bull, / on approaching the Lion's den, / saw the huge
황소는,   사자굴로 다가가다가

spits and giant caldrons, / and no sign whatever of the
커다란 꼬챙이와 큰 솥을 보았으나,   양의 흔적은 전혀 보이지 않았다,

sheep, / and, / without saying a word, / quietly took his
그래서,   아무 말 없이,   조용히 떠났다.

departure.

The Lion inquired / why he went off so abruptly /
사자는 물었다   황소가 왜 그렇게 갑자기 떠났는지

without a word of salutation / to his host, / who had not
인사 한 마디 없이   주인에게,   아무것도 주지 않은

given him / any cause for offense.
          기분을 상하게 할 만한 이유를.

"I have reasons enough," / said the Bull. "I see no
"내게는 충분한 이유가 있지,"   황소가 말했다.   "나는 아무 흔적도

indication / whatever of your having slaughtered a sheep,
보지 못했네   자네가 양을 잡았다는,

/ while I do see very plainly / every preparation / for
하지만 아주 분명하게 보았어   모든 준비를

your dining on a bull."
자네가 황소를 먹으려 하는."

slay 죽이다 | partake 먹다 | recline 눕다, 쉬다 | spit 꼬챙이 | caldron 가마솥 | abruptly 갑자기 | salutation
인사 | indication 표시, 암시 | slaughter 도살하다 | plainly 분명하게 | dine on ~을 먹다

The Lion and the Three Bulls
사자와 세 마리의 황소들

THREE BULLS / for a long time / pastured together. A
세 마리의 황소들이   오랫동안   함께 풀을 뜯고 있었다.

Lion lay in ambush / in the hope / of making them his
사자 한 마리가 숨어 있었다   바라면서   황소를 먹이로 삼기,

prey, / but was afraid / to attack them / while they kept
하지만 두려워했다   공격하기를   황소들이 함께 있는 동안.

together.

Having at last / by guileful speeches succeeded / in
마침내   교묘하게 속이는 말로   성공하자

separating them, / he attacked them / without fear / as
그들을 떼어 놓는데 성공하자, 사자는 황소들을 공격해   두려움 없이   황소가

they fed alone, / and feasted on them / one by one / at his
홀로 먹이를 먹고 있을 때, 잡아먹었다   한 마리씩 차례로

own leisure.
편하게.

Union is strength.
뭉치는 게 힘이다.

Key Expression

인식의 전치사 as

recognize A as B는 'A를 B라고 인식하다, 인정하다'의 의미를 가진 숙어
입니다.
이처럼 인식의 의미를 가진 다음의 동사 위에 전치사 as가 함께 쓰입니다.

recognize ㄱ
regard ㅓ
think of ㅓ
consider ㅓ A as B : A를 B로 간주하다[생각하다]
see ㅓ
view ㅓ
refer to ㄴ

ex) He recognized the Shepherd as the man who healed him.
그는 양치기가 자신을 도운 사람임을 알아보았다.

---

ambush 잠복, 매복 | guileful 교묘하게 속이는, 음흉한 | leisure 한가한 때 | roam 돌아다니다, 어슬렁거리다 |
suppliant 애원하는, 간청하는 | lap 무릎 | accusation 혐의, 비난 | condemned 비난 받은, 유죄 선고를 받은 |
cast (~에게) 표를 던지다 | impute 씌우다, ~의 탓으로 하다 | heal 치료하다 | pardon 사면하다, 용서하다

The Lion and the Shepherd
사자와 양치기

A LION, / roaming through a forest, / trod upon a thorn.
사자 한 마리가,   숲 속을 어슬렁거리다가,   가시를 밟았다.

Soon afterward / he came up to a Shepherd / and fawned
잠시 후   사자는 양치기에게 다가가서

upon him, / wagging his tail / as if to say, / "I am a
아양을 떨었다.   꼬리를 흔들며   마치 말하듯이,

suppliant, / and seek your aid."
"부탁합니다,   당신의 도움을 원해요"라고.

The Shepherd boldly examined the beast, / discovered
양치기는 대담하게 사자를 지켜보다가,   가시를 발견하고,

the thorn, / and placing his paw upon his lap, / pulled it
              사자의 발을 자신의 무릎에 놓고,   가시를 빼냈다:

out; / thus relieved of his pain, / the Lion returned / into
      이렇게 사자의 고통을 덜어 주었고,   사자는 돌아갔다

the forest.
숲 속으로.

Sometime after, / the Shepherd, / being imprisoned /
얼마 후에,   양치기는,   감옥에 갇혀

on a false accusation, / was condemned / "to be cast to
누명을 쓰고,   형을 선고 받았다   "사자에게 던져지는"

the Lions" / as the punishment / for his imputed crime.
              처벌로써   뒤집어 쓴 죄에 대한.

But / when the Lion was released / from his cage, / he
하지만   사자는 풀려나게 되자   우리에서,

recognized the Shepherd / as the man who healed him, /
양치기를 알아보았고   자신을 도운 사람이란 것을,

and instead of attacking him, / approached / and placed
그를 공격하는 대신   다가가서

his foot upon his lap.
그의 무릎에 발을 올려 놓았다.

The King, / as soon as he heard the tale, / ordered
왕은,   그 이야기를 듣자마자,

the Lion to be set free again / in the forest, / and the
사자를 다시 풀어 주라고 명령했고   숲 속에,

Shepherd to be pardoned / and restored to his friends.
양치기는 사면되어   친구들에게 돌아갔다.

The Lion And The Mouse
사자와 생쥐

A LION was awakened from sleep / by a Mouse /
사자가 잠에서 깨어났다   생쥐 때문에

running over his face. Rising up angrily, / he caught him
얼굴 위에서 뛰어다니던.   화를 내며 일어나서,   사자는 생쥐를 잡아

/ and was about to kill him, / when the Mouse piteously
죽이려 했다,   그때 생쥐는 애처롭게 간청하며,

entreated, / saying: / "If you would only spare my life, / I
말했다: "당신이 제 목숨을 살려 주신다면,

would be sure to repay / your kindness."
반드시 보답하겠습니다   당신의 친절에."

The Lion laughed / and let him go. It happened shortly
사자는 웃으면서   생쥐를 놓아 주었다.   이런 일이 일어나고 얼마 후에

after this / that the Lion was caught / by some hunters,
사자는 잡히게 되었다   사냥꾼들에게,

/ who bound him / by strong ropes / to the ground. The
사냥꾼은 사자를 묶었다   튼튼한 밧줄로   땅바닥에.

Mouse, / recognizing his roar, / came / and gnawed the
생쥐는,   사자의 울음 소리를 알아채고,   다가와서   밧줄을 끊어

rope / with his teeth, / and set him free, / exclaiming: /
이빨로,   사자를 풀어 주며,   소리쳤다:

"You ridiculed the idea / of my ever being able to help
"당신은 비웃었고   내가 도와줄 수 있으리라고,

you, / not expecting to receive / from me / any repayment
기대하지 않았지요   내게   당신의 호의에 보답하리

of your favor; / now you know / that it is possible / for
라고;   이제 아시겠죠   가능하다는 것을

even a Mouse / to confer benefits on a Lion."
생쥐라도   사자에게 은혜를 베푸는 것이."

---

piteously 애처롭게, 불쌍하게 | repay 보답하다 | roar 울부짖음, 포효 | ridicule 비웃다 | repayment 보답 |
favor 은혜, 친절 | confer 주다

The Lion, Jupiter, and the Elephant
사자, 제우스, 그리고 코끼리

THE LION wearied Jupiter / with his frequent
사자는 제우스를 피곤하게 했다   잦은 불평을 하며.

complaints. "It is true, / O Jupiter!" / he said, / "that
"사실입니다,   오 제우스여!"   사자는 말했다.

I am gigantic in strength, / handsome in shape, / and
"제가 힘이 세고,   모습이 멋있으며,

powerful in attack. I have jaws / well provided with
공격할 때 힘이 있다는 것이.   제게는 턱이 있고   이빨이 잘 나있는,

teeth, / and feet furnished with claws, / and I lord it over
발톱이 난 발이 있으며,   큰 소리를 칩니다

/ all the beasts of the forest, / and what a disgrace it is, /
숲 속의 모든 동물들에게,   그런데 참으로 수치스러운 일입니다,

that being such as I am, / I should be frightened / by the
그런 존재이면서도,   놀란다는 것이

crowing of a cock."
수탉 울음 소리에."

Jupiter replied, / "Why do you blame me / without a
제우스가 대답했다.   "넌 왜 나를 비난하느냐   아무 이유 없이?

cause? I have given you / all the attributes / which I
난 네게 주었다   모든 특성을

possess myself, / and your courage never fails you /
내 자신이 갖고 있던,   그리고 네 용기는 널 실망시키지 않았잖느냐

except in this one instance."
이 한 가지를 제외하고는."

On hearing this / the Lion groaned / and lamented very
이 말을 듣고　　　　　사자는 신음하며　　　　　매우 슬퍼했다

much / and, / reproaching himself / with his cowardice,
　　　그리고,　자신을 자책하면서　　　소심함으로,

/ wished that he might die. As these thoughts passed
죽고 싶었다.　　　　　　　이런 생각을 하고 있다가,

through his mind, / he met an Elephant / and came close
　　　　　　　　사자는 코끼리를 만났고　　　가까이 다가갔다

/ to hold a conversation with him. / After a time / he
말을 걸려고.　　　　　　　　　　　　잠시 후　　　　사자는

observed / that the Elephant shook his ears / very often, /
알게 되었고　코끼리가 귀를 흔들고 있음을　　　몹시 자주,

and he inquired / what was the matter / and why his ears
물었다　　　　무슨 일이 있는지　　　그리고 왜 귀를 움직이는지

moved / with such a tremor / every now and then.
　　그렇게 떨면서　　　가끔씩.

Just at that moment / a Gnat settled / on the head of the
바로 그때　　　각다귀 한 마리가 앉았고, 코끼리 머리 위에,

Elephant, / and he replied, / "Do you see / that little
　　코끼리가 대답했다,　　　"보이나　　　저 작고 윙윙거리는

buzzing insect? If it enters my ear, / my fate is sealed. I
벌레가?　　　그것이 내 귓속에 들어오면,　내 운명은 끝이야.

should die presently."
난 곧 죽게 되지."

The Lion said, / "Well, / since so huge a beast is afraid
사자가 말했다,　　"저런,　저렇게 거대한 동물이 무서워 하다니

/ of a tiny gnat, / I will no more complain, / nor wish
　작은 각다귀를,　난 더 이상 불평하지도,　　죽기를 바라지도

myself dead. I find myself, / even as I am, / better off /
않을 거야.　알았으니까,　나같은 존재라도,　더 낫다는 것을

than the Elephant."
코끼리보다."

---

weary 피곤하게 만들다 | gigantic 굉장히 큰 | jaw 턱 | lord it over ~에게 잘난 체 하다, 큰소리 치다 |
crowing 수탉의 울음 | attribute 속성, 특성 | lament 슬퍼하다 | cowardice 소심함, 비겁함 | tremor 떨림
seal 확정 짓다, 다짐하다 presently 곧, 즉시 | better off 더 부자인, 형편이 더 나은

The Lion, the Wolf, and the Fox
사자, 늑대, 그리고 여우

A LION, / growing old, / lay sick / in his cave. All
사자 한 마리가,   나이가 들어,   병들어 누웠다   굴 속에.

the beasts came to visit their king, / except the Fox.
모든 동물들이 왕을 방문했다,   여우만 제외하고.

The Wolf therefore, / thinking / that he had a capital
그래서 늑대는,   생각하면서   좋은 기회를 잡았다고,

opportunity, / accused the Fox to the Lion / of not paying
               사자에게 여우를 비난했다

any respect to him / who had the rule over them all / and
존경심을 표시하지 않고   모든 동물을 지배하는 자에게

of not coming to visit him.
찾아오지 않은 것에 대해.

At that very moment / the Fox came in / and heard these
바로 그 순간   여우가 들어왔고   늑대의 마지막 말을 들었다.

last words of the Wolf. The Lion roaring out / in a rage /
                         사자가 으르렁거리자   화를 내며

against him, / the Fox sought an opportunity / to defend
여우에게,   여우는 기회를 찾으려 하며   자신을 변호할

himself / and said, / "And who of all those who have
말했다,   "그런데 당신에게 왔던 동물들 중 누가

come to you / have benefited you / so much as I, / who
이득이 되었나요   저만큼,

have traveled / from place to place in every direction,
전 돌아다녔고   사방으로 이리저리,

/ and have sought and learnt / from the physicians / the
그리고 찾았고 알아냈으니까요   의사로부터

means of healing you?"
당신을 치료할 수 있는 방법을?"

The Lion commanded him / immediately / to tell him the
사자가 여우에게 명령했다   즉시   그 치료법을 말하라고,

cure, / when he replied, / "You must flay a wolf alive /
그러자 여우가 대답했다.   "당신은 늑대의 가죽을 산 채로 벗겨

and wrap his skin yet warm / around you."
아직 따뜻한 그 가죽으로 감싸야 합니다   당신의 몸을."

The Wolf was / at once / taken and flayed; / whereon the
늘대는   즉시   붙잡혀서 가죽이 벗겨졌다;   그러자 여우는,

Fox, / turning to him, / said / with a smile, / "You should
늘대에게 돌아서며,   말했다   웃으면서,

have moved your master / not to ill, / but to good, will."
"넌 주인을 감동시켰어야 했어   나쁜 의도가 아닌, 좋은 의도로."

The Lion, the Bear, and the Fox
사자, 곰, 그리고 여우

A LION and a Bear seized a Kid / at the same moment,
사자와 곰이 새끼 염소를 잡았다   동시에,

/ and fought fiercely / for its possession. When they had
그리고 맹렬하게 싸웠다   그 소유권을 놓고.

fearfully lacerated each other / and were faint / from the
그들은 서로에게 심한 상처를 입히고   지치자

long combat, / they lay down / exhausted with fatigue.
오랜 싸움으로,   드러누워 버렸다   피로에 지쳐.

A Fox, / who had gone round them / at a distance / several
여우 한 마리가, 그들 주위를 맴돌던   멀리서

times, / saw them both stretched / on the ground / with the
한참 동안, 그들 둘 다 뻗어 버린 것을 봤다   땅 위에

Kid lying untouched / in the middle. He ran in between
새끼 염소를 건드리지 않고 둔 채   가운데.   여우는 그들 사이로 달려들어가,

them, / and seizing the Kid / scampered off / as fast as he
새끼 염소를 잡아   도망쳐 버렸다

could.
최대한 빨리.

The Lion and the Bear saw him, / but not being able to get
사자와 곰은 여우를 봤지만,   일어나지 못하고,

up, / said, / "Woe be to us, / that we should have fought
말했다,   "우리가 어리석었어,   서로 싸우고 욕하다가

and belabored ourselves / only to serve the turn of a Fox."
결국 여우에게 기회를 주었으니."

capital 주요한, 멋진 | accuse 비난하다 | have the rule over ~을 지배하다 | defend 변호하다 | physician 의사, 내과
의사 | cure 치료법 | flay ~의 껍질을 벗기다 | whereon 무엇의 위에(=on what), 그 위에(=on which) | fearfully 몹시,
굉장히 | lacerate 찢다, 상처 입히다 | combat 싸움 | at a distance 멀리서 | belabor 욕하다, 공격하다 | turn 차례, 기회

135

It sometimes happens / that one man has all the toil, /
이따금 일어나곤 한다　　　　한 사람이 모든 고생을 하고,

and another all the profit.
다른 사람이 모든 이익을 차지하는 경우가.

The Lion, the Mouse, and the Fox
사자, 생쥐, 그리고 여우

A LION, / fatigued by the heat of a summer's day, / fell
사자 한 마리가,　여름날 더위에 지쳐서,

fast asleep / in his den. A Mouse ran over / his mane
잠들어 버렸다　굴 속에서.　생쥐 한 마리가 뛰어 다니다가　사자의 갈기와 귓가에서

and ears / and woke him from his slumbers. He rose up /
사자를 잠에서 깨우고 말았다.　사자는 일어나

and shook himself / in great wrath, / and searched every
몸을 흔들었고　몹시 화를 내며,　굴의 구석구석을 수색했다

corner of his den / to find the Mouse.
생쥐를 찾으려고.

A Fox seeing him said: / "A fine Lion you are, / to be
여우가 사자를 보고 말했다:　"당신같은 훌륭한 사자가,

frightened of a Mouse."
생쥐에 놀라다니."

"It's not the Mouse / I fear," / said the Lion; / "I resent /
"생쥐가 아니야　내가 두려워 하는 건," 사자가 말했다;　"화내는 거야

his familiarity and ill-breeding."
생쥐의 무례함과 버릇없음에."

Little liberties are great offenses.
약간의 방종이 큰 화를 부르는 법이다.

toil 고역, 고생 |mane (사자의) 갈기 |slumber 잠|resent ~에 대하여 화내다, 분개하다 |familiarity 무례함,
뻔뻔함 |ill-breeding 버릇없음 |liberty 자유 |enter into 시작하다, (논의를) 맺다 |secure 확보하다 |booty
노획품, 약탈품 |allot 할당하다 |due 적절한, 마땅한 |portion 몫, 할당 |treaty 협정 |modestly 겸손하게 |
division 분할 |accumulate 쌓다, 축적하다 |morsel 한 조각, 소량 |fraction 분할, 비율

The Lion, the Fox, and the Ass
사자, 여우, 그리고 당나귀

THE LION, the Fox and the Ass / entered into an
사자와 여우 그리고 당나귀가 / 협정을 맺었다

agreement / to assist each other / in the chase. Having
서로 돕자는 / 추적할 때.

secured a large booty, / the Lion on their return from the
커다란 노획물을 확보하자, / 사자는 숲에서 돌아오는 길에

forest / asked the Ass / to allot his due portion / to each
/ 당나귀에게 요청했다 / 적절한 몫을 나누라고

of the three partners / in the treaty.
세 명의 파트너 각자에게 / 조약을 맺은.

The Ass carefully divided the spoil / into three equal
당나귀는 조심스럽게 노획물을 나눴다 / 세 몫으로 똑같이

shares / and modestly requested the two others / to make
/ 그리고 겸손하게 다른 둘에게 요청했다

the first choice. The Lion, / bursting out into a great rage,
먼저 선택하라고. / 사자는, / 갑자기 크게 화를 내며,

/ devoured the Ass. Then he requested the Fox / to do
당나귀를 먹어 치웠다. / 그리고 나서 여우에게 요청했다

him the favor / to make a division.
부탁을 들어달라고 / 몫을 나눠 달라는.

The Fox accumulated / all that they had killed / into one
여우는 한데 모아서 / 자신들이 죽인 모든 것을

large heap / and left to himself / the smallest possible
하나의 큰 더미로 / 자신에게 남겼다 / 가장 작은 몫을.

morsel. The Lion said, / "who has taught you, / my very
사자가 말했다, / "누가 네게 가르쳤느냐,

excellent fellow, / the art of division? You are perfect to
완벽한 친구여, / 나누는 기술을? / 넌 몫을 완벽하게 나눴구나."

a fraction." He replied, / "I learned it from the Ass, / by
여우가 대답했다, / "당나귀에게서 배웠지요,

witnessing his fate."
그의 운명을 목격하고서."

Happy is the man / who learns from the misfortunes of
행복은 사람에게 찾아온다 / 다른 사람의 불행을 통해 깨달음을 얻은.

others.

The Lion in Love
사랑에 빠진 사자

A LION demanded the daughter of a woodcutter / in
사자가 나무꾼의 딸에게 요청했다

marriage. The Father, / unwilling to grant, / and yet
결혼해 달라고.   아버지는,   허락하고 싶지 않아서,

afraid to refuse his request, / hit upon this expedient
하지만 그 요구를 거절하기 두려워,   이런 방법을 생각해 냈다

/ to rid himself of his importunities. He expressed his
사자의 끈질긴 요청을 없앨.   그는 기꺼이 승낙하겠다고 말했고

willingness / to accept the Lion / as the suitor of his
사자를 받아들이겠다고   딸의 구혼자로

daughter / on one condition: / that he should allow him
한 가지 조건을 걸고: 사자가 나무꾼에게 허락해 줄 것을

/ to extract his teeth, / and cut off his claws, / as his
이를 빼고,   발톱을 자르도록,

daughter was fearfully afraid of both.
딸이 둘 다 무서워하기 때문에.

The Lion cheerfully assented / to the proposal. But when
사자는 기꺼이 동의했다   그 제안에.

the toothless, clawless Lion / returned to repeat his
하지만 이빨도, 발톱도 없는 사자가   자신의 요구를 되풀이 하려고 돌아왔을 때,

request, / the Woodman, / no longer afraid, / set upon
나무꾼은,   더 이상 무서워 하지 않고,

him with his club, / and drove him away / into the forest.
곤봉으로 공격해서,   쫓아버렸다   숲으로.

The Old Lion
늙은 사자

A LION, / worn out with years / and powerless from
사자 한 마리가,   나이가 들어 쇠약해지고   병으로 힘이 없어진,

disease, / lay on the ground / at the point of death. A
땅에 누워 있었다   죽어가면서.

Boar rushed upon him, / and avenged / with a stroke of
수돼지 한 마리가 사자에게 달려와,   복수했다   상아로 들이받으며

his tusks / a long-remembered injury.
오랫동안 기억해 온 상처에 대해.

Shortly afterwards / the Bull with his horns gored him
곧 이어   황소가 뿔로 사자를 들이받았다

/ as if he were an enemy. When the Ass saw / that the
마치 사자가 적인 것처럼.   당나귀가 알고서

huge beast could be assailed / with impunity, / he let
거대한 동물이 공격받고 있다는 것을   아무 보복도 없이,

drive at his forehead / with his heels.
사자의 이마를 공격했다   뒷발로.

The expiring Lion said, / "I have reluctantly brooked /
죽어가는 사자가 말했다,   "난 어쩔 수 없이 참았다

the insults of the brave, / but to be compelled to endure
용감한 동물들이 준 모욕은,   하지만 참아야 한다는 것은

/ such treatment from thee, / a disgrace to Nature, / is
너같은 녀석에게 그런 취급을 받는 것을,   자연의 수치이며,

indeed / to die a double death."
사실   두 번 죽은 것이나 마찬가지구나."

grant 허락하다 | hit upon ~생각해 내다 | expedient 방편, 처방 | importunity 집요함, (복수) 집요한 요구 | suitor[남자] 구혼자 | extract 뽑다, 빼내다 | assent to ~에 찬성하다 | set upon ~을 공격하다 | club 곤봉 | drive away 쫓아내다 | wear out (낡아서) 떨어지다, 지치게 하다 | with years 나이가 들어, 늙어서 | at the point of ~하려는 순간에 | boar 거세하지 않은 수퇘지 | rush upon 덤벼들다, 돌격하다 | avenge 복수하다 | tusk (코끼리의) 엄니, 상아 | gore 뿔로 받다 | assail 공격하다, 괴롭히다 | drive at ~을 겨누다 | heel 뒷다리, 발굽 | reluctantly 마지 못해, 억지로 | brook 참다 | insult 모욕 | be compelled to 강제로 ~하다, 할 수 없이 ~하다 | endure 참다

mini test 5

A. 다음 문장을 해석해 보세요.

(1) A lion, / greatly desiring to capture a Bull, / and yet afraid to attack him / on account of his great size, / resorted to a trick / to ensure his destruction.
→

(2) I see no indication / whatever of your having slaughtered a sheep.
→

(3) Sometime after, / the Shepherd, / being imprisoned / on a false accusation, / was condemned / "to be cast / to the Lions" / as the punishment / for his imputed crime.
→

(4) He expressed his willingness / to accept the Lion / as the suitor of his daughter / on one condition.
→

B. 다음 주어진 문장이 되도록 빈칸에 써 넣으세요.

(1) 그는 양치기가 자신을 도운 사람임을 알아보았다.

He recognized _____.

(2) 스스로 돕는 것이 최선이다.

→

(3) 그녀는 닷새 동안 아버지를 묻지 않은 채 내버려 두었다.

→

(4) 당신은 나쁜 의도가 아닌, 좋은 의도로, 주인을 감동시켰어야 했어요.

→

A. (1) 사자 한 마리가 간절히 황소를 잡고 싶어 하지만, 거대한 크기 때문에 공격하기 두려워하다가, 황소를 확실히 잡기 위한 계략을 사용했다. (2) 자네가 양을 잡았다는 아무 흔적도 보지 못했네. (3) 얼마 후, 양치기는 누명을 쓰고 감옥에 갇혀 유죄 선고를 받았고 그의 죄에 대해 "사자에게 던져지는" 처벌을 받았다. (4) 그는

C. 다음 주어진 문구가 알맞은 문장이 되도록 순서를 맞춰 보세요.

(1) 난 더 이상 불평하지도, 죽기를 바라지도 않을 거야.
(complain, / dead / wish / no / I will / myself / nor / more)

→

(2) 아버지는 그의 끈질긴 요청을 없애버릴 이런 방법을 생각해 냈다.
(his importunities / this expedient / hit / to / The Father /
upon / himself / of / rid)

→

(3) 얼마나 이런 날을 보기 원했던가.
(longed / I / this day / to / have / How / see)

→

(4) 저렇게 거대한 동물이 작은 각다귀를 무서워 하니까, 나는 더 이상 불평하지 않
을 거야.
(so / afraid / Since / gnat / beast / is / of / a / a / tiny / huge)

_____, I will

no more complain.

D. 다음 단어에 대한 맞는 설명과 연결해 보세요.

(1) taunt   ►   ◄ ① cuts something badly and
                                   deeply

(2) wrathful   ►   ◄ ② say unkind or insulting things

(3) amity   ►   ◄ ③ friendly relations between
                                   people or countries

(4) lacerate   ►   ◄ ④ raging or furious

한 가지 조건을 걸고 딸의 구혼자로 사자를 받아들이기를 기꺼이 승낙하겠다고 말했다. | B. (1) the
Shepherd as the man who healed him (2) Self-help is the best help. (3) She let him lie uninterred
for five days. (4) You should have moved your master not to ill, but to good, will. | C. (1) I will no
more complain, nor wish myself dead. (2) The Father hit upon this expedient to rid himself of his
importunities. (3) How I have longed to see this day. (4) Since so huge a beast is afraid of a tiny
gnat | D. (1) ② (2) ④ (3) ③ (4) ①

141

6

The Man and His Two Sweethearts
한 남자와 사랑하는 두 여자

A MIDDLE-AGED MAN, / whose hair had begun to
한 중년 남자가,   머리가 희어지기 시작한,

turn gray, / courted two women / at the same time. One
            두 여자에게 구애했다   동시에.

of them was young, / and the other well advanced in
한 명은 젊은 여자였고,   다른 한 명은 나이든 여자였다.

years.

The elder woman, / ashamed to be courted / by a man
나이든 여자는,   구애받는 것이 부끄러워서

younger than herself, / made a point, / whenever her
자신보다 어린 남자에게,   하곤 했다,   구혼자가 찾아올 때마다,

admirer visited her, / to pull out some portion of his
              검은 머리를 뽑는 일을.

black hairs. The younger, / on the contrary, / not wishing
               젊은 여자는,   반대로,

to become / the wife of an old man, / was equally zealous
되고 싶지 않아서   나이든 남자의 부인이   마찬가지로 열중했다

/ in removing every gray hair / she could find. Thus / it
흰머리를 뽑는 것에   발견하는 대로.   그리하여

came to pass that / between them both / he very soon
그 결과   두 여자 사이에서   그는 곧 알게 되었다

found / that he had not a hair left / on his head.
       머리카락이 한 가닥도 남지 않게 된 것을   자신의 머리에.

Those who seek to please / everybody MIDDLE-AGED /
만족시키려는 사람은   모든 중년을

please nobody.
아무도 만족시킬 수 없다

sweetheart 연인, 애인 | middle-aged 중년의 | court 구애하다, 환심을 사려고 하다 | admirer 구혼자(남성) |
on the contrary 이와 반대로 | zealous 열성적인 | come to pass 발생하다, ~한 결과가 되다 | go about
돌아다니다 | in quest of ~을 찾아서 | dip 담그다 | bestow 수여하다, 부여하다 | evil-disposed 악한 기질을
가진, 질이 나쁜

The Man Bitten by a Dog
개에게 물린 사람

A MAN / who had been bitten by a Dog / went about /
한 남자가   개에게 물린   돌아다녔다

in quest of / someone who might heal him. A friend, /
찾으려고   자신을 치료할 사람을.   한 친구가,

meeting him / and learning what he wanted, / said, / "If
그를 만나고   그가 원하는 것을 알고,   말했다

you would be cured, / take a piece of bread, / and dip it /
"치료 받고 싶다면,   빵 한 조각을 가져와서,   담궈 보게

in the blood from your wound, / and go and give it to the
자네 상처에서 흘린 피 속에,   그리고 그 빵 조각을 개에게 주도록 해

Dog / that bit you."
개   자네를 물었던."

The Man / who had been bitten / laughed at this advice /
그 남자는   개에게 물린   이 충고를 비웃으며

and said, / "why? If I should do so, / it would be / as if I
말했다,   "왜지? 내가 그렇게 해야 한다면,   그것은   마치 내가

should beg / every Dog in the town / to bite me."
애원하는 것 같잖아 이 마을의 모든 개에게   날 물으라고."

Benefits bestowed upon the evil-disposed / increase /
악한 의도로 부여 받은 도움은   증가시킨다

their means of injuring you.
당신을 상처 입히는 수단을.

Key Expression

make a point to 부정사 : 반드시 ~하다
make a point to 부정사는 '반드시 ~하다'라는 의미를 가진 숙어로 make a point of -ing와 같은 형태로 사용되기도 합니다. make a point를 사용한 다양한 표현을 함께 기억해 두세요.

▶ make a point : 1점을 얻다, 논지를 충분히 입증하다
▶ make a point of doing : 반드시 ~하다, ~을 주장[강조]하다
▶ make it a point to do 반드시 ~하다
▶ make a point that ~ : ~이라고 주장[강조]하다

ex) The elder woman, ashamed to be courted by a man younger than herself, made a point, whenever her admirer visited her, to pull out some portion of his black hairs.
나이든 여자는, 자신보다 어린 남자에게 구애받는 것이 부끄러워서, 구혼자가 찾아올 때마다 반드시 검은 머리를 뽑곤 했다.

143

The Man and His Wife
남자와 그의 부인

A MAN had a Wife / who made herself hated / by all the
한 남자에게 부인이 있었다   미움 받은   모든 사람들에게

members / of his household. Wishing to find out / if she
가족의.   알아내고 싶어서

had the same effect / on the persons in her father's house,
부인이 같은 결과를 얻게 될지   친정 사람들에게도,

/ he made some excuse / to send her home / on a visit to
그는 핑계를 대고   부인을 친정으로 보냈다   아버지를 방문하도록.

her father.

After a short time / she returned, / and when he inquired
얼마 후   부인이 돌아왔고,   그가 물어봤을 때

/ how she had got on / and how the servants had treated
부인이 어떻게 지냈는지   그리고 하인들이 어떻게 대했는지,

her, / she replied, / "The herdsmen and shepherds / cast
부인이 대답했다,   "목동과 양치기들은

on me looks of aversion."
내게 싫어하는 듯한 시선을 보냈어요."

He said, / "O Wife, / if you were disliked / by those /
그는 말했다,   "오 여보,   당신이 미움 받았다면   그런 사람들에게

who go out early in the morning / with their flocks / and
아침 일찍 나가서   가축을 끌고

return late in the evening, / what must have been felt
밤 늦게 돌아오는,   어떻게 느꼈겠소

towards you / by those / with whom you passed the /
사람들은   당신과 같이 지내는

whole day!"
하루종일!"

Straws show / how the wind blows.
지푸라기는 보여 준다   바람이 부는 방향을.

---

household 가족 | get on 지내다, 살아가다 | cast (시선을) 보내다, 던지다 | aversion 싫어함 | prowess 기량 |
strangle 목 졸라 죽이다 | erect 세우다, 만들다

The Man and the Lion
사람과 사자

A MAN and a Lion traveled together / through the
사람과 사자가 함께 여행했다　　　　　　　　　숲 속을.

forest. They soon began to boast / of their respective
그들은 곧 자랑하기 시작했다　　　　　각자의 우월함을

superiority / to each other / in strength and prowess.
서로에게　　　　　　힘과 기량 면에서의.

As they were disputing, / they passed a statue / carved in
그들이 언쟁하고 있을 때,　　　동상을 지나치게 되었다　　돌에 조각된,

stone, / which represented / "a Lion strangled by a Man."
그 동상은 묘사했다　　　"사람에게 목 졸려 죽은 사자"라고.

The traveler pointed to it / and said: / "See there! How
여행자는 동상을 가리키며　　　말했다:　　"저기 봐!

strong we are, / and how we prevail / over even the king
사람이 얼마나 강한지,　어떻게 이기는지　　　동물의 왕에게."

of beasts."

The Lion replied: / "This statue was made / by one of
사자가 대답했다:　　　"이 동상은 만들어졌네　　　너희 사람에 의해.

you men. If we Lions knew / how to erect statues, / you
만약 우리 사자들이 안다면　　동상을 세우는 방법을,

would see / the Man placed under the paw of the Lion."
자넨 보게 될 거야　사자의 앞발에 깔린 사람을."

One story is good, / till another is told.
한 이야기는 좋은 법이다,　　　다른 이야기가 나올 때까지는.

Key Expression

how to ~ : ~하는 방법
'how to + 동사원형'은 의문사와 to 부정사가 결합된 형태로 '어떻게 ~할지',
즉 '~하는 방법'이라는 의미를 나타냅니다. 이러한 '의문사 + to 부정사' 구문은 문
장 내에서 주어, 목적어, 보어의 기능을 하며 '의문사 + 주어 + should + 동사원
형' 형태의 절로 바꾸어 쓸 수 있습니다.

ex) If we Lions knew how to erect statues, you would see the Man placed under
the paw of the Lion.
만약 우리 사자들이 동상을 세우는 방법을 알고 있다면, 자넨 사자의 앞발에 깔
린 사람을 보게 될 거야.

The Man and the Satyr
남자와 사티로스

A MAN and a Satyr / once / drank together / in token of
남자와 사티로스가   한 번은 함께 술을 마셨다

a bond of alliance / being formed between them.
동맹의 의미로   그들 사이에 맺은.

One very cold wintry day, / as they talked, / the Man put
몹시 춥고 바람 불던 어느 날,   그들이 이야기 하고 있을 때,

his fingers to his mouth / and blew on them. When the
남자는 손가락을 입에 대고   불었다.

Satyr asked the reason for this, / he told him / that he did
사티로스가 그 이유를 묻자,   그는 말했나

it to warm his hands / because they were so cold.
손을 따뜻하게 하기 위한 것이라고   아주 추웠기 때문에.

Later on / in the day / they sat down to eat, / and the food
나중에   그날   그들은 앉아서 식사했는데,

prepared was quite scalding. The Man raised one of the
준비된 음식은 델 정도로 뜨거웠다.   그 남자는 음식을 조금 집어서

dishes / a little towards his mouth / and blew in it.
          입에 가져가며   불었다.

When the Satyr again inquired the reason, / he said / that
사티로스가 다시 한 번 그 이유를 묻자,   그는 말했다

he did it to cool the meat, / which was too hot. "I can no
고기를 식히기 위한 것이라고,   너무 뜨거웠기 때문에.

longer consider you / as a friend," / said the Satyr, / "a
"나는 더 이상 생각할 수 없네   자네를 친구라고,"   사티로스가 말했다,

fellow who with the same breath / blows hot and cold."
"똑같이 입김을 불면서   뜨겁게도 차갑게도 만드는 사람을."

The Man, the Horse, the Ox, and the Dog
사람, 말, 황소, 그리고 개

A HORSE, Ox, and Dog, / driven to great straits / by
말, 황소, 그리고 개가,   큰 공경에 빠진

the cold, / sought shelter / and protection from Man. He
추위 때문에,   피난처를 찾아   사람에게서 보호 받고자 했다.

received them kindly, / lighted a fire, / and warmed them.
사람은 그들을 친절하게 맞이했고,   불을 피워,   따뜻하게 해 줬다.

He let the Horse make free / with his oats, / gave the Ox /
그는 말에게 마음껏 먹게 했으며   자신의 귀리를,   황소에게는 줬다

an abundance of hay, / and fed the Dog with meat / from his
충분한 건초를,   그리고 개에게 고기를 먹였다

own table.
자신의 식탁에서 가져온.

Grateful for these favors, / the animals determined to repay
이 모든 친절을 감사히 여겨,   동물들은 그에게 보답하기로 결심했다

him / to the best of their ability. For this purpose, / they
최선을 다해.   이를 위해,

divided the term of his life / between them, / and each
동물들은 사람의 인생을 나누어   그들끼리,

endowed one portion of it / with the qualities / which chiefly
서로 각자의 부분에 부여했다   성질을

characterized himself.
자신의 특징을 잘 나타내는.

The Horse chose his earliest years / and gave them his own
말은 사람의 어린 시절을 택해   자신의 특성을 부여했다:

attributes: / hence every man is / in his youth / impetuous, /
그리하여 모든 사람들은   젊은 시기에   충동적이고,

headstrong, / and obstinate / in maintaining his own opinion.
고집이 세며,   완강해졌다   자신의 의견을 주장하는데 있어서.

The Ox took under his patronage / the next term of life,
황소는 자신이 돌보기로 했다   그 다음 시기를,

/ and therefore man in his middle age / is fond of work, /
그래서 중년의 사람은   일을 좋아하고,

devoted to labor, / and resolute / to amass wealth / and to
일에 전념하며,   의지가 강해졌다   부를 축적하고

husband his resources.
재산을 아껴 쓰려는.

Satyr 사티로스(고대 그리스 신화에서 숲의 신. 남자의 얼굴과 몸에 염소의 다리와 뿔을 가진 모습) | in token of
~의 표시로 | scalding 델 정도로 뜨거운 | strait 곤경, 곤궁 | make free with ~을 마음껏 먹다 | oat 귀리 |
abundance 풍부함 | repay 보답하다 | term 기간 | chiefly 주로, 우선, 특히 | characterize 특징을 나타내다 |
attribute 속성, 특성 | hence 그러므로, 따라서 | impetuous 충동적인 | headstrong 고집센 | obstinate 끈질긴
| maintain 주장하다 | patronage 후원, 보호 | devoted to ~에 헌신적인, ~에 전념하는 | resolute 의지가 굳은,
굳게 결심하고 있는 | amass 모으다 | husband 아껴 쓰다

The end of life was reserved / for the Dog, / wherefore
인생의 마지막 시기는 맡겨졌다   개에게,

the old man is often snappish, / irritable, / hard to please,
그렇기 때문에 노인은 종종 퉁명스럽고,   화를 잘 내며,   성미가 까다롭고

/ and selfish, / tolerant only of his own household, / but
이기적이게 되었다,   자신의 가족에게는 관대하지만,

averse / to strangers / and to all who do not administer /
배타적이다   낯선 사람과   주지 않는 모든 사람에게는

to his comfort or to his necessities.
위안이나 필요한 것을.

The Master and His Dogs
주인과 그의 개들

A CERTAIN MAN, / detained by a storm / in his
어떤 사람이,   폭풍우에 갇히게 되자

country house, / first of all killed his sheep, / and then
자신의 시골 집에서,   우선 양을 죽였고,   다음으로 염소를

his goats, / for the maintenance of his household. The
죽였다,   가족의 생계를 위해.

storm still continuing, / he was obliged to slaughter / his
폭풍이 여전히 계속되자,   어쩔 수 없이 죽였다

yoke oxen / for food.
소 한 쌍을   식량을 위해.

On seeing this, / his Dogs took counsel / together, / and
이를 보자,   개들은 회의를 열고   함께,

said, / "It is time / for us to be off, / for if the master
말했다, "시간이 됐어   우리가 떠나야 할,   왜냐하면 주인이 소를 살려두지

spare not his oxen, / who work for his gain, / how can we
않는다면,   자신의 소득을 위해 일하는,   어떻게 기대할 수

expect him / to spare us?"
있겠어   우리를 살려 주리라고?"

He is not to be trusted / as a friend / who mistreats his
신용받지 못한다   친구로서   가족을 저버리는 사람은.

own family.

Mercury and the Sculptor
머큐리와 조각가

MERCURY ONCE DETERMINED to learn / in what
한 번은 머큐리가 알아보기로 결심했다

esteem / he was held / among mortals. For this purpose /
어떤 평판을 자신이 받고 있는지 사람들 사이에서. 이를 위해

he assumed the character of a man / and visited / in this
그는 사람의 모습으로 변해 방문했고

disguise / a Sculptor's studio / having looked at various
변장한 채 한 조각가의 작업실을 다양한 조각상을 둘러보면서,

statues, / he demanded / the price of two figures of
그는 물었다 제우스와 주노의 조각상 가격을.

Jupiter and Juno.

When the sum at which they were valued was named, /
두 조각상의 가격의 총액을 말하자,

he pointed to a figure of himself, / saying to the Sculptor,
그는 자신의 조각상을 가리키며, 조각가에게 말했다.

/ "You will certainly want / much more / for this, / as it is
"당신은 분명히 원할 겁니다 훨씬 높은 값을 이것에는, 왜냐하면

the statue / of the Messenger of the Gods, / and author of
그것은 조각상이고 신들의 심부름꾼인, 당신에게 모든 소득을

all your gain." The Sculptor replied, / "Well, / if you will
얻게 해줄 테니." 조각가가 대답했다, "글쎄요, 당신이 이 두 조각

buy these, / I'll fling you that / into the bargain."
상을 사겠다면, 그 조각상도 드리겠습니다 덤으로."

---

reserve 남겨두다 | wherefore 그렇기 때문에 | snappish 통명스러운 | irritable 화를 잘 내는 | selfish
이기적인 | tolerant 관대한, 용서한 | averse to 몹시 싫어하여 | administer 주다, 베풀다 | detain 억류하다 |
maintenance 생계, 생활수단 | slaughter 도살, 도축 | mistreat 학대하다, 혹사하다 | Mercury 머큐리(로마
신화에서 신들의 전령이자 상업과 교역의 신, 그리스 신화의 헤르메스에 해당) | sculptor 조각가 | esteem 존경 |
mortal 인간 | disguise 가장, 위장 | studio 작업실 | figure 인물, 인물 조각 | Juno 주노(로마 신화에서 주피터의
아내이자 최고의 여신, 그리스 신화의 헤라에 해당) | messenger 심부름꾼, 전령 | fling 처분하다

149

Mercury and the Workmen
머큐리와 일꾼

A WORKMAN, / felling wood / by the side of a river,
한 일꾼이,　　　　　나무를 베던　　　　강가에서,

/ let his axe drop / by accident / into a deep pool. Being
도끼를 빠뜨렸다　　사고로　　　깊은 물 속에

thus deprived / of the means of his livelihood, / he sat
이렇게 빼앗기자　　　자신의 생계수단을,

down on the bank / and lamented his hard fate.
그는 강둑에 앉아　　　　자신의 가혹한 운명을 한탄했다.

Mercury appeared / and demanded the cause of his tears.
머큐리가 나타나서　　　우는 이유를 물었다.

After he told him his misfortune, / Mercury plunged into
일꾼이 자신의 불운에 대해 말하자,　　　머큐리는 물 속으로 들어갔다,

the stream, / and, / bringing up a golden axe, / inquired
　　　　　　그리고,　금도끼를 갖고 올라와서,　　　　물어봤다

/ if that were the one he had lost. On his saying / that it
그것이 그가 잃어버린 도끼인지.　　　그가 말하자　　　그것은 자신

was not his, / Mercury disappeared / beneath the water /
의 것이 아니라고,　머큐리는 사라졌고　　물 속으로

a second time, / returned / with a silver axe / in his hand,
다시 한 번,　　돌아왔다　은도끼를 갖고　　　손에,

/ and again asked the Workman / if it were his.
그리고 또 다시 물었다　　　그것이 그의 것인지.

When the Workman said / it was not, / he dived into the
일꾼이 말하자　　　　그것은 아니라고,　머큐리는 물 속으로 들어가

pool / for the third time / and brought up the axe / that
세 번째로　　　　그 도끼를 가지고 왔다

had been lost. The Workman claimed it / and expressed
그가 잃어버렸던.　일꾼은 맞다고 하며　　　기뻐했다

his joy / at its recovery.
다시 되찾은 것에.

---

by accident 우연히 | deprive 빼앗다 | livelihood 생계 (수단) | claim 주장하다 | weep 울다 | declare
선언하다 | knavery 나쁜 짓, 부정 행위

Mercury, / pleased with his honesty, / gave him / the
머큐리는, 그의 정직함을 기뻐하며, 그에게 줬다

golden and silver axes / in addition to his own. The
금도끼와 은도끼를 그의 도끼와 함께.

Workman, / on his return to his house, / related to his
일꾼은, 집으로 돌아오는 길에, 동료들에게 말했다

companions / all that had happened.
일어난 모든 일을.

One of them / at once / resolved / to try and secure / the
동료들 중 한 명은 즉시 결심했다 시도해서 얻겠다고

same good fortune / for himself. He ran to the river / and
같은 행운을 자신도. 그는 강으로 달려가

threw his axe / on purpose / into the pool / at the same
도끼를 빠뜨린 후 고의로 물 속에 같은 장소에서,

place, / and sat down on the bank / to weep.
강둑에 앉아서 울었다.

Mercury appeared to him / just as he hoped he would; /
머큐리가 그에게 나타났다 그가 바랐던 대로;

and having learned the cause of his grief, / plunged into
그리고 슬퍼하는 이유를 알게 되자, 물 속으로 들어가

the stream / and brought up a golden axe, / inquiring / if
금도끼를 갖고 올라와서, 물어봤다

he had lost it.
잃어버린 도끼인지.

The Workman seized it / greedily, / and declared /
일꾼은 그것을 잡아채고 탐욕스럽게, 선언했다

that truly it was the very same axe / that he had lost.
정말 바로 그 도끼라고 자신이 잃어버린.

Mercury, / displeased at his knavery, / not only took
머큐리는, 그의 거짓된 행동에 불쾌해 하며,

away the golden axe, / but refused to recover for him /
금도끼를 빼앗아 갔을 뿐 아니라, 되찾아 주는 것도 거절했다

the axe he had thrown / into the pool.
그가 던져 버렸던 도끼를 물 속에.

The Mouse, the Frog, and the Hawk
쥐, 개구리, 그리고 매

A MOUSE / who always lived on the land, / by an
쥐 한 마리가 　　항상 땅에서 살고 있던,

unlucky chance / formed an intimate acquaintance / with
불운한 기회로 　　친한 친구가 되었다

a Frog, / who lived for the most part / in the water. The
개구리와, 　거의 살고 있던 　　　물 속에서.

Frog, / one day / intent on mischief, / bound the foot of
개구리는, 　어느 날 　장난치려는 의도로, 　쥐의 다리를 단단히 묶었다

the Mouse tightly / to his own.
　　　　자신의 다리에.

Thus joined together, / the Frog first of all led / his
그렇게 함께 묶고, 　　개구리는 우선 이끌고 갔다

friend the Mouse / to the meadow / where they were
친구인 쥐를 　　풀밭으로 　　그들이 익숙했던

accustomed / to find their food. After this, / he gradually
　　음식을 찾느라고. 　　이런 후에, 　　개구리는 천천히 쥐를

led him / towards the pool / in which he lived, / until
이끌고 갔다 　연못으로 　　자신이 사는

reaching the very brink, / he suddenly jumped in, /
마침내 가장자리에 도착하자, 　개구리는 갑자기 뛰어 들었다,

dragging the Mouse with him.
쥐를 끌어당기며.

The Frog enjoyed the water / amazingly, / and swam
개구리는 물을 즐겼다 　　　　펑장히, 　　그리고 개골거리며

croaking about, / as if he had done a good deed. The
헤엄쳐 다녔다, 　마치 자신이 훌륭한 일을 해 냈다는 듯이.

unhappy Mouse was soon suffocated / by the water, /
불행한 쥐는 곧 질식해 죽어 버렸고 　　물 때문에,

and his dead body floated about / on the surface, / tied to
쥐의 시체가 떠다녔다 　　　　물 위에,

the foot of the Frog.
개구리의 발에 묶인 채.

intent 의도, 목적 | brink 가장자리 | suffocate 질식시키다 | hatch 부화시키다, (음모를) 꾸미다 | weasel 족제비
| defeat 패배 | discipline 규율, 훈련, 훈련시키다 | renowned 유명한, 명성 있는 | descent 혈통, 가문 | noted
유명한

A Hawk observed it, / and, / pouncing upon it / with his
매가 그것을 발견했고,   그리고,   쥐를 잡아채어

talons, / carried it aloft. The Frog, / being still fastened /
발톱으로,   높은 곳으로 가져갔다.   개구리는,   여전히 묶여 있었던

to the leg of the Mouse, / was also carried off a prisoner,
쥐의 발에,   역시 끌려가서,

/ and was eaten / by the Hawk.
먹히고 말았다   매에게.

Harm hatch, / harm catch.
해로운 짓을 꾸미면,   해를 당하는 법이다.

The Mice and the Weasels
쥐들과 족제비들

THE WEASELS and the Mice / waged a perpetual war
족제비들과 쥐들이   끊임없는 전쟁을 벌여서

/ with each other, / in which much blood was shed. The
서로,   많은 피를 흘렸다.

Weasels were / always the victors. The Mice thought
족제비들은   항상 승리했다.   쥐들은 생각했다

/ that the cause of their frequent defeats was / that
자신들의 잦은 패배의 원인은

they had no leaders / set apart from the general army
지도자가 없기 때문이라고   군대와 분리되어

/ to command them, / and / that they were exposed to
군대를 지휘할,   그리고   위험에 노출되기 때문이라고

dangers / from lack of discipline.
훈련이 부족해서.

They therefore chose as leaders / Mice / that were most
그래서 그들은 지도자로 선택했다   쥐를   가장 잘 알려져 있었던

renowned / for their family descent, / strength, / and
혈통이 좋고,   힘이 세며,   조언을

counsel, / as well as those most noted / for their courage
잘한다고,   가장 유명했을 뿐만 아니라   용기가 있다고

/ in the fight, / so that they might be better marshaled / in
전투에서,　　　　　　그래서 더 잘 결집되며

battle array / and formed / into troops, / regiments, / and
전투 대형으로　　　편성되도록　　　군대,　　　　연대,

battalions.
그리고 대대로.

When all this was done, / and the army disciplined, /
이 모든 작업이 완료되자,　　　　군대는 규율이 잡혔고,

and the herald Mouse had duly proclaimed war / by
전령 쥐가 정식으로 전쟁을 선포하자

challenging the Weasels, / the newly chosen generals /
족제비에게 도전하며,　　　　　새로 뽑힌 장군들은

bound their heads with straws, / that they might be more
머리에 밀짚을 묶었다.　　　　　　자신들이 눈에 잘 띄도록

conspicuous / to all their troops.
　　　　　　모든 군대에.

Scarcely had the battle begun, / when a great rout
전투가 시작되자마자,　　　　　쥐들은 완패했고,

overwhelmed the Mice, / who scampered off / as fast as
　　　　　　　　　　　　　도망쳤다

they could / to their holes.
최대한 빨리　　쥐구멍 속으로.

The generals, / not being able to get in / on account of
장군들은,　　　구멍에 들어갈 수 없어서

the ornaments / on their heads, / were all captured and
장식물 때문에　　머리에 두른,　　모두 잡혀 먹히고 말았다

eaten / by the Weasels.
　　　　족제비에게.

The more honor / the more danger.
명예를 얻으면 얻을수록　　위험도 커지는 법이다.

---

* 풍요의 뿔, 보고(라틴어의 '코르누코피아(cornucopia)'에서 유래한 말. 그리스 신화에서 제우스에게 젖을
먹여준 아말테아에게 선물한 무엇이든지 내놓는 마법의 뿔을 가리키는 풍요의 상징이다)

marshal 모으다, 결집시키다 | troop 군대 | regiment 연대 | battalion 대대 | herald 전령 | duly 적절한 절차에
따라, 때를 맞춰 | proclaim 선언하다 | general 장군 | straw 밀짚 | conspicuous 알아볼 수 있는, 눈에 잘 띄는
| rout 완패 | overwhelm 압도하다 | ornament 장식품, 장신구 | wheat-stock 밀의 줄기, 밀대 | hedgerow
생울타리 | ample 충분한, 풍부한 | dainty 맛있는, 맛있는 음식 | barley 보리 | fig 무화과 열매 | raisin 건포도 |
terms 말

The Town Mouse and the Country Mouse
도시 쥐와 시골 쥐

A COUNTRY MOUSE invited a Town Mouse, / an
시골 쥐가 도시 쥐를 초대했다.

intimate friend, / to pay him a visit / and partake of his
친한 친구인,　　　　자신을 한 번 찾아와서　　시골 음식을 함께 먹자고.

country fare.

As they were on the bare plowlands, / eating there wheat-
그들이 황량한 경작지에 있었을 때,　　　　　밀대와 뿌리를 먹으면서

stocks / and roots pulled up from the hedgerow, / the
　　　　생울타리에서 뽑아낸,

Town Mouse said / to his friend, / "You live here / the life
도시 쥐가 말했다　　친구에게,　　　"넌 이곳에서 사는 구나

of the ants, / while in my house / is the *horn of plenty. I
개미같은 삶을,　　하지만 내 집은　　　풍요로움이 가득하단다.

am surrounded / by every luxury, / and / if you will come
난 둘러싸여 있어　　화려한 것들에,　　그러니　네가 나랑 함께 간다면,

with me, / as I wish you would, / you shall have an ample
　　　　바라건대 너도,　　　　충분히 누리게 될 거야

share / of my dainties." The Country Mouse was easily
내 맛있는 음식을."　　시골 쥐는 쉽게 설득되어,

persuaded, / and returned to town / with his friend.
　　　　도시로 돌아왔다　　　　친구와 함께.

On his arrival, / the Town Mouse placed / before him /
도착하자마자,　　도시 쥐는 차려 놓았다　　그의 앞에

bread, / barley, / beans, / dried figs, / honey, / raisins, /
빵,　　보리,　　콩,　　말린 무화과,　　꿀,　　건포도를,

and, / last of all, / brought a dainty piece of cheese / from
그리고, 마지막으로,　　맛있는 치즈 한 조각을 가져왔다

a basket. The Country Mouse, / being much delighted / at
바구니에서.　시골 쥐는,　　　　몹시 기뻐서

the sight of such good cheer, / expressed his satisfaction /
그토록 맛있는 음식을 보고,　　　만족감을 표현하며

in warm terms / and lamented his own hard fate.
따뜻한 말로　　자신의 가혹한 운명을 한탄했다.

Just as they were beginning to eat, / someone opened the
그들이 식사를 시작하자마자,   누군가 문을 열었고,

door, / and they both ran off squeaking, / as fast as they
그들은 둘 다 찍찍거리며 달아났다,   최대한 빨리,

could, / to a hole / so narrow / that two could only find
구멍 속으로   매우 좁아서   둘이 겨우 들어갈 수 있었던

room / in it / by squeezing.
그 안에   바짝 붙어서.

They had scarcely begun their repast / again / when
그들이 식사를 시작하자마자   다시

someone else entered / to take something / out of a
다른 누군가가 들어왔고   뭔가를 가져가기 위해

cupboard, / whereupon the two Mice, / more frightened
찬장에서,   그러자 두 마리의 쥐는,   전보다 더욱 놀라,

than before, / ran away / and hid themselves.
도망쳐서   몸을 숨겼다.

At last / the Country Mouse, / almost famished, / said
마침내   시골 쥐는,   배가 고파 죽을 지경이 되어,

to his friend: / "Although you have prepared for me / so
친구에게 말했다: "네가 날 위해 준비했지만

dainty a feast, / I must leave you / to enjoy it / by yourself.
그렇게 맛있는 음식을,   난 떠나야 겠어   네가 즐기도록   혼자서.

It is surrounded / by too many dangers / to please me. I
그 음식은 둘러싸여 있어   너무 많은 위험에   즐길 수 없구나.

prefer / my bare plowlands / and roots from the hedgerow,
난 더 좋아   황량한 경작지와   생울타리에서 뽑아 낸 뿌리가,

/ where I can live / in safety, / and without fear."
그곳에서 난 살 수 있으니까   안전하고,   두려움 없이."

The Milk-Woman and Her Pail
우유 짜는 여자와 우유통

A FARMER'S daughter was carrying / her Pail of milk /
농부의 딸이 들고 가다가   우유통을

from the field to the farmhouse, / when she fell a-musing.
들판에서 집으로,   그때 공상에 빠져 들었다.

"The money / for which this milk will be sold, / will
"돈으로   이 우유를 팔아서 생긴,   살 거야

buy / at least three hundred eggs. The eggs, / allowing
     300개 이상의 달걀을.   달걀들은,   사고가 생길 것을

for all mishaps, / will produce / two hundred and fifty
감안하더라도,   부화되겠지   250마리의 닭으로.

chickens. The chickens will become ready for the market
              그 닭들이 시장에 팔 준비가 되면

/ when poultry will fetch / the highest price, / so that by
   그때 팔리겠지   높은 값으로,

the end of the year / I shall have money / enough from
그래서 올해 말 쯤이면   난 돈을 벌게 될 거야   충분한 몫의

my share / to buy a new gown. In this dress / I will go
     새 외투를 살 만큼.   이 옷을 입고

to the Christmas parties, / where all the young fellows /
크리스마스 파티에 가야지,   그곳에서 모든 남자들이

will propose to me, / but I will toss my head / and refuse
내게 청혼하면,   난 고개를 빳빳하게 들고

them every one."
그 모두를 거절할 거야."

At this moment / she tossed her head in unison / with her
이 순간   그녀는 고개를 들었고   생각과 동시에,

thoughts, / when down fell the milk pail to the ground, /
          그러자 우유통이 땅에 떨어지면서

and all her imaginary schemes perished / in a moment.
모든 상상이 사라져 버렸다   한 순간에.

---

repast 식사 | cupboard 찬장 | whereupon 그래서 | famished 굶어 죽게 된 | pail 우유통 | mishap 작은 사고
| fetch (특정 가격에) 팔리다 | toss 고개를 바짝 들다, 확 젖히다 | unison 조화, 화합, 일치 | perish 죽다, 소멸되다

The Miller, His Son, and Their Ass
방앗간 주인과 아들, 그리고 그들의 당나귀

A MILLER and his son were driving their Ass / to a
방앗간 집 부자가 당나귀를 몰고   근처 시장으로

neighboring fair / to sell him. They had not gone far /
향하고 있었다   당나귀를 팔려고.   얼마 가지 않아

when they met / with a troop of women / collected round
그들은 만났다   여자들의 무리를   우물 주위에 모여,

a well, / talking and laughing.
       웃으며 이야기 하고 있던.

"Look there," / cried one of them, / "did you ever see
"저기 좀 봐,"   그들 중 한 명이 소리쳤다,   "저런 사람들 본 적 있니,

such fellows, / to be trudging along the road on foot
              길을 따라 느릿느릿 걷고 있다니

/ when they might ride?" The old man hearing this, /
당나귀를 탈 수 있는데?"   아버지는 이 말을 듣고,

quickly made his son mount the Ass, / and continued to
재빨리 아들을 당나귀에 태운 후,   계속 걸어갔다

walk along / merrily / by his side.
           즐겁게   그 옆에서.

Presently / they came up / to a group of old men / in
잠시 후   그들은 마주쳤다   노인들 무리와

earnest debate. "There," / said one of them, / "it proves
열띤 논쟁을 벌이고 있던. "저기,"   한 노인이 말했다,

what I was a-saying. What respect is shown to old age
"내가 말하던 것이 사실이잖아.   노인에게 존경심을 보이냐고

/ in these days? Do you see / that idle lad riding / while
요즘에는?   보이지   저 게으른 녀석이 타고 있는 것이

his old father has to walk? Get down, / you young
늙은 아버지는 걷게 하면서?   썩 내리렴,   어린 망나니 같으니,

scapegrace, / and let the old man rest / his weary limbs."
            그리고 노인더러 쉬게 해야지   지친 다리를."

---

miller 방앗간 주인, 일꾼 | fair 시장 | trudge 느릿느릿 걷다, 터버터벅 걷다 | idle 게으른 | scapegrace 망나니,
쓸모없는 놈

Upon this / the old man made his son dismount, / and
이 말을 듣고   아버지는 아들을 내리게 한 후,   자신이

got up himself. In this manner / they had not proceeded
당나귀에 올라탔다.   이런 방법으로   얼마 가지 못했을 때

far / when they met a company of women and children: /
그들은 여자들과 아이들 무리를 만나게 되었다:

"Why, / you lazy old fellow," / cried several tongues / at
"어머나,   게으른 노인이군요,"   몇몇 사람들이 소리쳤다

once, / "how can you ride / upon the beast, / while that
갑자기,   "어떻게 탈 수 있죠   그 당나귀 위에,

poor little lad there / can hardly keep pace / by the side
거기 있는 불쌍한 어린 소년은   따라가기 힘들어 하는데   옆에서?"

of you?" The good-natured Miller / immediately took up
본성이 착한 아버지는   즉시 아들을 태웠다

his son / behind him. They had now almost reached the
자신의 뒤에.   그들은 마을에 거의 도착하게 되었다.

town.

"Pray, / honest friend," / said a citizen, / "is that Ass your
"이보시오,   정직한 양반."   한 사람이 말했다,   "그 당나귀는 당신들 거요?"

own?"

"Yes," / replied the old man.
"그렇소,"   아버지가 대답했다.

"O, / one would not have thought so," / said the other, /
"오,   누구도 그렇게 생각하지 않을 거요,"   다른 사람이 말했다,

"by the way you load him. Why, / you two fellows are
"당신들이 타고 가는 모습을 보면.   저런,   당신들 둘이 들고 가는 것이 더 낫겠소

better able to carry / the poor beast / than he you."
그 불쌍한 동물을   당나귀가 당신들을 태우기 보다."

"Anything to please you," / said the old man; / "we can
"원하신다면,"   아버지가 말했다;

but try."
"할 수밖에요."

---

dismount 내리다 |proceeded 전진하다, 진행하다 |pray 고어에서 질문이나 부탁을 할 때 please와 같은 의미로 쓰는
말 |alight (말·차·배 등에서) 내리다 |endeavor 노력하다, 시도하다 |vexed 화[짜증]가 난 |convince 확신하다

So, / alighting with his son, / they tied the legs of the
그래서, 아들과 함께 내려서,　　　　　그들은 당나귀 다리를 한데 묶은 후

Ass together / and with the help of a pole / endeavored to
　　　　　장대를 이용하여

carry him / on their shoulders / over a bridge / near the
들고 가려고 했다　어깨에 메고　　　　　　다리 위를

entrance to the town.
마을 입구 근처에 있는.

This entertaining sight brought / the people in crowds /
이런 재미있는 광경을 보자　　　　　　　모여 있던 사람들은

to laugh at it, / till the Ass, / not liking the noise / nor
그 모습을 비웃었고,　그러자 당나귀는,　그 웃음소리도 거슬려서

the strange handling that he was subject to, / broke the
또한 자신을 지고 가는 이상한 모습도,　　　　　줄을 끊었고

cords / that bound him / and, / tumbling off the pole, /
　　　묶여 있던　　　　그리고,　장대에서 굴러 떨어져,

fell into the river.
강 속으로 빠지고 말았다.

Upon this, / the old man, / vexed and ashamed, / made
이 광경을 보고,　아버지는,　　화가 나고 부끄러워서,

the best of his way home / again, / convinced that /
최대한 빨리 집으로 돌아오며　다시,　확신했다

by endeavoring to please everybody / he had pleased
모두를 만족시키려고 애쓰다가는　　　　　　아무도 만족시킬 수 없으며,

nobody, / and lost his Ass / in the bargain.
　　　　당나귀도 잃고 만다는 것을　팔려던.

Key Expression

물주구문의 해석은 부사구처럼 한다

무생물 주어로 시작하는 문장을 '물주구문'이라고 부릅니다. 이러한 문장은 종종 무생물 주어의 행동을 '~때문에, ~로 인해'와 같이 부사구처럼 해석하는 것이 자연스러워요.

ex) This entertaining sight brought the people in crowds to laugh at it.
　　이런 재미있는 광경은 모여 있던 사람들이 그 모습을 비웃게 만들었다.
　　(→ 이런 재미있는 광경을 보자 모여 있던 사람들은 그 모습을 비웃었다.)

The Dancing Monkeys
춤추는 원숭이

A PRINCE had some Monkeys trained / to dance. Being
한 왕자가 원숭이 몇 마리를 훈련시켰다   춤추도록.

naturally great mimics / of men's actions, / they showed
본래 잘 흉내 내기 때문에   사람의 행동을,

themselves most apt pupils, / and when arrayed in their
원숭이들은 영리한 학생의 모습을 보여 줬고,   값비싼 옷과 가면으로 치장했을 때에는,

rich clothes and masks, / they danced / as well as any of
춤췄다   어느 신하 못지 않게 잘.

the courtiers.

The spectacle was often repeated / with great applause,
그 쇼는 종종 되풀이 되었고   많은 박수를 받으며,

/ till on one occasion / a courtier, / bent on mischief, /
마침내 한 번은   어느 신하가,   장난으로,

took from his pocket a handful of nuts / and threw them /
주머니에서 땅콩 한 줌을 꺼내어   그들에게 던져 주었다

upon the stage.
무대 위에.

The Monkeys at the sight of the nuts / forgot their
땅콩을 본 원숭이들은   춤추기를 잊고

dancing / and became / (as indeed they were) / Monkeys
되어 버렸다   (실제 자신들의 모습인)   원숭이가

/ instead of actors. Pulling off their masks / and tearing
배우가 아니라.   가면을 벗어 버리고   옷을 찢으며,

their robes, / they fought with one another / for the nuts.
원숭이들은 서로 싸웠다   땅콩을 차지하려고.

The dancing spectacle / thus / came to an end / amidst
그 춤추는 쇼는   이렇게   끝나고 말았다

the laughter and ridicule / of the audience.
웃음과 조소 속에서   관객들의.

naturally본래, 선천적으로 | apt영리한, 이해가 빠른 | pupil학생 | array치장하다 | courtier신하 | tear찢다
| robe의복 | come to an end끝나다 | amidst~하는 가운데 | ridicule조소 | fondle귀여워하다, 사랑스럽게
만지다 | nurture키우다, 양육하다 | affection애정 | neglect소홀히 다루다, 무시하다, 무관심 | caress
어루만지다, 귀여워하다 | smother질식시키다 | despised무시당한 | rear기르다 | bound~로 향하는 | coast
해안 | tempest폭풍 | wreck난파시키다

The Monkeys and Their Mother
원숭이들과 어미 원숭이

THE MONKEY, / it is said, / has two young ones / at
원숭이는,　　　　흔히 말하기를,　새끼 두 마리를 낳는다

each birth. The Mother fondles one / and nurtures it
한 번에.　　어미 원숭이는 한 마리를 귀여워 하여　돌보지만

/ with the greatest affection and care, / but hates and
많은 애정과 관심을 쏟으며,　　　　　　다른 한 마리는 싫어하며

neglects the other.
소홀히 다룬다.

It happened once / that the young one / which was
한 번은 일어났다　　새끼 원숭이가

caressed and loved / was smothered / by the too great
보살핌과 사랑을 받던　질식해 버리는 일이

affection of the Mother, / while the despised one was
어미의 너무 지나친 애정 때문에,　반면 버림 받은 원숭이는 양육되고 키워졌다

nurtured and reared / in spite of the neglect / to which it
　　　　　　무관심에도 불구하고

was exposed.
당하고 있던.

The best intentions will not always ensure success.
최선의 의도가 항상 성공을 보장하는 것은 아니다.

The Monkey and the Dolphin
원숭이와 돌고래

A SAILOR, / bound on a long voyage, / took with him
한 선원이,　　긴 항해를 떠나는,　　　　원숭이를 데리고 갔다

a Monkey / to amuse him / while on shipboard. As he
원숭이　자신을 즐겁게 해 줄　항해 동안.

sailed off the coast of Greece, / a violent tempest arose /
그리스 해안을 떠나 항해하고 있을 때,　심한 폭풍우가 일어나

in which the ship was wrecked / and he, / his Monkey, /
배가 난파되었고　　　　　　그 선원과,　원숭이와,

and all the crew / were obliged to swim / for their lives.
모든 선원들은　　헤엄쳐야만 했다　　살기 위해.

A Dolphin saw the Monkey / contending with the waves, /
돌고래 한 마리가 원숭이를 보고 / 파도와 싸우고 있는,

and supposing him to be a man / (whom he is always said
사람으로 착각하고 / (사람은 항상 친구라고 들었기에),

to befriend), / came / and placed himself under him, / to
다가가 / 원숭이의 아래로 가서,

convey him / on his back / in safety / to the shore.
데려가 주었다 / 등에 태우고 / 안전하게 / 해안가에.

When the Dolphin arrived / with his burden / in sight of
돌고래가 도착했을 때 / 원숭이와 함께 / 육지가 보이는 곳에

land / not far from Athens, / he asked the Monkey / if
아테네에서 멀지 않은, / 원숭이에게 물어봤다

he were an Athenian. The latter replied / that he was, /
아테네 사람이냐고. / 원숭이는 대답했다 / 그렇다고,

and that he was descended / from one of the most noble
그리고 자신은 후손이라고 / 가장 고귀한 가문의

families / in that city. The Dolphin then inquired / if he
그 도시에서. / 그러자 돌고래가 물었다

knew the Piraeus / (the famous harbor of Athens).
파이리어스를 아는지 / (아테네의 유명한 항구인).

Supposing that a man was meant, / the Monkey answered
그것이 사람을 뜻한다고 생각하여, / 원숭이는 대답했다

/ that he knew him very well / and that he was an intimate
그를 잘 알고 있으며 / 친한 친구라고.

friend. The Dolphin, / indignant at these falsehoods, /
돌고래는, / 이런 거짓말에 화가 나서,

dipped the Monkey / under the water / and drowned him.
원숭이를 빠뜨려 / 물 속에 / 익사시켰다.

The Monkey and the Camel
원숭이와 낙타

THE BEASTS of the forest / gave a splendid entertainment
숲 속의 동물들이 / 멋진 여흥을 베풀었다

/ at which the Monkey stood up and danced. Having vastly
그곳에서 원숭이가 일어나 춤췄다. / 모인 동물들을 매우

delighted the assembly, / he sat down / amidst universal
즐겁게 해 주고 나서, / 자리에 앉았다

applause.
박수갈채를 받으며.

The Camel, / envious of the praises / bestowed on the
낙타는,   칭찬을 시샘하며   원숭이에게 쏟아진

Monkey / and desiring to divert to himself / the favor
자신에게 향하게 하고 싶어서

of the guests, / proposed to / stand up / in his turn / and
손님들의 호의를,   제안했다   일어나서   자신의 차례에

dance / for their amusement.
춤추겠다고 즐겁게 해 주기 위해.

He moved about / in so utterly ridiculous a manner / that
낙타는 돌아다녔고   매우 우스꽝스러운 모습으로

the Beasts, / in a fit of indignation, / set upon him with
동물들은,   화가 나서,   그를 곤봉으로 때리며

clubs / and drove him out of the assembly.
모임에서 쫓아내 버렸다.

It is absurd / to ape our betters.
어리석은 짓이다   사람들의 장점을 흉내만 내는 것은.

The Mountain in Labor
흔들리는 산

A MOUNTAIN was / once / greatly agitated. Loud
어느 산이   한 번은   심하게 흔들렸다.

groans and noises were heard, / and crowds of people
우르릉 쾅쾅 소리가 들렸고,   사람들이 다가왔다

came / from all parts / to see what was the matter. While
모든 곳에서   무슨 일인지 보기 위해.

they were assembled / in anxious expectation / of some
사람들이 모여들었을 때   걱정 어린 기대감으로

terrible calamity, / out came a Mouse.
끔찍한 일이 생겼을 거라는,   쥐 한 마리가 나타났다.

Don't make much ado about nothing.
아무것도 아닌 일에 법석을 떨지 마라.

contend with ~와 싸우다 | convey 운반하다 | descend ~의 자손이다 | noble 고귀한 | indignant 화가 난
| falsehood 거짓(말) | splendid 멋진, 훌륭한 | vastly 몹시, 매우 | envious 시기하는 | divert 딴 데로 돌리다
| utterly 아주, 완전히 | fit 흥분, 발작 | indignation 분노, 분개 | drive out 몰아내다 | absurd 우스꽝스러운,
터무니없는 | ape 흉내내다 | labor 심한 요동 | agitated 동요하는 | calamity 재앙, 재난

The Mules and the Robbers
노새와 강도들

TWO MULES / well-laden with packs / were trudging
두 마리의 노새가　　　짐을 잔뜩 실은　　　　　　터벅터벅 걷고 있었다.

along. One carried panniers / filled with money, / the
한 마리는 바구니를 운반하고 있었고　돈이 가득 든,

other sacks / weighted with grain.
다른 바구니에는　　곡식으로 가득 차 있었다.

The Mule carrying the treasure / walked with head erect,
귀중품을 운반하는 노새는　　　　　　고개를 똑바로 들고 걸어가며,

/ as if conscious of the value of his burden, / and tossed
마치 자신의 짐의 가치를 아는 듯이,

up and down / the clear-toned bells fastened / to his neck.
아래위로 흔들었다　　맑은 소리가 나는 종을　　　　목에 묶인.

His companion followed / with quiet and easy step.
동료 노새는 뒤따라갔다　　　　조용하고 느긋한 발걸음으로.

All of a sudden / Robbers rushed upon them / from their
갑자기　　　　강도들이 그들을 덮쳤고　　　　숨어 있는 곳에서

hiding-places, / and in the scuffle with their owners, /
나와,　　　　　노새 주인들과 싸우다가,

wounded with a sword / the Mule carrying the treasure,
칼로 상처를 입히고　　　　귀중품을 운반하던 노새를,

/ which they greedily seized / while taking no notice
탐욕스럽게 빼앗았다　　　　반면 곡식에는 신경 쓰지 않은 채.

of the grain. The Mule / which had been robbed / and
노새는　　　　강도를 당해 상처 입은

wounded bewailed his misfortunes.
자신의 불운을 슬퍼했다.

The other replied, / "I am indeed glad / that I was
다른 노새가 대답했다,　　　"난 정말로 기쁘구나

thought so little of, / for I have lost nothing, / nor am I
내가 그렇게 무시당한 것이,　왜냐하면 아무것도 잃지 않았고,

hurt with any wound."
아무 상처도 입지 않아 안 아프니까."

The North Wind and the Sun
북풍과 태양

THE NORTH WIND and the Sun disputed / as to which
북풍과 태양이 논쟁을 벌이다가

was the most powerful, / and agreed / that he should be
누가 가장 힘이 센지에 관해,　　　　합의했다　　　　승자가 되어야 한다고

declared the victor / who could first strip / a wayfaring
　　　　　　　　　　　먼저 벗길 수 있는 쪽이

man of his clothes.
여행자의 옷을.

The North Wind first tried his power / and blew / with
북풍이 먼저 힘을 시도했고　　　　　　　　바람을 불었다

all his might, / but the keener his blasts, / the closer the
온 힘을 다해,　　　그러나 바람이 거셀수록,

Traveler wrapped his cloak around him, / until at last, /
여행자는 외투를 더욱 꼭 감쌌고,　　　　　　　마침내,

resigning all hope of victory, / the Wind called upon the
승자가 되겠다는 희망을 포기하고,　　　태양에게 요구했다

Sun / to see what he could do.
　　무엇을 할 수 있는지 보여 달라고.

The Sun suddenly shone out / with all his warmth. The
태양은 갑자기 빛을 쪼였다　　　　온 열기를 다해.

Traveler / no sooner felt his genial rays / than he took
여행자는　　　따뜻한 빛을 느끼자마자　　　　벗었고

off / one garment after another, / and at last, / fairly
　　옷을 하나씩,　　　　　　　마침내,

overcome with heat, / undressed and bathed / in a stream
열기를 이겨내지 못하자,　　　옷을 벗고 목욕했다　　　개울에서

/ that lay in his path.
　가는 길에 있던.

Persuasion is better than Force.
설득이 힘보다 나은 법이다.

---

mule 노새 |well-laden with ~을 잔뜩 실은 |pannier 바구니 |sack 주머니 |fastened 고정된 |companion
친구, 동행자 |scuffle 난투 |bewail 몹시 슬퍼하다 |think little of ~을 전혀 생각하지 않다, ~을 무시하다 |
strip 벗기다 |wayfaring 여행 중인 |keen 격렬한, 격심한 |blast 돌풍 |cloak 망토 |resign 포기하다, 그만두다
|genial 따뜻한, 상냥한 |garment 옷, 의복 |fairly 아주, 완전히 |bath 목욕하다

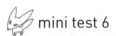
A. 다음 문장을 해석해 보세요.

(1) The elder woman, / ashamed to be courted / by a man / younger than herself, / made a point, / whenever her admirer visited her, / to pull out / some portion of his black hairs.
→

(2) If you were disliked / by those / who go out early in the morning / with their flocks / and return late in the evening, / what must have been felt towards you / by those / with whom you passed the / whole day!
→

(3) For this purpose, / they divided the term of his life / between them, / and each endowed one portion of it / with the qualities / which chiefly characterized himself.
→

(4) This entertaining sight brought / the people in crowds / to laugh at it.
→

B. 다음 주어진 문장이 되도록 빈칸에 써 넣으세요.

(1) 나는 더 이상 자네를 친구라고 생각할 수 없네.

→

(2) 당신이 이 두 조각상을 사겠다면, <u>그 조각상도 덤으로 드리겠습니다.</u>

If you will buy these,   .

(3) 개구리는 <u>마치 좋은 일을 하는 듯</u> 개골거리며 헤엄쳐 다녔다.

The Frog swam croaking about,   .

A. (1) 나이든 여자는 자신보다 어린 남자에게 구애받는 것이 부끄러워서, 구혼자가 찾아올 때마다 반드시 검은 머리를 뽑곤 했다. (2) 당신이 아침 일찍 나가서 가축을 끌고 밤 늦게 돌아오는 사람들에게도 미움을 받는다면, 당신과 하루종일 같이 보내는 사람들은 어떻게 느꼈겠소! (3) 이를 위해, 동물들은 사람의 인생을 나누어,

(4) 명예를 얻으면 얻을수록 위험도 커지는 법이다.

→

C. 다음 주어진 문구가 알맞은 문장이 되도록 순서를 맞춰 보세요.

(1) 그는 말에게 자신의 귀리를 마음껏 먹게 했다.
   [let / He / the Horse / make / free / with / his oats]

   →

(2) 우리가 떠나야 할 시간이 됐어.
   [to / time / is / It / off / for / be / us]

   →

(3) 전투가 시작되자마자, 쥐들은 완패했다.
   [when / had / a great rout / the battle / Scarcely / the Mice / begun, / overwhelmed]

   →

(4) 당신들이 그를 타고 가는 모습을 보면 누구도 그렇게 생각하지 않을 텐데.
   [would / load / One / not / so, / the / thought / you / have / by / him / way]

   →

D. 의미가 서로 비슷한 것끼리 연결해 보세요.

(1) bestow   ▶   ◀ ① skill

(2) prowess   ▶   ◀ ② avert

(3) disguise   ▶   ◀ ③ present

(4) divert   ▶   ◀ ④ camouflage

Answer

서로 각자의 부분에 자신의 특징을 잘 나타내는 성질을 부여했다. (4) 이런 재미있는 광경을 보자 모여 있던 사람들은 그 모습을 비웃었다. | B. (1) I can no longer consider you as a friend. (2) I'll fling you that into the bargain (3) as if he had done a good deed (4) The more honor the more danger. | C. (1) He let the Horse make free with his oats. (2) It is time for us to be off. (3) Scarcely had the battle begun, when a great rout overwhelmed the Mice. (4) One would not have thought so, by the way you load him. | D. (1) ③ (2) ① (3) ④ (4) ②

169

7

The Oak and the Reeds
참나무와 갈대

A VERY LARGE OAK was uprooted / by the wind /
매우 큰 참나무가 뿌리채 뽑혀서   바람에

and thrown across a stream. It fell among some Reeds, /
개울 건너편으로 떨어졌다.   참나무는 갈대들 사이에 떨어졌고,

which it thus addressed: / "I wonder / how you, / who are
그러자 참나무는 갈대에게 이렇게 말했다: "궁금하구나   어떻게 너희들은,

so light and weak, / are not entirely crushed / by these
그토록 가볍고 약한,   전혀 부러지지 않는지

strong winds."
이런 강한 바람에도."

They replied, / "You fight and contend with the wind,
갈대들이 대답했다,   "당신은 바람과 싸우고 맞서잖아,

/ and consequently you are destroyed; / while we on
그래서 결과적으로 뽑히는 거야: 반면 우리는 그와 반대로

the contrary / bend before the least breath of air, / and
아주 약한 바람 앞에서도 휘어지지,

therefore / remain unbroken, / and escape."
그래서   부러지지 않은 채,   있는 거야."

Stoop to conquer.
승리하려면 몸을 굽혀라.

The Oak and the Woodcutters
떡갈나무와 나무꾼

THE WOODCUTTER cut down a Mountain Oak / and
나무꾼이 산에 있는 참나무를 베어

split it in pieces, / making wedges of its own branches /
여러 조각으로 쪼개어,   그 가지로 쐐기를 만들었다

for dividing the trunk.
나무의 몸통을 나누기 위해.

---

reed 갈대 |contend 싸우다, 맞서다 |stoop 구부리다 |split 나누다, 쪼개다 |wedge 쐐기 |aimed at ~을
목표로 한 |foliage 잎 |despoil 빼앗다 |denude 벗기다

The Oak said / with a sigh, / "I do not care about / the
참나무가 말했다   한숨을 쉬며,   "난 신경 쓰지 않아

blows of the axe / aimed at my roots, / but I do grieve / at
도끼를 내려치는 것에는   내 뿌리를 겨냥해서,   하지만 슬프구나

being torn in pieces / by these wedges / made from my
여러 조각으로 쪼개지는 것은   이 쐐기를 사용해서

own branches."
내 자신의 가지로 만들어진."

Misfortunes springing from ourselves / are the hardest to
우리 자신에게서 비롯된 불행은   가장 참기 힘들다.

bear.

The Olive-Tree and the Fig-Tree
올리브 나무와 무화과 나무

THE OLIVE-TREE ridiculed the Fig-Tree / because, /
올리브 나무가 무화과 나무를 비웃었다   왜냐하면,

while she was green / all the year round, / the Fig-Tree
자신은 푸르지만   1년 내내,   무화과 나무는 잎 색깔

changed its leaves / with the seasons.
을 바꾸기 때문이었다   계절에 따라.

A shower of snow fell upon them, / and, / finding the
함박눈이 나무들 위로 내렸다.   그리고,   잎이 무성한 올리브

Olive full of foliage, / it settled upon its branches / and
나무를 발견하고,   그 가지 위에 내려앉아

broke them down / with its weight, / at once despoiling
가지를 부러뜨리고 말았고   그 무게 때문에,   곧 나무의 아름다움을 빼앗아

it of its beauty / and killing the tree. But finding the Fig-
죽여 버렸다.   하지만 무화과 나무를 발견하고는

Tree / denuded of leaves, / the snow fell through / to the
잎이 다 떨어져 버린,   눈은 곧장 떨어졌고

ground, / and did not injure it at all.
땅으로,   그래서 나무를 전혀 해치지 않았다.

The Ox and the Frog
황소와 개구리

AN OX / drinking at a pool / trod on a brood of young
황소 한 마리가 연못에서 물을 마시던 새끼 개구리 형제들을 밟아

frogs / and crushed one of them to death.
그 중 한 마리를 으스러뜨려 죽이고 말았다.

The Mother coming up, / and missing one of her sons, /
어미 개구리가 나타나, 아들 중 한 마리가 없어진 것을 알고,

inquired of his brothers / what had become of him.
개구리들에게 물었다 그 개구리가 어떻게 되었는지.

"He is dead, / dear Mother; / for just now / a very huge
"그 애는 죽었어요, 엄마; 왜냐하면 방금 아주 거대한 동물이

beast / with four great feet / came to the pool / and
커다란 네 발을 가진 연못에 다가와서

crushed him to death / with his cloven heel."
그 애를 밟아 죽였거든요 갈라진 뒷발굽으로."

The Frog, / puffing herself out, / inquired, / "if the beast
개구리는, 자신의 몸을 부풀리며, 물었다, "만약 그 동물이

was / as big as that in size."
크기가 이 정도로 크다면."

"Cease, / Mother, / to puff yourself out," / said her son,
"그만두세요, 엄마, 몸을 부풀리는 것을," 아들 개구리가 말했다,

/ "and do not be angry; / for you would, / I assure you, /
"그리고 화내지 마세요; 왜냐하면 엄마는, 확신하건대,

sooner burst / than successfully imitate / the hugeness of
먼저 터져 버릴 거예요 성공적으로 흉내 내기 전에 그 괴물의 거대한 크기를."

that monster."

The Oxen and the Butchers
황소들과 푸줏간 주인

THE OXEN / once upon a time / sought to destroy the
황소들이 옛날 옛적에 푸줏간 주인들을 죽이려고 했다,

Butchers, / who practiced a trade / destructive to their
일을 하는 자신의 종족을 파괴시키는.

race. They assembled / on a certain day / to carry out
황소들은 모여서 어느 날 목표를 실행하기 위해,

their purpose, / and sharpened their horns / for the contest.
빨을 갈았다   싸움을 위해.

But one of them / who was exceedingly old / (for many a
하지만 황소들 중 하나가   아주 나이가 많았던

field had he plowed) / thus spoke: / "These Butchers, / it is
(많은 밭을 갈아왔던)   이렇게 말했다: "이 푸줏간 주인들은,

true, / slaughter us, / but they do so / with skillful hands,
사실,   우리들을 죽이지만,   그 일을 한다   숙련된 손길로,

/ and with no unnecessary pain. If we get rid of them, /
불필요한 고통 없이.   만약 우리가 그들을 없앤다면,

we shall fall into / the hands of unskillful operators, / and
넘어가고 말 거야   서툰 일꾼들의 손에,

thus suffer a double death: / for you may be assured, / that
그래서 두 배의 고통을 겪겠지: 왜냐하면 확신하건대,

though all the Butchers should perish, / yet will men never
모든 푸줏간 주인들이 사라지더라도,   사람들은 고기를 원할 수밖에

want beef."
없으니까."

Do not be in a hurry / to change one evil for another.
서두르지 마라   악한 것을 다른 것으로 바꾸는데.

Key Expression

동사 + to death : ~해 죽[이]다

동사 + to death 형태의 표현은 '~해 죽[이]다'라는 식으로 해석합니다. '~해
죽이다'의 경우에는 능동태를, '~해 죽다'의 경우에는 수동태가 주로 쓰입니다.

▶ crush to death : 으스러뜨려 죽이다
▶ beat to death : 때려 죽이다
▶ shoot to death : 쏘아 죽이다
▶ stone to death : 돌을 던져 죽이다
▶ burn to death : 태워 죽이다
▶ be bored to death : 지루해 죽다
▶ be scared to death : 무서워 죽다
▶ be frozen to death : 얼어 죽다

ex) An ox drinking at a pool trod on a brood of young frogs and crushed one of
them to death.
연못에서 물을 마시던 황소 한 마리가 새끼 개구리 형제들을 밟아 그 중 한
마리를 으스러뜨려 죽이고 말았다.

clove 쪼개다, 가르다 | heel 뒤꿈치, 뒷발굽 | puff 부풀리다 | cease 중단하다 | butcher 정육점 주인, 도살업자
race 종족 | get rid of 제거하다 | operator 작업자

The Oxen and the Axle-Trees
황소들과 차축

A HEAVY WAGON was being dragged / along a
무거운 마차가 끌려가고 있었다

country lane / by a team of Oxen. The Axle-trees
시골길을 따라   황소 무리에 의해.   차축은 소리를 내며

groaned / and creaked terribly; / whereupon the Oxen,
심하게 삐걱거렸다;   그러자 황소들은,

/ turning round, / thus addressed the wheels: / "Hullo
돌아보면서,   바퀴들에게 이렇게 말했다: "어이 거기!

there! Why do you make so much noise? We bear all the
왜 그렇게 큰 소리를 내는 거야?   우리는 모든 중노동을 참고

labor, / and we, / not you, / ought to cry out."
있는데,   그러니 우리가,   네가 아닌,   울어야 한다고."

Those who suffer most / cry out the least.
가장 고통받는 자들은   가장 작은 소리를 낸다.

The Owl and the Birds
올빼미와 새들

AN OWL, / in her wisdom, / counseled the Birds / that
올빼미 한 마리가,   지혜로운,   새들에게 조언했다

when the acorn first began to sprout, / to pull it all up
도토리가 첫 싹을 틔우기 시작할 때,   전부 뽑아버려서

/ out of the ground / and not allow it to grow. She said
땅에서   자라지 못하게 하라고.   올빼미는 말했다

/ acorns would produce mistletoe, / from which an
도토리는 겨우살이를 만들어 내고,   겨우살이에서는 치명적인 독인,

irremediable poison, / the bird-lime, / would be extracted
새 잡는 끈끈이가,   추출되어

/ and by which they would be captured.
그것으로 인해 새들이 붙잡힐 것이고.

The Owl next advised them / to pluck up the seed of the
그 다음 올빼미는 충고했다   아마의 씨앗을 뽑으라고,

flax, / which men had sown, / as it was a plant / which
인간들이 뿌려 놓은,   그것은 식물이기 때문에

boded no good to them.
새들에게 나쁜 징조가 될.

And, / lastly, / the Owl, / seeing an archer approach,
그리고,   마지막으로, 올빼미는,   궁수가 다가오는 것을 보고,

/ predicted / that this man, / being on foot, / would
예언했다   이 사람이,   걸어다니는,   만들어 낼 것이라고

contrive / darts armed with feathers / which would fly
깃털로 무장한 화살을   더 빠르게 날아올

faster / than the wings of the Birds themselves.
새들의 날개짓보다.

The Birds gave no credence / to these warning words, /
새들은 전혀 신경 쓰지 않고   이런 경고의 말을,

but considered / the Owl to be beside herself / and said
오히려 생각하며   올빼미가 제정신이 아니라고   말했다

/ that she was mad. But afterwards, / finding her words
미쳤다고.   하지만 나중에,   올빼미의 말이 사실임을 알게

were true, / they wondered / at her knowledge / and
되자,   새들은 놀랐고   올빼미의 지식에

deemed her / to be the wisest of birds.
올빼미를 여겼다   가장 지혜로운 새라고.

Hence / it is that when she appears / they look to her /
그 후로   올빼미가 나타날 때면   새들은 올빼미에게 기대한다

as knowing all things, / while she no longer gives them
모든 것을 알고 있기에,   하지만 올빼미는 더 이상 충고를 하지 않고,

advice, / but in solitude laments / their past folly.
홀로 탄식한다   새들의 과거의 어리석음을.

---

axle-tree(수레의) 굴대, 차축 | creak삐걱거리다 | hullo(=hello) | acorn도토리 | sprout싹이 나다 |
mistletoe겨우살이(그 줄기를 크리스마스 장식에 쓰곤 하는 덩굴식물로, 크리스마스 때 겨우살이 아래서 키스를 하는
전통이 있다) | irremediable치료할 수 없는 | extract추출하다 | pluck뽑다 | flax아마(亞麻) | sow씨뿌리다 |
bode~의 징조가 되다, 예언하다 | archer궁수 | contrive고안하다 | dart화살 | credence믿음, 신임 | beside
oneself제정신이 아닌 | deem생각하다, 여기다 | look to기대하다, ~에 기대를 걸다 | solitude고독

175

The Panther and the Shepherds
표범과 양치기

A PANTHER, / by some mischance, / fell into a pit.
표범 한 마리가, 불운하게도, 구덩이에 빠져 버렸다.

The Shepherds discovered him, / and some threw sticks
양치기들이 표범을 발견했는데, 몇몇은 막대기를 던지고

/ at him / and pelted him with stones, / while others, /
표범에게 돌로 공격했지만, 다른 이들은,

moved with compassion / towards one about to die / even
동정심을 느껴 막 죽어가는 동물에게

though no one should hurt him, / threw in some food / to
아무도 표범을 상처 입히지는 않았지만, 약간의 음식을 던져 주었다

prolong his life.
목숨을 부지하기 위한.

At night / they returned home, / not dreaming of any
밤이 되어 양치기들은 집으로 돌아갔지만, 위험할 것이라고 전혀 생각하지 않고,

danger, / but supposing / that on the morrow / they would
생각하면서 그 다음 날

find him dead.
표범이 죽은 걸 발견할 거라고.

The Panther, / however, / when he had recruited his
표범은, 그러나, 미약한 힘을 짜내어,

feeble strength, / freed himself with a sudden bound /
갑자기 뛰어올라 탈출했고

from the pit, / and hastened to his den / with rapid steps.
구덩이로부터, 서둘러 굴로 돌아갔다 빠른 걸음으로.

After a few days / he came forth / and slaughtered the
며칠 후 표범이 나와 소떼를 공격했고,

cattle, / and, / killing the Shepherds / who had attacked
그리고, 양치기들을 죽였다 자신을 공격했던

him, / raged with angry fury. Then / they who had
사납게 화를 내며. 그러자 표범의 목숨을 살려준 사람들은,

spared his life, / fearing for their safety, / surrendered to
안전할 수 있을지 두려워 하며,

him their flocks / and begged only for their lives.
표범에게 가축을 내어 주고 살려만 달라고 애원했다.

To them / the Panther made this reply: / "I remember
그들에게   표범은 이렇게 대답했다: "나도 똑같이 기억하네

alike those / who sought my life with stones, / and those
             돌을 던져 내 목숨을 노린 자들과,

who gave me food aside, / therefore, / your fears. I return
내게 음식을 준 자들을,   그러니,   당신들의 두려움도. 난 적으로

as an enemy / only to those who injured me."
여기고 복수하지   날 해친 자들에게만."

mischance 불운 | pit 구덩이 | pelt (던지며) 공격하다 | prolong 연장시키다, 연장하다 | morrow 그 다음 날 |
recruit 모집하다, 뽑다 | feeble 아주 약한, 미미한 | come forth 나오다 | surrender 항복하다, 포기하다, 내주다

The Peasant and the Apple-Tree
농부와 사과나무

A PEASANT had / in his garden / an Apple-Tree /
한 농부는 갖고 있었다   정원에   사과나무 한 그루를

which bore no fruit / but only served as a harbor / for the
열매를 맺지 못하고   휴식처 역할만 하는

sparrows and grasshoppers. He resolved to cut it down,
제비와 베짱이들의.   그는 나무를 베기로 결심하고,

/ and taking his axe in his hand, / made a bold stroke / at
손에 도끼를 들고,   세게 내리쳤다

its roots.
나무 뿌리를.

The grasshoppers and sparrows entreated him / not to
베짱이와 제비들은 농부에게 간청했다

cut down the tree / that sheltered them, / but to spare it,
나무를 베지 말고   자신들을 쉬게 해 주는,   살려 달라고,

/ and they would sing to him / and lighten his labors. He
그러면 농부에게 노래를 불러서   힘든 노동을 덜어 주겠다고.

paid no attention to their request, / but gave the tree a
농부는 그들의 요구에 주의를 기울이지 않고,   나무를 두 번 그리고 세 번 내리쳤다

second and a third blow / with his axe.
도끼로.

When he reached the hollow of the tree, / he found a hive
농부가 나무의 텅 빈 속에 이르렀을 때,   꿀이 가득 찬 벌집을

full of honey. Having tasted the honeycomb, / he threw
발견했다.   벌집을 맛보고 나서,   농부는 도끼를

down his axe, / and looking on the tree as sacred, / took
내던지고,   나무를 신성하게 여기며,

great care of it.
잘 돌봐주었다.

Self-interest alone moves some men.
사리사욕 만으로 사람들의 마음을 움직이기도 한다.

---

peasant 농부 | bear (열매를) 맺다 | harbor 피난처, 은신처 | sparrow 제비 | hive 벌집 | honeycomb 벌집
look on 여기다 | sacred 성스러운, 신성한 | self-interest 사리사욕, 사리 추구

The Peacock and the Crane
공작새와 두루미

A PEACOCK / spreading its gorgeous tail / mocked a
공작새 한 마리가　　멋진 꼬리를 펼치고 있던　　　두루미를 조롱했다

Crane / that passed by, / ridiculing the ashen hue of its
지나가던,　　잿빛 깃털을 비웃으며

plumage / and saying, / "I am robed, / like a king, / in gold
말했다.　　"난 옷을 입었지.　　왕처럼,

and purple / and all the colors of the rainbow; / while you
황금색과 자주색　　그리고 온갖 무지개색으로;

have not a bit of color / on your wings."
반면 넌 색이 없구나　　날개에."

"True," / replied the Crane; / "but I soar to the heights of
"맞아,"　　두루미가 대답했다;　　"하지만 난 하늘 높이 날아올라

heaven / and lift up my voice / to the stars, / while you walk
목소리를 높이지　　별까지 들리도록,　　반면 넌 아래에서 걸어다

below, / like a cock, / among the birds of the dunghill."
니잖니,　　수탉처럼,　　지저분한 장소에 사는 새들 속을."

Fine feathers don't make fine birds.
멋진 깃털이 멋진 새를 만들지 않는다.

The Philosopher, the Ants, and Mercury
철학자, 개미, 그리고 머큐리

A PHILOSOPHER witnessed / from the shore / the
한 철학자가 목격했다　　바닷가에서

shipwreck of a vessel, / of which the crew and passengers
부서진 배 한 척을,　　선원과 승객들이

/ were all drowned. He inveighed / against the injustice
모두 익사해 버린.　　그는 비난했다　　신의 부당한 처사에 대해,

of Providence, / which would for the sake of one criminal
한 명의 범죄자 때문에

/ perchance sailing in the ship / allow so many innocent
어쩌면 그 배에 타고 있었을지 모르는　　수많은 무고한 사람들을 죽게 만들었다고.

persons to perish.

As he was indulging / in these reflections, / he found
몰두하고 있을 때　　　이런 깊은 생각에,

himself / surrounded by a whole army of Ants, / near
그는 발견했다　수많은 개미떼에 둘러싸여 있다는 것을,

whose nest / he was standing. One of them climbed up /
개미 집 근처에서　그가 서 있던.　　개미 한 마리가 기어 올라와

and stung him, / and he immediately trampled them all
그를 물자,　　그는 즉시 모두 밟아 죽였다

to death / with his foot.
　　발로.

Mercury presented himself, / and striking the
머큐리가 나타나,　　　철학자를 때리면서

Philosopher / with his wand, / said, / "And are you
지팡이로,　　　말했다,

indeed to make yourself / a judge of the dealings of
"그러면 네가 정말로 되겠다는 거냐　신의 섭리를 심판하는 사람이,

Providence, / who hast thyself in a similar manner /
네 자신도 같은 방법으로

treated these poor Ants?"
이 개미들을 다뤘으면서?"

Key Expression

make oneself~

make와 재귀대명사를 사용한 5형식 문장은 우리말로 직역하면 자연스러운 해석이 되지 않죠. 다음과 같이 해석해 보세요.

▶ make oneself + 동사원형 : (자신을 ~하게 만들다) → ~하다

▶ make oneself + 명사 : (자신을 ~로 만들다) → ~가 되다

▶ make oneself + 형용사 : (자신을 ~한 사람으로 만들다) → ~하게 되다, ~한 사람이 되다

▶ make oneself + 과거분사 : (자신을 ~되게 만들다) → ~받게 되다, (동사의 반대 의미의 해석으로) ~하게 되다

ex) And are you indeed to make yourself a judge of the dealings of Providence?
　그러면 네가 정말로 신의 섭리를 심판하는 사람이 되겠다는 것인가?

peacock 공작 | gorgeous 화려한, 멋진 | ashen 잿빛의 | dunghill 똥 더미, 더러운 곳 | philosopher 철학자 |
shipwreck 난파선 | inveigh 통렬히 비난하다, 독설을 퍼붓다 | providence (신의) 섭리 | criminal 범죄자 |
perchance 아마, 어쩌면 | trample 짓밟다 | wand 지팡이 | hast have의 제2인칭·단수·직설법·현재형

181

The Thirsty Pigeon
목마른 비둘기

A PIGEON, / oppressed by excessive thirst, / saw a goblet
비둘기 한 마리가,   심한 갈증에 시달리던,   물이 담긴 포도주 잔을

of water / painted on a signboard. Not supposing it to be
보았다   간판 위에 그려진.   그것이 그림일 뿐이라고 생각하지 못한 채,

only a picture, / she flew towards it / with a loud whir / and
              비둘기는 그것을 향해 날아갔고   요란한 날갯짓으로   자신도

unwittingly / dashed against the signboard, / jarring herself
모르는 사이에   간판에 부딪혀,   심하게 다치고 말았다.

terribly. Having broken her wings / by the blow, / she fell to
         날개가 부러지고   충격으로 인해,   비둘기는 땅으로

the ground, / and was caught / by one of the bystanders.
떨어져,   붙잡혔다   구경꾼에 의해.

Zeal should not outrun discretion.
열의가 신중함을 앞서서는 안 된다.

The Two Pots
두 개의 항아리

A RIVER carried down / in its stream / two Pots, / one
강이 실어가고 있었다   물살에   항아리 두 개를,

made of earthenware / and the other of brass. The Earthen
하나는 흙으로 만든 것이었고   다른 하나는 청동으로 만든 것이었다.

Pot said to the Brass Pot, / "Pray keep at a distance / and do
흙 항아리가 청동 항아리에게 말했다, "제발 떨어져 줘

not come near me, / for if you touch me ever / so slightly,
그리고 가까이 다가오지 마,   왜냐하면 네가 날 건드리기라도 하면   살짝이라도,

/ I shall be broken in pieces, / and besides, / I by no means
내가 산산조각이 날 테니까,   게다가,   난 결코 가고 싶지 않거든

wish to come / near you."
              네 가까이에."

Equals make the best friends.
평등한 지위가 친한 친구를 만든다.

pigeon 비둘기 | oppress 압박하다 | goblet 고블릿(유리나 금속으로 된 포도주잔) | signboard 간판 | whir
윙윙거리는 소리 | unwittingly 자신도 모르게, 부지불식간에 | dash 내동댕이치다, 부딪치다 | jar 충격을 주다 |
zeal 열의, 열성 | outrun 더 빨리[멀리] 달리다 | discretion 신중함 | earthenware 도자기 | brass 청동

The Raven and the Swan
갈까마귀와 백조

A RAVEN saw a Swan / and desired to secure for /
갈까마귀가 백조를 보고 갖고 싶어 했다

himself / the same beautiful plumage. Supposing / that
자신도 똑같이 아름다운 깃털을. 생각해서

the Swan's splendid white color arose / from his washing
백조의 멋진 흰 깃털이 생긴 것이라고 물에서 씻기 때문에

in the water / in which he swam, / the Raven left the
헤엄치는, 갈까마귀는 제단을 떠나

altars / in the neighborhood / where he picked up his
근처의 생계를 꾸리고 있던,

living, / and took up residence / in the lakes and pools.
둥지를 마련했다 호수와 연못에.

But cleansing his feathers / as often as he would, / he
하지만 아무리 깃털을 씻어도 최대한 자주,

could not change their color, / while through want of
자신의 색을 바꿀 수 없었고, 오히려 먹이 부족으로

food / he perished.
죽고 말았다.

Change of habit cannot alter Nature.
습관을 바꾼다고 본성을 바꿀 수 없다

Key Expression

suppose it to be ~ : 그것이 ~이라고 상상하다[생각하다]

생각이나 판단의 의미를 가진 동사들은 5형식으로 사용될 때 'to be ~'의 목적보어를 취합니다. 이때 to be는 종종 생략되기도 합니다.

think ┐
believe ┤
consider ┤ + 목적어 + to be + 명사/형용사
know ┤
suppose ┘

ex) Not supposing it to be only a picture, she flew towards it with a loud whir.
그것이 그림일 뿐이라고 생각하지 못한 채, 비둘기는 요란한 날갯짓으로 그것을 향해 날아갔다.

altar 제단 | cleanse 씻다 | want 결핍, 부족

The Salt Merchant and His Ass
소금 장수와 당나귀

A PEDDLER drove his Ass / to the seashore / to buy salt.
한 장사꾼이 당나귀를 몰고 갔다   바닷가로   소금을 사려고.

His road home / lay across a stream / into which his Ass,
집으로 가는 길에   개울이 가로질러 놓여 있었는데   개울로 들어가다 당나귀는,

/ making a false step, / fell by accident / and rose up again
발을 헛딛어서,   실수로 넘어졌고   다시 일어나보니

/ with his load considerably lighter, / as the water melted
짐이 꽤 가벼워져 있었다.   물에 소금이 녹았기 때문에.

the sack.

The Peddler retraced his steps / and refilled his panniers /
장사꾼은 가던 길을 되돌아서   바구니를 채워왔다

with a larger quantity of salt / than before. When he came
더 많은 양의 소금으로   전보다.

again to the stream, / the Ass fell down / on purpose / in
그가 다시 개울에 도착하자,   당나귀가 넘어졌고   일부러

the same spot, / and, / regaining his feet / with the weight
같은 지점에서,   그리고,   다시 일어나면서

of his load much diminished, / brayed triumphantly / as if
짐의 무게가 훨씬 가벼워진 채.   의기양양하게 울었다

he had obtained / what he desired.
마치 자신이 얻었다는 듯   원하던 것을.

The Peddler saw through his trick / and drove him for
장사꾼은 당나귀의 속임수를 꿰뚫어 보고   세 번째로 끌고 가서

the third time / to the coast, / where he bought a cargo of
해변으로.   스펀지 한 짐을 샀다

sponges / instead of salt. The Ass, / again playing the fool,
소금 대신.   당나귀는,   또 다시 어리석은 짓을 하면서,

/ fell down / on purpose / when he reached the stream,
넘어졌다   일부러   개울에 도달했을 때,

/ but the sponges became swollen with water, / greatly
그러나 스펀지가 물 때문에 부풀어 올라서,

increasing his load. And thus / his trick recoiled / on him,
짐이 훨씬 무거워졌다.   그래서 이렇게   당나귀의 잔꾀는 되돌아왔다   자신에게,

/ for he now carried / on his back / a double burden.
왜냐하면 이제 지게 되었으니까   등에   두 배의 짐을.

The Seagull and the Kite
갈매기와 솔개

A SEAGULL / having bolted down / too large a fish, /
갈매기 한 마리가   급하게 삼킨   너무 큰 물고기를,

burst its deep gullet-bag / and lay down / on the shore
식도가 터져서   쓰러져   바닷가에

/ to die. A Kite saw him / and exclaimed: / "You richly
죽었다. 솔개가 갈매기를 보고   소리쳤다:

deserve your fate; / for a bird of the air / has no business
"넌 정말 당할 만해;   왜냐하면 하늘을 나는 새는   먹이를 찾아서는 안 되지

to seek its food / from the sea."
바다에서."

Every man should be content to / mind his own business.
모든 사람은 만족해야 한다   자신의 일에 신경 쓰는 것에.

The Serpent and the Eagle
뱀과 독수리

A SERPENT and an Eagle were struggling / with
뱀과 독수리가 다투고 있었다

each other / in deadly conflict. The Serpent had the
서로   목숨을 건 싸움으로. 뱀이 유리해져서,

advantage, / and was about to strangle the bird.
새를 목 졸라 죽이려 했다.

A countryman saw them, / and running up, / loosed
시골 농부가 그것들을 보고,   달려가서,

the coil of the Serpent / and let the Eagle go free. The
뱀의 똬리를 풀고   독수리를 놓아 주었다.

Serpent, / irritated at the escape of his prey, / injected his
뱀은,   자신의 먹이가 달아난 것에 화가 나서,   독을 넣었다

poison / into the drinking horn of the countryman.
뿔로 된 농부의 물병 속에.

---

peddler 행상인(=pedlar) | melt 녹이다 | retrace (왔던 길을) 되짚어 가다 | refill 다시 채우다 | diminish
줄어들다, 감소하다 | bray (나귀 등이) 시끄럽게 울다 | recoil (총이 발사할 때) 반동이 생기다 | seagull 갈매기 |
bolt down 급하게 먹다 | gullet 식도 | richly 매우 | have no business to ~할 권리가 없다, ~해서는 안 되다 |
serpent 뱀 | deadly 치명적인 | strangle 교살하다, 목졸라 죽이다 | coil 똬리 | inject 주입하다

The rustic, / ignorant of his danger, / was about to drink,
시골 농부가, 자신의 위험을 모른 채, 막 물을 마시려 하자,

/ when the Eagle struck his hand / with his wing, / and, /
그때 독수리가 그의 손을 치고 날개로, 그리고,

seizing the drinking horn / in his talons, / carried it aloft.
물병을 빼앗아 발톱으로, 하늘 높이 가져가 버렸다.

The Shepherd's Boy and the Wolf
양치기 소년과 늑대

A SHEPHERD-BOY, / who watched a flock of sheep / near
한 양치기 소년이, 양떼를 지키고 있던

a village, / brought out the villagers / three or four times
마을 근처에서, 마을 사람들을 불러냈다 서너 번이나

/ by crying out, / "Wolf! Wolf!" / and when his neighbors
소리쳐서, "늑대다! 늑대다!"라고 그리고 이웃들이 도우러 왔을 때,

came to help him, / laughed at them / for their pains.
비웃었다 그들의 수고를.

The Wolf, / however, / did truly come / at last. The
늑대는, 그러나, 진짜 나타났다 마침내.

Shepherd-boy, / now really alarmed, / shouted / in an agony
양치기 소년은, 이제 정말 놀라서, 소리쳤다 두려움에 괴로워

of terror: / "Pray, / do come and help me; / the Wolf is
하며: "제발, 와서 도와주세요; 늑대가 양을 죽이고 있어요;"

killing the sheep;" / but no one paid any heed / to his cries, /
하지만 아무도 주의를 기울이지도 않았고 그의 외침에,

nor rendered any assistance. The Wolf, / having no cause of
도와주지도 않았다. 늑대는, 두려워 할 이유가 없었기 때문에,

fear, / at his leisure / lacerated or destroyed the whole flock.
마음 내키는 대로 모든 양떼를 찢어 죽였다.

There is no believing a liar, / even when he speaks the truth.
거짓말쟁이를 믿을 수 없다, 심지어 진실을 말할 때에도.

---

rustic 시골 사람 | heed 주의 | render 주다, 만들다 | lacerate 찢다 | inadvertently 무심코, 우연히, 부주의로 |
fray 닳게 하다, 해어지게 하다, 비비다 | garment 의류, 옷

The Shepherd and the Sheep
양치기와 양떼

A SHEPHERD / driving his Sheep to a wood, / saw an
한 양치기가   양떼를 몰고 숲으로 가던,

oak of unusual size / full of acorns, / and spreading his
유난히 큰 참나무를 보고   도토리가 가득 열린,   자신의 외투를 펼쳐 놓고

cloak / under the branches, / he climbed up into the tree /
나뭇가지 아래,   나무 위로 올라가서

and shook them down.
흔들어 떨어뜨렸다.

The Sheep / eating the acorns inadvertently / frayed and
양떼는   무심코 도토리를 먹다가   외투를 해어지고

tore the cloak. When the Shepherd came down / and
찢어지게 해 버렸다.   양치기가 내려와

saw / what was done, / he said, / "O you most ungrateful
보고   일어난 일을,   말했다,   "오 배은망덕한 동물들아!

creatures! You provide wool / to make garments / for
너희는 양털을 주면서   옷을 만들도록

all other men, / but you destroy / the clothes of him who
다른 모든 사람들에게는,   찢어 놓는구나   너희들을 먹이는 사람의 옷은."

feeds you."

The She-Goats and Their Beards
암염소와 턱수염

THE SHE-GOATS / having obtained a beard / by
암염소들이   턱수염을 얻자

request to Jupiter, / the He-Goats were sorely displeased
제우스에게 부탁하여,   숫염소들은 몹시 불쾌해 하며

/ and made complaint / that the females equaled them /
불평했다   암컷들이 똑같아졌다고

in dignity.
위엄에서.

"Allow them," / said Jupiter, / "to enjoy an empty honor /
"그들에게 허락하거라,"   제우스가 말했다,   "공허한 명예를 즐기도록

and to assume the badge of your nobler sex, / so long as
그리고 너희들의 고귀한 성별의 상징을 가지도록,

they are not your equals / in strength or courage."
그들이 너희들과 대등하지 않은 한   힘이나 용기에서."

It matters little / if those who are inferior to us / in merit
중요하지 않다   우리보다 못한 자들이   장점에서

/ should be like us / in outside appearances.
우리와 같아진다고 해도   외모에 있어서.

The Shipwrecked Man and the Sea
조난자와 바다

A SHIPWRECKED MAN, / having been cast / upon a
한 조난 당한 사람이,   내던져진

certain shore, / slept / after his buffetings / with the deep.
어느 해변에,   잠들었다 사투를 벌인 뒤   깊은 바다와.

After a while / he awoke, / and looking upon the Sea, /
잠시 후   그가 깨어나서,   바다를 내려다보며,

loaded it with reproaches.
비난을 퍼부어댔다.

beard 턱수염 | sorely 몹시 | dignity 위엄, 품위 | badge 증표, 상징 | shipwrecked 난파한, 파괴된 | cast 던지다
| buffeting 난타, 난기류에 의한 큰 진동 | entice 유인하다 | induce 설득하다, 유도하다 | plow 헤치고 나아가다 |
lash 채찍으로 때리다, 자극하다 | help oneself 음식물을 마음대로 먹다 | the means of living 생계 수단

He argued / that it enticed men / with the calmness of
그는 주장했다   바다가 사람들을 유혹했다고   고요해 보이는 겉모습으로,

its looks, / but when it had induced them / to plow its
하지만 사람들을 끌어들여   바닷물을 가르게

waters, / it grew rough / and destroyed them.
할 때에는,   거칠어져서   사람들을 파괴해 버린다고.

The Sea, / assuming the form of a woman, / replied to
바다가,   여자의 모습으로 꾸민 채,   그에게 대답했다:

him: / "Blame not me, / my good sir, / but the winds, /
"날 비난하지 말고,   제발,   바람을 비난하세요,

for I am / by my own nature / as calm and firm / even as
왜냐하면 전   본래   고요하고 요동이 없지만

this earth; / but the winds suddenly falling on me / create
이 땅처럼;   바람이 갑자기 제게 불어와서   이런 파도

these waves, / and lash me into fury."
를 만들어 내고,   화내도록 채찍질 하니까요."

The Sick Stag
병든 수사슴

A SICK STAG lay down / in a quiet corner of its
병든 수사슴이 누워 있었다   풀밭 한 쪽 조용한 구석에.

pasture-ground. His companions came / in great
동료들이 왔다   많은 수의

numbers / to inquire after his health, / and each one
수사슴의 건강을 알아보기 위해,   그리고 제각기 먹어 버렸다

helped himself / to a share of the food / which had been
몫의 먹이를   놓여 있던

placed / for his use; / so that he died, / not from his
수사슴이 먹으려고;   그래서 수사슴은 죽었다,   병 때문이 아니라,

sickness, / but from the failure of the means of living
끼니를 때우는데 실패하여.

Evil companions bring / more hurt than profit.
악한 동료들은 가져다 준다   이익보다는 더한 상처를.

The Stag in the Ox-Stall
외양간의 수사슴

A STAG, / roundly chased / by the hounds / and blinded
수사슴 한 마리가, 대대적으로 쫓기던   사냥개에   눈이 멀어버렸고

/ by fear to the danger / he was running into, / took
위험에 대한 공포로   자신이 맞닥뜨린,   피신처를 찾아

shelter / in a farmyard / and hid himself / in a shed /
농장 안에서   몸을 숨겼다   우리 속에

among the oxen.
황소들 사이에.

An Ox gave him / this kindly warning: / "O unhappy
한 황소가 수사슴에게   친절하게 경고했다: "오 불행한 동물이여!

creature! Why should you thus, / of your own accord,
넌 왜 이렇게,   자진해서,

/ incur destruction / and trust yourself / in the house
파멸을 초래하고   네 자신을 맡기느냐   적의 집 안에?"

of your enemy?" The Stag replied: / "Only allow me,
수사슴이 대답했다: "허락만 해 주시오,

/ friend, / to stay / where I am, / and I will undertake
친구여,   머물도록   지금 있는 곳에,   그러면 찾도록 하겠네

to find / some favorable opportunity / of effecting my
유리한 기회를   빠져 나갈 수 있는."

escape."

At the approach of the evening / the herdsman came
저녁이 다가오자   목동이 가축의 먹이를 주러 왔지만,

to feed his cattle, / but did not see the Stag; / and
수사슴을 보지 못했다;

even the farm-bailiff / with several laborers / passed
그리고 농장 관리인조차   일꾼들과 함께

through the shed / and failed to notice him. The Stag, /
우리를 지나쳤지만   발견하지 못하고 말았다.   수사슴은,

congratulating himself / on his safety, / began to express
자신을 축하하며   안전해진 것에 대해,   진심어린 감사를 표현하기

his sincere thanks / to the Oxen / who had kindly helped
시작했다   황소들에게   친절하게 도와준

him / in the hour of need.
곤경에 빠졌을 때.

One of them again answered him: / "We indeed wish
황소들 중 한 마리가 다시 대답했다: "우리는 정말 네가 무사하길

you well, / but the danger is not over. There is one other
바라지만,   위험은 아직 끝나지 않았어.   또 한 명이 있어

/ yet / to pass through the shed, / who has as it were / a
아직   우리를 지나갈,   그는 이른바   100개

hundred eyes, / and until he has come and gone, / your
의 눈을 가진 사람이야,   그가 왔다 가기 전까지,

life is still in peril."
네 목숨은 여전히 위험해."

At that moment / the master himself entered, / and
그 순간   주인이 직접 들어와,

having had to complain / that his oxen had not been
불평을 해대며   소들이 충분히 먹이를 먹지 않았다고,

properly fed, / he went up to their racks / and cried out:
선반으로 다가가   외쳤다:

/ "why is there / such a scarcity of fodder? There is not
"왜 있는 거지   저렇게 부족한 사료가?

half enough straw / for them to lie on. Those lazy fellows
지푸라기가 절반도 안 되잖아   소들이 눕기에.   게으른 녀석들이

/ have not even swept / the cobwebs away."
쓸지도 않았구나   거미줄도."

While he thus examined everything / in turn, / he spied
그가 이렇게 모든 것들을 검사하는 동안   차례로,

the tips of the antlers / of the Stag peeping out of the
사슴 뿔의 끝을 알아챘다   지푸라기 밖으로 빠져 나온.

straw. Then / summoning his laborers, / he ordered / that
그러자   일꾼들을 불러,   명령했다

the Stag should be seized / and killed.
수사슴을 잡아   죽이라고.

---

roundly 강력하게, 대대적으로 | shed 헛간, 가축우리 | incur 초래하다 | undertake 착수하다, 약속하다 |
herdsman 목동 | farm-bailiff 농장 관리인 | rack 받침대, 선반 | scarcity 부족, 결핍 | fodder 사료 | cobweb
거미줄 | spy 알아채다 | antler 사슴뿔

The Stag, the Wolf, and the Sheep
수사슴, 늑대, 그리고 양

A STAG asked a Sheep / to lend him / a measure of
수사슴이 양에게 부탁하며   빌려 달라고   밀 한 포대를,

wheat, / and said / that the Wolf would be his surety.
말했다   늑대가 자신의 보증인이라고.

The Sheep, / fearing some fraud was intended, / excused
양은,   속임수가 있지 않을까 걱정하여,

herself, / saying, / "The Wolf is accustomed / to seize
핑계를 대며,   말했다,   "늑대는 익숙하지   자신이 원하는

what he wants / and to run off; / and you, / too, / can
것을 빼앗아   도망가는데;   그리고 너도,   또한,

quickly outstrip me / in your rapid flight. How then shall
금새 날 앞지를 수 있지   빨리 달리면.   그러니 내가 어떻게 널 찾

I be able to find you, / when the day of payment comes?"
을 수 있겠니,   갚을 날이 다가왔을 때?"

Two blacks do not make one white.
검은 것이 두 개 있다고 흰 것을 만들어 낼 수 없다. (악을 악으로 갚는다고 선이 되지는 않는다.)

The Stag at the Pool
연못에 빠진 수사슴

A STAG overpowered by heat / came to a spring to
수사슴 한 마리가 더위에 지쳐   물을 마시러 샘에 왔다.

drink. Seeing his own shadow / reflected in the water, /
자신의 그림자를 보고   물에 비친,

he greatly admired / the size and variety of his horns, /
사슴은 대단히 감탄하면서도   자신의 뿔의 크기와 다양한 모습에,

but felt angry with himself / for having such slender and
자신에게 화가 났다   무척 가늘고 약한 다리를 가졌다는 것에.

weak feet.

While he was thus contemplating himself, / a Lion
수사슴이 이렇게 자신을 응시하는 동안,

appeared at the pool / and crouched to spring upon him.
사자 한 마리가 연못에 다가와   수사슴을 덮치려고 쭈그려 앉았다.

The Stag immediately took to flight, / and exerting his
수사슴은 갑자기 달아나며,　　　　　　　　　최대한의 스피드를 냈고,

utmost speed, / as long as the plain was smooth and open /
　　　　　　들판이 잔잔하고 펼쳐진 동안에는

kept himself easily at a safe distance / from the Lion. But
쉽게 거리를 유지할 수 있었다　　　　　　사자로부터.

entering a wood / he became entangled by his horns, / and
하지만 숲에 들어서자　　수사슴은 뿔 때문에 얽혀 버렸고,

the Lion quickly came up to him / and caught him.
사자가 재빨리 다가가　　　　　　　　　수사슴을 잡았다.

When too late, / he thus reproached himself: / "Woe is
너무 늦었을 때,　　　　수사슴은 자신을 이렇게 책망했다:　　"슬프도다!

me! How I have deceived myself! These feet / which
　　난 내 자신을 속여왔구나!　　　　　　내 다리를

would have saved me / I despised, / and I gloried / in these
날 구해 준　　　　　　멸시하고,　　　자랑하다니

antlers / which have proved my destruction."
내 뿔을　　　날 파멸시킨."

What is most truly valuable / is often underrated.
진정으로 가치 있는 것은　　　　　　종종 과소평가 받곤 한다.

The Swallow and the Crow
제비와 까마귀

THE SWALLOW and the Crow had a contention / about
제비와 까마귀가 논쟁을 벌였다

their plumage. The Crow put an end to the dispute / by
자신들의 깃털에 대해.　　까마귀는 논쟁을 종결지었다

saying, / "Your feathers are all very well / in the spring, /
말하면서,　　　"네 깃털은 무척 아름답지　　　　봄에는,

but mine protect me / against the winter."
하지만 내 깃털은 나를 지켜줘　　겨울에."

Fair weather friends are not worth much.
좋은 날의 친구는 그리 가치 있는 것이 아니다.

surety 보증인 | fraud 사기, 속임수 | excuse oneself 핑계를 대다, 변명하다 | outstrip 능가하다 | overpower
제압하다 | contemplate 생각하다, 응시하다 | crouch (몸을) 쭈그리다, 쭈그리고 앉다 | take to flight 도망치다 |
swallow 제비 | contention 논쟁, 언쟁 | put an end 끝맺다

193

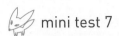

mini test 7

A. 다음 문장을 해석해 보세요.

(1) We bear all the labor, / and we, / not you, / ought to cry out.
→

(2) He inveighed / against the injustice of Providence, / which would for the sake of one criminal perchance / sailing in the ship / allow so many innocent persons to perish.
→

(3) Supposing / that the Swan's splendid white color arose / from his washing in the water / in which he swam, / the Raven left the altars / in the neighborhood / where he picked up his living, / and took up residence / in the lakes and pools.
→

(4) "Allow them," / said Jupiter, / "to enjoy an empty honor / and to assume the badge of your nobler sex, / so long as they are not your equals / in strength or courage."
→

B. 다음 주어진 문장이 되도록 빈칸에 써 넣으세요.

(1) 연못에서 물을 마시던 황소 한 마리가 <u>새끼 개구리 형제들을 밟아서 그 중 한 마리를 으스러뜨려 죽이고 말았다.</u>

An ox drinking at a pool _____.

(2) 난 나를 해친 자들에게만 적으로서 복수하지.

→

(3) 하늘의 새는 바다에서 먹이를 찾아서는 안 된다.

→

(4) 심지어 진실을 말할 때에도, <u>거짓말쟁이를 믿을 수 없다.</u>

_____, even when he speaks the truth.

A. (1) 우리는 모든 중노동을 참고 있으니, 네가 아니라 우리가 울어야 해. (2) 그는 배에 탄 한 명의 범죄자 때문에 수많은 무고한 사람들을 죽게 만들었을지 모르는 신의 부당함에 대해 비난했다. (3) 백조의 멋진 흰 깃털은 백조가 헤엄치는 물 속에서 씻기 때문이라고 생각하여, 갈까마귀는 생계를 꾸리고 있던 근처의 제단을 떠나 호수

C. 다음 주어진 문구가 알맞은 문장이 되도록 순서를 맞춰 보세요.

(1) 농부는 그들의 요구에 주의를 기울이지 않았다.
(their / paid / He / to /no / request / attention)

→

(2) 네가 정말로 신의 섭리를 심판하는 사람이 되겠다는 것인가?
(Providence / a judge / to make / indeed / of / Are you / the dealings / of / yourself)

→

(3) 제발 멀리 떨어져서 가까이 오지 말아 줘.
(Pray / keep / near / come / me / and / do not / a distance / at)

→

(4) <u>그것이 그림일 뿐이라고 생각하지 못한 채</u>, 비둘기는 요란한 날갯짓으로 그것을 향해 날아갔다.
(Not / a picture / supposing / only / it / be / to)

_____, she flew towards it with a loud.

D. 다음 단어에대한맞는 설명과 연결해 보세요.

(1) sprout ▶   ◀ ① not enough

(2) undertake ▶   ◀ ② kill someone by squeezing their throat tightly

(3) strangle ▶   ◀ ③ produce new shoots or leaves

(4) scarcity ▶   ◀ ④ accept responsibility for something

와 연못에 둥지를 마련했다. (4) 제우스가 말했다. "그들이 힘이나 용기에서 너희들과 대등하지 않은 한 그들에게 공허한 명예를 즐기고 너희들의 고귀한 성별의 상징을 갖도록 허락하라." | B. (1) trod on a brood of young frogs and crushed one of them to death (2) I return as an enemy only to those who injured me, (3) A bird of the air has no business to seek its food from the sea, (4) There is no believing a liar | C. (1) He paid no attention to their request, (2) Are you indeed to make your-self a judge of the dealings of Providence? (3) Pray keep at a distance and do not come near me, (4) Not supposing it to be only a picture | D. (1) ③ (2) ④ (3) ② (4) ②

8

The Thief and His Mother
도둑과 어머니

A BOY / stole a lesson-book / from one of his
한 소년이 교과서를 훔친 학교 친구의

schoolfellows / and took it home / to his Mother. She not
집으로 가져왔다 어머니에게.

only abstained from beating him, / but encouraged him.
어머니는 아들을 때리지 않고 오히려 격려했다.

He next time / stole a cloak / and brought it to her, / and
소년은 다음으로 망토를 훔쳐서 어머니에게 가져왔고,

she again commended him. The Youth, / advanced to
어머니는 다시 아들을 칭찬했다. 젊은이는, 성인이 된,

adulthood, / proceeded to steal / things of still greater
계속 훔쳤다 더 값 나가는 물건들을.

value. At last / he was caught / in the very act, / and
마침내 그는 붙잡혔고 바로 그 행동으로,

having his hands bound behind him, / was led away / to
손이 뒤로 묶인 채, 끌려갔다

the place of public execution.
공개 처형 장소로.

His Mother followed / in the crowd / and violently beat
어머니는 따라가며 군중 속에서 심하게 가슴을 쳤다

her breast / in sorrow, / whereupon the young man said, /
슬픔에 잠긴 채, 그러자 젊은이가 말했다,

"I wish to say something to my Mother / in her ear." She
"어머니께 이야기 하고 싶어요 귓속말로."

came close to him, / and he quickly seized her ear / with
어머니가 그에게 다가가자, 그는 재빨리 어머니의 귀를 잡고

his teeth / and bit it off.
이빨로 물어뜯어 버렸다.

---

lesson-book 교과서 | abstain from -ing ~을 하지 않다 | commend 칭찬하다 | execution 처형 |
whereupon 그것에 대해 | disgraceful 치욕스러운

The Mother upbraided him / as an unnatural child, /
어머니는 아들을 비난했고   나쁜 아이라고,

whereon he replied, / "Ah! If you had beaten me / when
그러자 그가 대답했다,   "아!   어머니가 저를 때렸더라면

I first stole / and brought to you / that lesson-book, / I
처음으로 훔쳐서   가져갔을 때   교과서를,

should not have come to this, / nor have been thus led /
저는 이 자리에 오지도,   이렇게 당하지도 않았을 거예요

to a disgraceful death."
수치스러운 죽음을."

Key Expression 🔎

should have p.p. : ~했어야 했는데

should have p.p.는 '~했어야 했는데'라는 뜻으로 과거에 하지 않은 일에 대한 유감, 후회, 비난을 담고 있는 표현입니다.
should 대신에 ought to를 사용할 수 있습니다.

▶ I should have p.p~ = I am sorry that I didn't ~

이처럼 조동사 + have p.p 구문의 의미를 비교 정리해 둘 필요가 있습니다.

▶ 과거 사실에 대한 추측
   – must have p.p : ~였음에 틀림없다
   – may : ~ 였을 것 같다
   – might might have p.p : ~였을 지도 모른다
   – cannot have p.p : ~였을리가 없다

▶ 과거 사실에 대한 유감
   – should / ought to have p.p : ~했어야 했는데
   – could have p.p : ~할 수 있었는데
   – would have p.p : ~ 했을텐데
   – would rather have p.p : ~하는 게 나았을텐데
   – need not have p.p : ~할 필요는 없었는데

ex) If you had beaten me when I first stole and brought to you that lesson-book,
I should not have come to this, nor have been thus led to a disgraceful
death.
교과서를 처음으로 훔쳐서 가져갔을 때 어머니가 저를 때렸더라면, 저는 이
자리에 오지도, 이렇게 수치스러운 죽음을 당하지도 않았을 거예요.

The Thief and the Innkeeper
도둑과 여관 주인

A THIEF hired a room / in a tavern / and stayed a while
한 도둑이 방을 빌려서 / 여관에 / 한동안 머물렀다

/ in the hope of stealing / something which should enable
/ 훔치고 싶어 하며 / 뭔가 방값을 치를 수 있을 만한 것을.

him to pay his reckoning.

When he had waited some days / in vain, / he saw the
며칠을 기다렸을 때 / 소득 없이,

Innkeeper dressed / in a new and handsome coat / and
그는 여관 주인을 보았다 / 새로 산 멋진 코트를 입고

sitting before his door. The Thief sat down beside him /
자신의 방문 앞에 앉아 있는. / 도둑은 주인 옆에 앉아

and talked with him.
이야기를 나눴다.

As the conversation began to flag, / the Thief yawned
대화가 시들해지자, / 도둑은 심하게 하품하며

terribly / and at the same time / howled like a wolf. The
/ 동시에 / 늑대 울음 소리를 냈다.

Innkeeper said, / "why do you howl / so fearfully?"
여관 주인이 말했다, / "왜 우는 겁니까 / 그렇게 무섭게?"

"I will tell you," / said the Thief, / "but first let me ask
"말씀 드리죠," / 도둑이 말했다, / "하지만 먼저 부탁합니다

you / to hold my clothes, / or I shall tear them to pieces.
내 옷을 잡아 달라고, / 그렇지 않으면 찢어 버릴 테니까요.

I know not, / sir, / when I got this habit of yawning, / nor
난 몰라요, / 선생님, / 언제 이렇게 하품하는 버릇이 생겼는지도,

whether these attacks of howling / were inflicted on me
이러한 울부짖음이 / 내게 나타나는 것인지도

/ as a judgment / for my crimes, / or for any other cause;
/ 판단 근거로 / 내가 저지를 범죄나, / 다른 이유 때문에;

/ but this I do know, / that when I yawn / for the third
/ 하지만 알아요, / 내가 하품하면 / 세 번째로,

time, / I actually turn into a wolf / and attack men."
정말 늑대로 변해서 / 사람들을 공격할 것을."

With this speech / he commenced a second fit of yawning
이렇게 말하며   그는 두 번째 하품을 하고

/ and again howled / like a wolf, / as he had at first. The
다시 울음 소리를 냈다   늑대처럼,   처음 했었던 대로.

Innkeeper, / hearing his tale / and believing what he said,
여관 주인은,   그의 이야기를 듣고   그가 한 말을 믿으며,

/ became greatly alarmed and, / rising from his seat, /
몹시 놀라서,   자리에서 일어나,

attempted to run away.
달아나려고 했다.

The Thief laid hold of his coat / and entreated him to
도둑은 그의 코트를 잡고   머물러 달라고 애원했다,

stop, / saying, / "Pray wait, / sir, / and hold my clothes, /
말하면서,   "기다려 주세요,   선생님, 그리고 내 옷을 잡아 주세요,

or I shall tear them to pieces / in my fury, / when I turn
그렇지 않으면 난 옷을 찢어 버릴지 몰라요   사나워져서,   늑대로 변해 버리면."

into a wolf." At the same moment / he yawned the third
동시에   그는 세 번째 하품을 하며

time / and set up a terrible howl.
끔찍한 울음 소리를 냈다.

The Innkeeper, / frightened lest he should be attacked, /
여관 주인은,   공격을 당할까봐 겁이 나서,

left his new coat / in the Thief's hand / and ran / as fast as
새 코트를 놔 둔 채   도둑의 손 안에   달아났다   최대한 빨리

he could / into the inn / for safety. The Thief made off /
여관으로   안전을 위해.   도둑은 달아나서

with the coat / and did not return again / to the inn.
코트를 갖고   다시는 돌아오지 않았다   여관으로.

Every tale is not to be believed.
모든 이야기가 믿을 만한 것은 아니다.

---

innkeeper 여관 주인 | tavern 여관 | reckoning 계산 | flag (흥미·기력 등이) 떨어지다, 시들해지다 | yawn
하품하다 | tale 이야기 | lest ~하지 않도록

The Tortoise and the Eagle
거북이와 독수리

A TORTOISE, / lazily basking in the sun, / complained
거북이 한 마리가,　　느긋하게 일광욕을 하다가,

to the sea-birds / of her hard fate, / that no one would
바다 새들에게 불평했다　자신의 괴로운 운명을,　아무도 나는 법을 가르쳐 주지

teach her to fly. An Eagle, / hovering near, / heard her
않는다고.　독수리 한 마리가,　주위를 날아다니다,　거북이의 한탄을 듣고

lamentation / and demanded / what reward she would
물어봤다　어떤 보답을 주겠느냐고

give him / if he would take her aloft / and float her in the
그에게 주겠냐고　하늘 높이 데려가　공중에서 날게 해 준다면.

air.

"I will give you," / she said, / "all the riches of the Red
"당신께 드릴게요,"　거북이가 말했다,　"홍해의 모든 보물을."

Sea." "I will teach you to fly / then," / said the Eagle; /
"나는 법을 가르쳐 주겠소　그러면,"　독수리가 말했다;

and taking her up / in his talons / he carried her / almost
그리고는 거북이를 들고　발톱으로　데려갔다가

to the clouds / suddenly he let her go, / and she fell on
구름 가까이에　갑자기 놓아 주었고,　그러자 거북이는 높은 산 위에

a lofty mountain, / dashing her shell to pieces. The
떨어져,　등 껍질이 산산조각이 나고 말았다.

Tortoise exclaimed / in the moment of death: / "I have
거북이는 소리쳤다　죽음의 순간에:

deserved my present fate; / for what had I to do / with
"이렇게 되도 싸지;　뭘 하겠어

wings and clouds, / who can with difficulty move about /
날개와 구름이 있다고 해도,　힘들게 기어 다니는 내가

on the earth?"
땅 위를?"

If men had all they wished, / they would be often ruined.
사람들은 원하는 것을 모두 가진다면,　종종 파멸하곤 한다.

bask 햇볕을 쪼이다

The Thieves and the Cock
도둑들과 수탉

SOME THIEVES broke into a house / and found nothing
도둑 일당이 어느 집에 침입하여   수탉 한 마리 밖에 발견하지

but a Cock, / whom they stole, / and got off / as fast as
못하자,   수탉을 훔쳐,   달아났다   최대한 빨리.

they could.

Upon arriving at home / they prepared to kill the Cock,
집에 도착하자마자   도둑들은 수탉을 죽일 준비했고,

/ who thus pleaded / for his life: / "Pray spare me; / I am
그러자 수탉은 애원했다   목숨을 살려 달라고: "제발 살려 주세요;

very serviceable to men. I wake them up / in the night /
난 사람들에게 매우 쓸모 있어요.   사람들을 깨우죠   밤에

to their work."
일하러 가도록."

"That is the very reason / why we must the more
"그것이 바로 이유야   우리가 널 죽여야만 하는,"

kill you," / they replied; / "for when you wake your
도둑들이 대답했다;   "네가 이웃들을 깨우면,

neighbors, / you entirely put an end to our business."
우리 사업을 끝장내는 것이니까."

The safeguards of virtue / are hateful / to those with evil
덕의 수호자는   증오스러운 법이다   악한 의도를 가진 이한테.

intentions.

The Three Tradesmen
세 명의 상인

A GREAT CITY was besieged, / and its inhabitants
어느 거대한 도시가 포위되어,   주민들이 소집되었다

were called together / to consider the best means / of
가장 좋은 방법을 생각하기 위해

protecting it from the enemy.
적으로부터 도시를 보호할.

A Bricklayer earnestly recommended bricks / as affording
벽돌공은 벽돌을 추천했다

the best material / for an effective resistance. A Carpenter,
최고의 재료로　　　　　효과적인 저항을 위한.　　　　　목수는,

/ with equal enthusiasm, / proposed timber / as a
같은 열망으로,　　　　　　목재를 제안했다

preferable method of defense.
방어를 위한 최선의 수단으로.

Upon which / a Currier stood up and said, / "Sirs, / I
이에 대해　　　제혁공이 일어나 말했다,　　　　　"여러분,

differ from you altogether: / there is no material / for
전 의견이 전혀 다릅니다:　　　　재료는 없어요

resistance / equal to a covering of hides, / and nothing so
저항을 위해　　　가죽 덮개만한;

good as leather."
그러니 가죽만큼 좋은 것은 없어요."

Every man for himself.
모두가 자신만을 위한다.

Key Expression 🍋

부정주어를 사용한 최상급

형용사나 부사에는 최상급 단어가 따로 있지만, 부정주어와 원급/비교급을 사용해서 최상급 표현을 할 수도 있습니다.

▶ 부정어 ~ so[as] 원급 as … : …만큼 ~한 것은 없다
▶ 부정어 ~ 비교급 than any other 단수명사 : …보다 더 ~한 것은 없다

ex) There is no material for resistance equal to a covering of hides; and nothing so good as leather.
저항을 위한 재료로 가죽으로 덮개만한 재료는 없어요; 그러니 가죽만큼 좋은 것은 없어요.

serviceable 쓸 만한 | put an end 끝내다 | tradesman 상인 | besiege 포위하다 | bricklayer 벽돌공 |
resistance 저항 | carpenter 목수 | timber 목재 | preferable 더 좋은, 나은 | hide 가죽, 피혁 | leather 가죽

The Boasting Traveler
뽐내는 여행자

A MAN / who had traveled / in foreign lands boasted
한 사람이　　　외국을 여행했던　　　　몹시 뽐냈다,

very much, / on returning to his own country, / of the
고국으로 돌아오자마자,

many wonderful and heroic feats / he had performed / in
수많은 놀랍고 영웅적인 행동에 대해　　　　자신이 했던

the different places / he had visited. Among other things,
여러 나라에서　　　　방문했던.　　　무엇보다도,

/ he said that / when he was at Rhodes / he had leaped
그는 말했다　　로도스에 있을 때　　　무척 먼 거리를 뛰었는데

to such a distance / that no man of his day could leap /
당시 아무도 뛸 수 없었다고

anywhere near him / as to that, / there were in Rhodes
그의 주변조차　　　　그만큼,　　　로도스의 많은 사람들이

many persons / who saw him do it / and whom he could
자신의 행동을 봤으며

call as witnesses.
증인으로 부를 수도 있다고.

One of the bystanders interrupted him, / saying: / "Now,
구경꾼 중 한 명이 끼어 들어,　　　　　　말했다:

my good man, / if this be all true / there is no need of
"자, 잘난 양반,　　　그 말이 모두 사실이라면　　증인을 부를 필요 없어요.

witnesses. Suppose this to be Rhodes, / and leap for us."
여기가 로도스라고 생각하고,　　　우리를 위해 뛰어 보시오."

The Two Travelers and the Axe
두 여행자와 도끼

TWO MEN were journeying together. One of them
두 사람이 함께 여행하고 있었다.　　　　　　한 사람이 도끼를 주워 들고

picked up an axe / that lay upon the path, / and said, /
길 위에 놓여 있던,　　　　　말했다,

boast　뽐내다, 자랑하다 |feat　위업, 개가 |Rhodes　로도스 섬(에게 해에 있는 그리스령 섬) |nay　옛글투의 no |
mode　방식 |seaside　해변 |summit　정상 |cliff　절벽 |look over　훑어보다, 살펴보다

"I have found an axe." / "Nay, my friend," / replied the
"내가 도끼를 발견했어." "아니지, 친구여," 다른 사람이 대답했다,

other, / "do not say 'I,' / but 'We' have found an axe."
"'내가'라고 하지 말고, '우리'가 발견했다고 해야지."

They had not gone far / before they saw the owner of
그들은 얼마 가지 않아 도끼 주인을 봤다

the axe / pursuing them, / and he who had picked up the
차신들을 좇아오는, 그러자 도끼를 주웠던 사람이 말했다,

axe said, / "We are undone." / "Nay," / replied the other,
"우리는 끝장이군." "아니지," 다른 사람이 대답했다,

/ "keep to your first mode of speech, / my friend; / what
"처음 말했던 대로 하게나, 친구여;

you thought right then, / think right now. Say 'I,' / not
그때 자네가 생각한 것이 맞군, 지금 생각해 보니. '내'라고 하게나

'We' are undone."
'우리'가 끝난 것이 아니라."

He who shares the danger / ought to share the prize.
위험을 함께 하는 사람은 상도 함께 받아야 한다.

The Seaside Travelers
해변의 여행자들

SOME TRAVELERS, / journeying along the seashore, /
여행자 몇 명이, 해변을 따라 여행하다가,

climbed to the summit of a tall cliff, / and looking over
높은 절벽 꼭대기에 올라갔고, 바다를 살펴보다가,

the sea, / saw in the distance / what they thought was a
멀리 있는 것을 보게 되었다 큰 배처럼 보이는 것을.

large ship. They waited / in the hope of seeing / it enter
그들은 기다렸다 보게 될 것을 기대하며 그 배가 항구로

the harbor, / but as the object on which they looked / was
들어오는 것을. 하지만 그들이 본 물체가

driven nearer to shore / by the wind, / they found / that it
해변 가까이 밀려왔을 때 바람에, 그들은 알았다

could at the most / be a small boat, / and not a ship.
그것이 기껏해야 작은 보트일 뿐, 배가 아니라는 것을.

When however / it reached the beach, / they discovered /
하지만   그 배가 해변에 닿자,   그들은 발견했다

that it was only a large faggot of sticks, / and one of them
그것이 그저 커다란 나뭇가지임을,

said to his companions, / "We have waited / for no purpose,
그러자 한 사람이 동료들에게 말했다,   "우리는 기다렸구나   헛되이,

/ for after all / there is nothing to see / but a load of wood."
왜냐하면 결국   아무것도 없었으니   나뭇가지 더미 밖에."

Our mere anticipations of life / outrun its realities.
인생의 작은 기대는   현실보다 클 때가 있다.

The Traveler and Fortune
여행자와 행운

A TRAVELER / wearied from a long journey / lay down, /
한 여행자가   긴 여행에 지친   누워서,

overcome with fatigue, / on the very brink of a deep well.
피로를 달래고 있었다,   깊은 우물의 끝에서.

Just as he was about to fall / into the water, / Dame
그가 막 떨어지려고 할 때   물 속으로,   운명의 여신이,

Fortune, / it is said, / appeared to him / and waking him
소위,   그에게 나타나   꿈 속에서 걸어 나와

from his slumber / thus addressed him: / "Good Sir, / pray
이렇게 말했다: "이봐요,

wake up: / for if you fall into the well, / the blame will
일어나세요: 왜냐하면 당신이 떨어진다면,   내게 비난을 퍼부을 테고,

be thrown on me, / and I shall get an ill name / among
그러면 난 악명을 얻게 될 테니   사람들 사이에서;

mortals; / for I find / that men are sure to impute / their
알고 있으니까   사람들은 분명히 덮어 씌운다는 걸

calamities to me, / however much by their own folly / they
자신들의 불행을 내게,   자기 잘못이라 하더라도

have really brought them / on themselves."
정말 불행을 가져온 것이   자신들에게."

Everyone is / more or less / master of his own fate.
모든 이들은   대부분   자신의 운명에 책임이 있다.

The Travelers and the Plane-Tree
여행자들과 플라타너스

TWO TRAVELERS, / worn out / by the heat of the
두 명의 여행자가,　　　지쳐서　　　여름날 태양의 열기로,

summer's sun, / laid themselves down / at noon / under the
　　　　　　누워 있었다　　　정오에

widespreading branches of a Plane-Tree.
넓게 펼쳐진 플라타너스 가지 아래에.

As they rested / under its shade, / one of the Travelers said
그들이 쉬고 있을 때　　나무 그늘 아래에서,　　한 명이 다른 한 명에게 말했다,

to the other, / "What a singularly useless tree / is the Plane!
　　　　"아주 쓸모 없는 나무구나　　　　플라타너스는!

It bears no fruit, / and is not of the least service to man."
열매도 맺지 않고,　　　사람한테 전혀 도움이 안 되잖아."

The Plane-Tree, / interrupting him, / said, / "You
플라타너스가,　　　끼어 들며,　　　말했다,

ungrateful fellows! Do you, / while receiving benefits /
"은혜를 모르는 사람들이군요!　당신들은,　　나로부터 혜택을 입으면서

from me / and resting under my shade, / dare to describe
내게　　　내 그늘 아래에서 쉬면서,　　　감히 날 말할 수 있나요

me / as useless, / and unprofitable?"
　　쓸모없고,　　도움도 안 된다고?"

Some men underrate their best blessings.
어떤 사람들은 최고의 축복을 과소평가하곤 한다.

Key Expression

more or less : 거의, 대략, 다소
more or less는 거의, 대략, 혹은 다소라는 뜻을 가진 숙어입니다.
한편 more or less가 부정주어와 함께 쓰여서 nothing more or less
(than) 혹은 neither more nor less (than)로 쓰이면 '많지도 적지도 않게
정확하게'라는 뜻이 됩니다.

ex) Everyone is more or less master of his own fate.
　　모든 이들은 대부분 자신의 운명에 책임이 있다.

anticipation 예상, 기대 | brink 직전, 끝 | Dame Fortune 운명의 여신 | slumber 잠 | plane-tree 플라타너스
| singularly 아주, 몹시, 특이하게

The Traveler and His Dog
여행자와 개

A TRAVELER / about to set out on a journey / saw his
한 여행자가   막 여행을 떠나려는   개가 서 있는 것을

Dog stand / at the door / stretching himself. He asked him
봤다   문 앞에서   기지개를 켜며.   그는 개에게 엄하게

sharply: / "Why do you stand there gaping? Everything is
물었다: "왜 거기에서 멍하니 서 있는 거냐?   모든 것이 준비되었으니

ready / but you, / so come with me / instantly." The Dog, /
너만 빼고,   함께 가자   즉시."   개는,

wagging his tail, / replied: / "O, master! I am quite ready; /
꼬리를 흔들며,   대답했다: "오, 주인님!   전 준비됐어요;

it is you for whom I am waiting."
주인님을 기다리고 있었다고요."

The loiterer often blames / delay / on his more active friend.
게으른 사람은 종종 탓으로 돌린다   지체된 것을   더 적극적인 친구에게.

The Widow and the Sheep
과부와 양

A CERTAIN poor widow had / one solitary Sheep. At
어떤 가난한 과부에게   단 한 마리의 양이 있었다.

shearing time, / wishing to take his fleece / and to avoid
털을 깎을 때가 되자,   양털도 얻고   비용도 줄이고자,

expense, / she sheared him herself, / but used the shears so
비용도 줄이고자,   그녀는 직접 양털을 깎았다,   하지만 가위질이 서툴러서

unskillfully / that with the fleece / she sheared the flesh.
양털과 함께   살까지 베고 말았다.

The Sheep, / writhing with pain, / said, / "Why do you hurt
양은,   고통에 몸부림치며,   말했다,   "왜 절 이토록 아프게 하세요,

me so, / Mistress? What weight can my blood add / to the
주인님?   제 피가 얼마나 무게를 더하겠어요

wool? If you want my flesh, / there is the butcher, / who will
양털에?   제 살을 원하신다면,   정육점 주인이 있잖아요,   절 죽일

stretch oneself 기지개를 켜다 | gape 멍하니 바라보다 | instantly 즉각, 즉시 | loiter 어정거리다, 빈둥거리다 |
widow 과부 | solitary 단 하나의 | shear 털을 깎다 | shears 큰 가위 | writhe 온몸을 비틀다, 몸부림치다 | in
an instant 곧, 당장, 즉시 | outlay 경비, 지출 | alliance 동맹 | distribute 나누어 주다, 분배하다

kill me / in an instant; / but if you want my fleece and wool,
즉시;   하지만 제 털을 원하신다면,

/ there is the shearer, / who will shear and / not hurt me."
털 깎는 사람이 있어요,   제 털을 깎으면서   다치지 않게 할."

The least outlay / is not always the greatest gain.
최소의 경비가   언제나 최대의 이익이 되는 것은 아니다.

The Wild Ass and the Lion
야생 당나귀와 사자

A WILD ASS and a Lion / entered into an alliance / so that
야생 당나귀와 사자가   동맹을 맺었다

they might capture the beasts of the forest / with greater
숲 속 동물들을 잡으려고   훨씬 쉽게.

ease. The Lion agreed to assist the Wild Ass / with his
사자는 야생 당나귀를 돕기로 동의했고

strength, / while the Wild Ass gave the Lion the / benefit of
힘으로,   야생 당나귀는 사자에게 주기로 했다

his greater speed.
빠른 속도로 인한 이득을.

When they had taken / as many beasts as their necessities
그들이 잡자   필요한 만큼의 동물들을,

required, / the Lion undertook to distribute the prey, / and
            사자는 사냥감을 분배하는 일을 맡았고,

for this purpose / divided it into three shares. "I will take
이를 위해   사냥감을 세 몫으로 나눴다.   "내가 첫 번째 몫을

the first share," / he said, / "because I am King: / and the
갖겠어,"   사자가 말했다,   "왜냐하면 나는 왕이니까:

second share, / as a partner with you / in the chase: / and
두 번째 몫은,   너와 함께 파트너가 되었으니   추격에서:

the third share / (believe me) / will be a source of great evil
세 번째 몫은   (분명히)   네게는 큰 재앙의 원천이 될 거야,

to you, / unless you willingly resign it to me, / and set off /
           만약 네가 내게 기꺼이 양보하고,   달아나지 않으면

as fast as you can."
최대한 빨리."

Might makes right.
힘이 권리를 만든다.   209

The Old Woman and the Wine-Jar
노파와 포도주 단지

AN OLD WOMAN found an empty jar / which had lately
한 노파가 빈 단지를 발견했다   최근까지 가득 차 있었고

been full / of prime old wine / and which still retained / the
최상급의 오래된 포도주로   여전히 남아 있는

fragrant smell of its former contents. She greedily placed
포도주의 향기로운 냄새가.   그녀는 탐욕스럽게 단지를 가져가서

it / several times / to her nose, / and drawing it backwards
몇 번이나   코에,   앞뒤로 가져가면서

and forwards / said, / "O most delicious! How nice / must
말했다.   "오 정말 달콤하구나!   얼마나 훌륭했을까

the Wine itself have been, / when it leaves behind / in the
포도주 자체는,   남겨 놓았으니

very vessel / which contained it / so sweet a perfume!"
그릇에   포도주를 담았던   이토록 달콤한 향기를!"

The memory of a good deed lives.
훌륭한 행동의 기억은 살아있다.

The Wolf and the Sheep
늑대와 양

A WOLF, / sorely wounded and bitten / by dogs, / lay sick /
늑대 한 마리가,   심하게 상처입고 물린   개들에게,   아파서 누웠다

and maimed / in his lair. Being in want of food, / he called
불구가 되어   굴 속에.   먹을 것이 부족해서,

to a Sheep / who was passing, / and asked him / to fetch
늑대는 양을 불러   지나가던,   부탁했다   물을 좀 갖다

some water / from a stream / flowing close beside him.
달라고   냇가에서   근처의 흐르는.

---

prime 최고급의, 훌륭한 | leave behind 남겨 두고 가다 | vessel (액체를 담는) 용기, 그릇 | maimed 불구의
| draught 한 모금, 마실 것 | doubtless 확실히, 틀림 없이 | evil-disposed 악한 기질을 가진 | bark 짖다
| dismiss 보내다, 물러가게 하다 | treaty 협정 | reconciliation 화해 | beguile 구슬리다 | at one's own
pleasure 마음 내키는대로, 자유로이

"For," / he said, / "if you will bring me drink, / I will find
"왜냐하면," 늑대가 말했다, "네가 물을 갖다 주면, 방법을 찾을 테

means / to provide myself with meat." / "Yes," / said the
니까 고기를 마련할." "그래," 양이 말했다,

Sheep, / "if I should bring you the draught, / you would
"네게 물을 갖다 주면,

doubtless / make me provide the meat also."
넌 틀림없이 내게 고기도 내놓으라고 하겠지."

Hypocritical speeches / are easily seen through.
위선적인 말은 쉽게 들통나기 마련이다.

The Wolves and the Sheep
늑대들과 양들

"WHY SHOULD there always be / this fear and
"왜 항상 있는 거지 이런 공포와 살육이

slaughter / between us?" / said the Wolves to the Sheep.
우리 사이에는?" 늑대들이 양들에게 말했다.

"Those evil-disposed Dogs / have much to answer for.
"저 사악한 개들에게 책임이 있어.

They always bark / whenever we approach you / and
개들은 항상 짖으면서 우리가 너희들에게 다가갈 때마다

attack us / before we have done any harm. If you would
공격하거든 아무런 해도 끼치기 전에.

only dismiss them / from your heels, / there might soon
너희들이 개들을 쫓아낸다면 발끝으로,

be treaties of peace and reconciliation / between us."
곧 평화와 화해 조약이 성립될 거야 우리 사이에."

The Sheep, / poor silly creatures, / were easily beguiled
양들은, 불쌍하고 어리석은 짐승인, 쉽게 속아 넘어가서

/ and dismissed the Dogs, / whereupon the Wolves
개들을 쫓아 버렸고, 그러자 늑대들은 죽여 버렸다

destroyed / the unguarded flock / at their own pleasure.
지키는 이 없는 양떼들을 마음대로.

The Wolf in Sheep's Clothing
양의 가죽을 쓴 늑대

ONCE UPON A time / a Wolf resolved / to disguise
옛날 옛적에   한 늑대가 결심했다   모습을 변장하기로

his appearance / in order to secure food more easily.
            먹이를 보다 쉽게 확보하기 위해.

Encased in the skin of a sheep, / he pastured with the
양의 가죽을 덮어쓰고,   늑대는 양떼와 함께 풀을 뜯었다

flock / deceiving the shepherd / by his costume.
양치기를 속이고   겉모습으로.

In the evening / he was shut up / by the shepherd / in
저녁에   늑대는 갇혔고   양치기에 의해

the fold; / the gate was closed, / and the entrance made
우리 속에;   문이 닫히자,   입구는 안전하게 봉인되었다.

thoroughly secure. But the shepherd, / returning to the
                하지만 양치기는,   우리로 돌아와

fold / during the night / to obtain meat / for the next day,
밤중에   고기를 얻으려고   다음 날을 위한,

/ mistakenly caught up the Wolf / instead of a sheep, /
실수로 늑대를 잡아   양 대신,

and killed him instantly.
즉시 죽여 버렸다.

Harm seek, / harm find.
해로움을 추구하면,   해로움을 당한다.

Key Expression

in order to ~ : ~하기 위하여

in order to는 to 부정사를 이용한 숙어로 '~하기 위하여'라는 의미입니다. to
뒤에는 동사원형이 오며 부정할 때에는 in order not to로 사용합니다.

ex) Once upon a time a Wolf resolved to disguise his appearance in order to
secure food more easily.
옛날 옛적에 한 늑대가 먹이를 보다 쉽게 확보하기 위해 모습을 변장하기로
결심했다.

The Wolves and the Sheepdogs
늑대들과 양치기 개들

THE WOLVES thus addressed the Sheepdogs: / "why
늑대들이 양치기 개들에게 이렇게 말했다:

should you, / who are like us / in so many things, / not
"왜 너희들은,   우리와 같은데   많은 점에서,

be entirely of one mind / with us, / and live with us / as
완전히 한 마음이 되지 못하고   우리와,   같이 살지 못하는 걸까

brothers should? We differ from you / in one point only.
형제들이 그러하듯?   우리는 너희와 달라   단 한 가지 점만.

We live in freedom, / but you bow down to / and slave /
우리는 자유롭게 살지만,   너희들은 복종하고,   노예처럼 일하지

for men, / who in return for your services / flog you with
사람들을 위해,   그런데 사람들은 너희들의 봉사에 대한 보답으로   채찍으로 때리고

whips / and put collars on your necks.
         목에 굴레를 씌웠지.

They make you also guard their sheep, / and while they
사람들은 또한 너희에게 양을 지키게 하고,   양고기를 먹으면서

eat the mutton / throw only the bones to you. If you
         뼈다귀만 던져줄 뿐이지.

will be persuaded by us, / you will give us the sheep,
너희가 우리에게 동의한다면,   우리에게 양을 넘겨 주고,

/ and we will enjoy them in common, / till we all are
  함께 즐기게 될 거야,   배불리 먹을 때까지."

surfeited."

The Dogs listened favorably / to these proposals, / and,
개들은 호의적으로 들었고   이 제안을,   그래서,

/ entering the den of the Wolves, / they were set upon /
  늑대의 굴로 들어가자,   공격을 받아

and torn to pieces.
갈기갈기 찢기고 말았다.

---

encase 감싸다, 둘러싸다 | fold 양의 우리(들판에서 양을 안전하게 놓아먹일 수 있도록 울타리나 담을 친 구역)
| sheepdog 양치기 개, 목양견 | bow down to 굽히고 들어가다 | in return for ~의 대가로, 답례로 | flog
채찍으로 때리다 | collar (개의) 목줄 | mutton 양고기 | surfeit 과식하다 | favorably 호의적으로

The Wolf and the Fox
늦대와 여우

AT ONE TIME / a very large and strong Wolf was born /
한 번은   매우 크고 힘센 늑대가 태어났다

among the wolves, / who exceeded all his fellow-wolves /
늑대들 사이에서,   그 늑대는 모든 동료들을 능가했다

in strength, size, and swiftness, / so that they unanimously
힘, 크기, 그리고 민첩함에서,   그래서 늑대들은 만장일치로 결정했다

decided / to call him "Lion." The Wolf, / with a lack of sense
          "사자"라고 부르기로. 그 늑대는,   분별력이 부족해서

/ proportioned to his enormous size, / thought / that they
자신의 커다란 몸집에 맞는,   생각했다

gave him this name / in earnest, / and, / leaving his own
늑대들이 이런 이름을 지어줬다고   진심으로,   그래서,   늑대 무리를 떠나,

race, / consorted exclusively with the lions.
오직 사자들과 어울렸다.

An old sly Fox, / seeing this, / said, / "May I never make
어느 늙고 교활한 여우가, 이를 보고,   말했다,   "부디 난 절대 웃음거리가 되지 않기를

myself so ridiculous / as you do / in your pride and self-
          네가 그런 것처럼   자만심과 허영심으로;

conceit; / for even though you have the size of a lion / among
왜냐하면 네가 사자의 몸집을 가지고 있을지라도   늑대 무리

wolves, / in a herd of lions / you are definitely a wolf."
에서는,   사자 무리에서   넌 분명 늑대일 뿐이니까."

Key Expression ♪

may를 사용한 소망 표현
기원이나 소망을 나타낼 때 조동사 may를 사용하여 표현할 수 있습니다. may를
사용한 기원문의 형태는 다음과 같아요.
동사원형을 사용하고 ?로 끝나지 않는 점에서 may 의문문과 구분합니다.

▶ May + 주어 + 동사원형 : 부디 ~이기를
▶ May + 주어 + never + 동사원형 : 부디 ~이 아니기를

ex) May I never make myself so ridiculous as you do in your pride and self-
    conceit.
    부디 나는 네가 그런 것처럼 자만심과 허영심으로 웃음 거리가 되지 않기를.

The Wolf and the Shepherd
늑대와 양치기

A WOLF / followed a flock of sheep / for a long time /
늑대 한 마리가   양떼를 따라다니면서도   오랫동안

and did not attempt to injure / one of them. The Shepherd
해치려는 시도는 하지 않았다   한 마리도.   양치기는

/ at first stood / on his guard against him, / as against an
처음에   늑대를 경계하며,   적을 상대하듯이,

enemy, / and kept a strict watch over / his movements.
철저하게 감시했다   늑대의 행동을.

But when the Wolf, / day after day, / kept in the company
하지만 늑대가,   날마다,   양들과 친하게 지내면서

of the sheep / and did not make the slightest effort / to
조금도 시도하지 않자

seize them, / the Shepherd began to look upon him / as
양을 잡으려고,   양치기는 늑대를 여기기 시작했다

a guardian of his flock / rather than as a plotter of evil /
양떼를 지켜주는 수호자로   사악한 음모를 꾸미는 자가 아니라

against it; / and when occasion called him / one day / into
양떼에 대해;   그래서 일 때문에 불려지자   어느 날

the city, / he left the sheep entirely / in his charge. The
도시로,   양치기는 양떼를 맡겼다   완전히 늑대의 책임 하에.

Wolf, / now that he had the opportunity, / fell upon the
늑대는,   기회를 잡았기 때문에,   양들을 공격하여,

sheep, / and destroyed the greater part of the flock.
꽤 많은 양을 죽였다.

When the Shepherd returned / to find his flock destroyed,
양치기가 돌아와서   양들이 죽은 것을 보고,

/ he exclaimed: / "I have been rightly served; / why did I
소리쳤다: "이런 일을 당하는 게 당연해;   내가 왜 내 양들을

trust my sheep / to a Wolf?"
맡겼을까   늑대에게?"

---

unanimously 만장일치로 | proportioned 균형잡힌, 비례하는 | consort (나쁜 무리와) 어울리다 | exclusively
오로지 | sly 교활한 | self-conceit 자만심, 허영심 | look upon A as B A를 B로 여기다 | guardian 보호자,
수호자 | plotter 음모자 | charge 책임, 담당 | rightly 당연히, 마땅히 | trust 맡기다

The Wolf and the Horse
늑대와 말

A WOLF / coming out of a field of oats / met a Horse /
늑대 한 마리가   귀리 밭에서 나오던   말을 만나

and thus addressed him: / "I would advise you / to go
이렇게 말했다: "네게 충고하겠어

into that field. It is full of fine oats, / which I have left
저 밭에 들어가 보라고. 그곳에는 좋은 귀리가 가득하고,   난 건드리지 않은 채 두었지

untouched / for you, / as you are a friend / whom I would
난   널 위해,   넌 친구이고   난 듣고 싶으니까

love / to hear enjoying good eating."
즐기며 잘 먹는 소리를."

The Horse replied, / "If oats had been the food of wolves,
말이 대답했다,   "귀리가 늑대의 먹이였다면,

/ you would never have indulged your ears / at the cost of
넌 네 귀를 만족시키려 하지 않았겠지

your belly."
배를 희생시키면서."

Men of evil reputation, / when they perform a good
나쁜 평판을 듣는 사람들은,   좋은 행동을 했을 때,

deed, / fail to get credit for it.
신용을 얻지 못한다.

The Wolf and the Lion
늑대와 사자

ROAMING BY the mountainside / at sundown, / a Wolf
산기슭을 어슬렁거리다가   해질 무렵,   늑대는 봤고

saw / his own shadow become greatly extended and
자신의 그림자가 늘어나면서 확대되는 것을,

magnified, / and he said to himself, / "Why should I, /
혼잣말을 했다,   "왜 나는,

being of such an immense size / and extending nearly an
저렇게 엄청난 크기에   길이는 1에이커까지 늘어나는데,

acre in length, / be afraid of the Lion? Ought I not to be
사자를 두려워하는 거지?   인정받아야 하지 않을까

acknowledged / as King of all the collected beasts?"
모든 동물의 왕으로서?"

While he was indulging / in these proud thoughts, / a Lion
그가 빠져 있을 때   이런 자신만만한 생각들에,

fell upon him / and killed him. He exclaimed / with a too
사자가 늑대를 공격했고   죽여 버렸다.   늑대는 소리쳤다

late repentance, / "Wretched me! This overestimation of
너무 늦은 한탄을 하며,   "비참하구나!   내 자신에 대한 과대평가가

myself / is the cause of my destruction."
날 파멸시킨 원인이구나."

The Wolf and The Lamb
늑대와 양

WOLF, / meeting with a Lamb / astray from the fold, /
늑대가,   양을 만나자   양 우리에서 벗어난,

resolved / not to lay violent hands on him, / but to find some
결심했다   폭력을 쓰지 않고,   합리화 할 구실을 찾겠다고

plea to justify / to the Lamb / the Wolf's right to eat him.
    양에게   늑대는 양을 잡아먹을 권리가 있다고.

---

indulge 마음껏 하다, 충족시키다 | at the cost of ~을 희생하여 | belly 배 | mountainside 산비탈 |
sundown 일몰, 해질녘 | magnify 확대하다 | immense 엄청난, 어마어마한 | acre 에이커(약 4,050평방미터에
해당하는 크기의 땅) | repentance 후회 | overestimation 과대 평가 | astray 벗어난, 길을 잃은 | plea 이유,
구실 | justify 정당화하다, 합리화하다

He thus / addressed him: / "Sirrah, / last year / you
늑대는 그래서 양에게 말했다 : "이봐, 작년에

grossly insulted me."
내게 몹시 창피를 줬지,"

"Indeed," / bleated the Lamb / in a mournful tone of
"사실은," 양은 매애 하고 울었다 슬픔에 잠긴 목소리로,

voice, / "I was not then born."
"전 그때 태어나지도 않았다고요."

Then said the Wolf, / "You feed in my pasture."
그러자 늑대가 말했다. "넌 내 풀밭에서 풀을 뜯었지."

"No, good sir," / replied the Lamb, / "I have not yet
"아니에요, 아저씨." 양이 대답했다, "전 아직 풀을 맛보지도

tasted grass."
못했는 걸요."

Again said the Wolf, / "You drink of my well."
다시 늑대가 말했다. "넌 내 샘에서 물을 마시잖아."

"No," / exclaimed the Lamb, / "I never yet drank water,
"아니에요." 양이 소리쳤다, "전 아직 물을 마신 적이 없어요,

/ for as yet / my mother's milk is both food and drink to
왜냐하면 아직 엄마 젖이 제게는 음식이고 물이니까요."

me."

Upon which / the Wolf seized him / and ate him up, /
이 말을 듣고 늑대는 양을 잡아서 먹어 버렸다,

saying, / "Well! I won't remain supperless, / even though
말하면서, "음! 저녁을 굶을 수는 없지, 네가 반박하더라도

you refute / every one of my imputations."
내 비난을 전부."

The tyrant will always find / a pretext for his tyranny.
폭군은 언제나 찾는 법이다 자신의 폭정에 대한 구실을.

---

grossly 지독히, 심하게 | bleat (양·염소가) 매애 하고 울다 | mournful 애처로운, 구슬픈 | refute 반박하다,
부인하다 | imputation 죄를 남에게 돌림, 전가 | tyrant 폭군, 독재자 | pretext 구실, 핑계 | tyranny 폭압, 독재

The Wolf and the Crane
늑대와 두루미

A WOLF / who had a bone stuck / in his throat / hired a
어느 늑대가   가시가 박힌   목 안에   두루미를

Crane, / for a large sum, / to put her head into his mouth
고용했다,   많은 보수로,   머리를 자신의 입 속에 넣어

/ and draw out the bone.
가시를 꺼내 달라고.

When the Crane had extracted the bone / and demanded
두루미가 가시를 빼내고는   약속한 보수를 요구하자,

the promised payment, / the Wolf, / grinning and
                            늑대는,

grinding his teeth, / exclaimed: / "Why, / you have surely
웃으며 이를 갈면서,   소리쳤다: "이봐,   넌 이미 받았잖아

already had / a sufficient recompense, / in having been
                충분한 보상을,

permitted to draw out your head / in safety / from the
네 머리를 꺼낸 것으로   안전하게

mouth and jaws of a wolf."
늑대의 입 속에서."

In serving the wicked, / expect no reward, / and be
악한 사람의 일을 할 때에는,   보수를 바라지 말고,

thankful / if you escape injury for your pains.
감사하라   고통에서 벗어날 수만 있다면.

The Wolf, the Fox, and the Ape
늑대, 여우, 그리고 원숭이

A WOLF accused a Fox of theft, / but the Fox entirely
늑대가 여우를 도둑질의 혐의로 고발했지만,   여우는 혐의를 전면 부인했다.

denied the charge. An Ape undertook to adjudge / the
                                원숭이가 판결하는 일을 맡게 되었다

matter / between them.
        둘 사이의 문제를.

When each had fully stated his case / the Ape announced
각자 자신의 입장을 충분히 이야기 하자   원숭이가 이런 판결을 발표했다:

this sentence: / "I do not think / you, Wolf, / ever lost /
"난 생각하지 않아   자네, 늑대가,   잃어버렸다고는

what you claim; / and I do believe / you, Fox, / to have
주장하는 것을;   그리고 난 믿고 있지   자네, 여우가,   훔쳤다고도

stolen / what you so stoutly deny."
그토록 단호하게 부정하는 것을."

The dishonest, / if they act honestly, / get no credit.
정직하지 못한 사람은,   정직하게 행동하더라도,   신뢰를 얻지 못한다.

accuse A of B : A를 B의 혐의로 고발하다

accuse A of B는 'A를 B의 혐의로 고발하다'라는 의미로 쓰이는 동사구입니다. 이처럼 정보, 경고, 확신의 의미를 가진 동사에서 of가 '~에 관하여'라는 의미로 사용됩니다. 아래의 동사들은 4형식 동사로 착각하기 쉬우니 꼭 기억하세요. 단, 비슷한 고발과 비난의 뜻이지만 blame은 blame A for B와 같이 for를 사용한다는 점을 기억하세요.

▶ advice A of B : A에게 B를 충고하다
▶ assure A of B: A에게 B를 확신시키다
▶ convince A of B : A에게 B를 확신시키다
▶ inform A of B : A에게 B를 알리다
▶ remind A of B : A에게 B를 상기시키다
▶ warn A of B : A에게 B를 경고하다

ex) A Wolf accused a Fox of theft, but the Fox entirely denied the charge.
   늑대가 여우를 도둑질의 혐의로 고발했지만, 여우는 그 혐의를 전면 부인했다.

throat 목구멍 | sum 금액 | extract 뽑다 | grin (소리 없이) 활짝 웃다 | grind 갈다 | recompense 보상 | theft 도둑질 | adjudge 판결하다 | sentence (형의) 선고 | claim 주장하다 | stoutly 단호하게

 mini test 8

A. 다음 문장을 해석해 보세요.

(1) If you had beaten me / when I first stole / and brought to you / that lesson-book, / I should not have come to this, / nor have been thus led / to a disgraceful death.
→

(2) A man / who had traveled / in foreign lands boasted very much, / on returning to his own country, / of the many wonderful and heroic feats / he had performed / in the different places / he had visited.
→

(3) They waited / in the hope of seeing / it enter the harbor, / but as the object on / which they looked was driven nearer to shore / by the wind, / they found / that it could at the most / be a small boat, / and not a ship.
→

(4) I find / that men are sure to impute / their calamities to me, / however much by their own folly / they have really brought them / on themselves.
→

B. 다음 주어진 문장이 되도록 빈칸에 써 넣으세요.

(1) 어머니께 귓속말로 뭔가 말하고 싶어요.

→

(2) 나뭇가지 더미 밖에 보이는 건 아무것도 없었다.

→

(3) 모든 이들은 대부분 자신의 운명에 책임이 있다.

→

(4) 내가 모든 동물의 왕으로서 인정받아야 하지 않을까?

→

C. 다음 주어진 문구가 알맞은 문장이 되도록 순서를 맞춰 보세요.

(1) 그녀는 아들을 때리지도 않고 오히려 격려했다.
(not / from / She / encouraged / only / beating / him, / but / him / abstained)

→

(2) 그들은 얼마 가지 않아 자신들을 쫓아오는 도끼 주인을 봤다.
(far / had / They / not / gone / before)

_____ they saw the owner of the axe

pursuing them.

(3) 부디 나는 네가 그런 것처럼 자만심과 허영심으로 웃음거리가 되지 않기를.
(never / so / May / I / myself / as / you / ridiculous)

_____ in your

pride and self-conceit.

(4) 모든 이야기가 믿을 만한 것은 아니다.
(Every / believed / tale / be / to / is)

→

D. 의미가 서로 비슷한 것끼리 연결해 보세요.

(1) bask   ▶   ◀ ① enclose

(2) besiege   ▶   ◀ ② satisfy

(3) indulge   ▶   ◀ ③ excuse

(4) pretext   ▶   ◀ ④ sunbathe

Answer

〈Aesop's Fables〉를 다시 읽어 보세요.

The Aethiop

THE PURCHASER of a black servant was persuaded that the color of his skin arose from dirt contracted through the neglect of his former masters. On bringing him home he resorted to every means of cleaning, and subjected the man to incessant scrubbings. The servant caught a severe cold, but he never changed his color or complexion.

What's bred in the bone will stick to the flesh.

The Ant and the Dove

AN ANT went to the bank of a river to quench its thirst, and being carried away by the rush of the stream, was on the point of drowning.

A Dove sitting on a tree overhanging the water plucked a leaf and let it fall into the stream close to her. The Ant climbed onto it and floated in safety to the bank.

Shortly afterwards a birdcatcher came and stood under the tree, and laid his lime-twigs for the Dove, which sat in the branches.

The Ant, perceiving his design, stung him in the foot. In pain the birdcatcher threw down the twigs, and the noise made the Dove take wing.

The Ants and the Grasshopper

THE ANTS were spending a fine winter's day drying grain collected in the summertime. A Grasshopper, perishing with famine, passed by and earnestly begged for a little food.

The Ants inquired of him, "Why did you not treasure up food during the summer?" He replied, "I had not leisure enough. I passed the days in singing."

They then said in derision: "If you were foolish enough to sing all the summer, you must dance supperless to bed in the winter."

The Apes and the Two Travelers

TWO MEN, one who always spoke the truth and the other who told nothing but lies, were traveling together and by chance came to the land of Apes.

One of the Apes, who had raised himself to be king, commanded them to be seized and brought before him, that he might know what was said of him among men. He ordered at the same time that all the Apes be arranged in a long row on his right hand and on his left, and that a throne be placed for him, as was the custom among men.

After these preparations he signified that the two men should be brought before him, and greeted them with this salutation: "what sort of a king do I seem to you to be, O strangers?"

The Lying Traveler replied, "You seem to me a most mighty king." "And what is your estimate of those you see around me?"

"These," he made answer, "are worthy companions of yourself, fit at least to be ambassadors and leaders of armies." The Ape and all his court, gratified with the lie, commanded that a handsome present be given to the flatterer.

On this the truthful Traveler thought to himself, "If so great a reward be given for a lie, with what gift may not I be rewarded, if, according to my custom, I tell the truth?" The Ape quickly turned to him. "And pray how do I and these my friends around me seem to you?" "Thou art," he said, "a most excellent Ape, and all these thy companions after thy example are excellent Apes too."

The King of the Apes, enraged at hearing these truths, gave him over to the teeth and claws of his companions.

The Ass and the Frogs

AN ASS, carrying a load of wood, passed through a pond. As he was crossing through the water he lost his footing, stumbled and fell, and not being able to rise on account of his load, groaned heavily.

Some Frogs frequenting the pool heard his lamentation, and said, "What would you do if you had to live here always as we do, when you make such a fuss about a mere fall into the water?"

Men often bear little grievances with less courage than they do large misfortunes.

The Ass Carrying the Image

AN ASS once carried through the streets of a city a famous wooden Image, to be placed in one of its Temples. As he passed along, the crowd made lowly prostration before the Image.

The Ass, thinking that they bowed their heads in token of respect for himself, bristled up with pride, gave himself airs, and refused to move another step.

The driver, seeing him thus stop, laid his whip lustily about his shoulders and said, "O you perverse dull-head! It is not yet come to this, that men pay worship to an Ass."

They are not wise who give to themselves the credit due to others.

The Ass, the Cock, and the Lion

AN ASS and a Cock were in a straw-yard together when a Lion, desperate from hunger, approached the spot. He was about to spring upon the Ass, when the Cock (to the sound of whose voice the Lion, it is said, has a singular aversion) crowed loudly, and the Lion fled away as fast as he could.

The Ass, observing his trepidation at the mere crowing of a Cock summoned courage to attack him, and galloped after him for that purpose. He had run no long distance, when the Lion, turning about, seized him and tore him to pieces.

False confidence often leads into danger.

The Ass and His Shadow

A TRAVELER hired an Ass to convey him to a distant place. The day being intensely hot, and the sun shining in its strength, the Traveler stopped to rest, and sought shelter from the heat under the Shadow of the Ass.

As this afforded only protection for one, and as the Traveler and the owner of the Ass both claimed it, a violent dispute arose between them as to which of them had the right to the Shadow. The owner maintained that he had let the Ass only, and not his Shadow. The Traveler asserted that he had, with the hire of the Ass, hired his Shadow also.

The quarrel proceeded from words to blows, and while the men fought, the Ass galloped off.

In quarreling about the shadow we often lose the substance.

The Ass and the Lapdog

A MAN had an Ass, and a Maltese Lapdog, a very great beauty. The Ass was left in a stable and had plenty of oats and hay to eat, just as any other Ass would. The Lapdog knew many tricks and was a great favorite with his master, who often fondled him and seldom went out to dine without bringing him home some tidbit to eat.

The Ass, on the contrary, had much work to do in grinding the corn-mill and in carrying wood from the forest or burdens from the farm. He often lamented his own hard fate and contrasted it with the luxury and idleness of the Lapdog, till at last one day he broke his cords and halter, and galloped into his master's house, kicking up his heels without measure, and frisking and fawning as well as he could.

He next tried to jump about his master as he had seen the Lapdog do, but he broke the table and smashed all the dishes upon it to atoms. He then attempted to lick his master, and jumped upon his back.

The servants, hearing the strange hubbub and perceiving the danger of their master, quickly relieved him, and drove out the Ass to his stable with kicks and clubs and cuffs.

The Ass, as he returned to his stall beaten nearly to death, thus lamented: "I have brought it all on myself! Why could I not have been contented to labor with my companions, and not wish to be idle all the day like that useless little Lapdog!"

The Bald Man and the Fly

A FLY bit the bare head of a Bald Man who, endeavoring to destroy it, gave himself a heavy slap.

Escaping, the Fly said mockingly, "You who have wished to revenge, even with death, the Prick of a tiny insect, see what you have done to yourself to add insult to injury?"

The Bald Man replied, "I can easily make peace with myself, because I know there was no intention to hurt. but you, an ill-favored and contemptible insect who delights in sucking human blood, I wish that I could have killed you even if I had incurred a heavier penalty."

The Bat And The Weasels

A BAT who fell upon the ground and was caught by a Weasel pleaded to be spared his life. The Weasel refused, saying that he was by nature the enemy of all birds. The Bat assured him that he was not a bird, but a mouse, and thus was set free.

Shortly afterwards the Bat again fell to the ground and was caught by another Weasel, whom he likewise entreated not to eat him. The Weasel said that he had a special hostility to mice. The Bat assured him that he was not a mouse, but a bat, and thus a second time escaped.

It is wise to turn circumstances to good account.

The Bear and the Two Travelers

TWO MEN were traveling together, when a Bear suddenly met them on their path.

One of them climbed up quickly into a tree and concealed himself in the branches. The other, seeing that he must be attacked, fell flat on the ground, and when the Bear came up and felt him with his snout, and smelt him all over, he held his breath, and feigned the appearance of death as much as he could. The Bear soon left him, for it is said he will not touch a dead body.

When he was quite gone, the other Traveler descended from the tree, and jocularly inquired of his friend what it was the Bear had whispered in his ear. "He gave me this advice," his companion replied. "Never travel with a friend who deserts you at the approach of danger."

Misfortune tests the sincerity of friends.

The Bee and Jupiter

A BEE from Mount Hymettus, the queen of the hive, ascended to Olympus to present Jupiter some honey fresh from her combs. Jupiter, delighted with the offering of honey, promised to give whatever she should ask.

She therefore besought him, saying, "Give me, I pray thee, a sting, that if any mortal shall approach to take my honey, I may kill him." Jupiter was much displeased, for he loved the race of man, but could not refuse the request because of his promise.

He thus answered the Bee: "You shall have your request, but it will be at the peril of your own life. For if you use your sting, it shall remain in the wound you make, and then you will die from the loss of it."

Evil wishes, like chickens, come home to roost.

The Bitch and Her Whelps

A BITCH, ready to whelp, earnestly begged a shepherd for a place where she might litter.

When her request was granted, she besought permission to rear her puppies in the same spot. The shepherd again consented. but At last the Bitch, protected by the bodyguard of her Whelps, who had now grown up and were able to defend themselves, asserted her exclusive right to the place and would not permit the shepherd to approach.

The Blind Man and the Whelp

A BLIND MAN was accustomed to distinguishing different animals by touching them with his hands. The whelp of a Wolf was brought him, with a request that he would feel it, and say what it was. He felt it, and being in doubt, said: "I do not quite know whether it is the cub of a Fox, or the whelp of a Wolf, but this I know full well. It would not be safe to admit him to the sheepfold."

Evil tendencies are shown in early life.

The Boy and the Filberts

A BOY put his hand into a pitcher full of filberts. He grasped as many as he could possibly hold, but when he tried to pull out his hand, he was prevented from doing so by the neck of the pitcher. Unwilling to lose his filberts, and yet unable to withdraw his hand, he burst into tears and bitterly lamented his disappointment.

A bystander said to him, "Be satisfied with half the quantity, and you will readily draw out your hand."

Do not attempt too much at once.

The Boy and the Nettles

A BOY was stung by a Nettle. He ran home and told his Mother, saying, "Although it hurts me very much, I only touched it gently."

"That was just why it stung you," said his Mother. "The next time you touch a Nettle, grasp it boldly, and it will be soft as silk to your hand, and not in the least hurt you."

Whatever you do, do with all your might.

The Boy Bathing

A BOY bathing in a river was in danger of being drowned. He called out to a passing traveler for help, but instead of holding out a helping hand, the man stood by unconcernedly, and scolded the boy for his imprudence. "Oh, sir!" cried the youth, "Pray help me now and scold me afterwards."

Counsel without help is useless.

The Brother and the Sister

A FATHER had one son and one daughter, the former remarkable for his good looks, the latter for her extraordinary ugliness.

While they were playing one day as children, they happened by chance to look together into a mirror that was placed on their mother's chair.

The boy congratulated himself on his good looks; the girl grew angry, and could not bear the self-praises of her Brother, interpreting all he said (and how could she do otherwise?) into reflection on herself.

She ran off to her father, to be avenged on her Brother, and spitefully accused him of having, as a boy, made use of that which belonged only to girls.

The father embraced them both, and bestowing his kisses and affection impartially on each, said, "I wish you both would look into the mirror every day: you, my son, that you may not spoil your beauty by evil conduct; and you, my daughter, that you may make up for your lack of beauty by your virtues."

The Buffoon and the Countryman

A RICH NOBLEMAN once opened the theaters without charge to the people, and gave a public notice that he would handsomely reward any person who invented a new amusement for the occasion. Various public performers contended for the prize.

Among them came a Buffoon well known among the populace for his jokes, and said that he had a kind of entertainment which had never been brought out on any stage before. This report being spread about made a great stir, and the theater was crowded in every part.

The Buffoon appeared alone upon the platform, without any apparatus or confederates, and the very sense of expectation caused an intense silence. He suddenly bent his head towards his bosom and imitated the squeaking of a little pig so admirably with his voice that the audience declared he had a porker under his cloak, and demanded that it should be shaken out. When that was done and nothing was found, they cheered the actor, and loaded him with the loudest applause.

A Countryman in the crowd, observing all that has passed, said, "So help me, Hercules, he shall not beat me at that trick!" and at once proclaimed that he would do the same thing on the next day, though in a much more natural way.

On the morrow a still larger crowd assembled in the theater, but now partiality for their favorite actor very generally prevailed, and the audience came rather to ridicule the Countryman than to see the spectacle. Both of the performers appeared on the stage.

The Buffoon grunted and squeaked away first, and obtained, as on the preceding day, the applause and cheers of the spectators. Next the Countryman commenced, and pretending that he concealed a little pig beneath his clothes (which in truth he did, but not suspected by the audience) contrived to take hold of and to pull his ear causing the pig to squeak.

The Crowd, however, cried out with one consent that the Buffoon had given a far more exact imitation, and clamored for the Countryman to be kicked out of the theater.

On this the rustic produced the little pig from his cloak and showed by the most positive proof the greatness of their mistake. "Look here," he said, "This shows what sort of judges you are."

The Bull and the Goat

A BULL, escaping from a Lion, hid in a cave which some shepherds had recently occupied. As soon as he entered, a He-Goat left in the cave sharply attacked him with his horns.

The Bull quietly addressed him: "Butt away as much as you will. I have no fear of you, but of the Lion. Let that monster go away and I will soon let you know what is the respective strength of a Goat and a Bull."

It shows an evil disposition to take advantage of a friend in distress.

2

The Camel

WHEN MAN first saw the Camel, he was so frightened at his vast size that he ran away. After a time, perceiving the meekness and gentleness of the beast's temper, he summoned courage enough to approach him.

Soon afterwards, observing that he was an animal altogether deficient in spirit, he assumed such boldness as to put a bridle in his mouth, and to let a child drive him.

Use serves to overcome dread.

The Cat and Venus

A CAT fell in love with a handsome young man, and entreated Venus to change her into the form of a woman. Venus consented to her request and transformed her into a beautiful damsel, so that the youth saw her and loved her, and took her home as his bride.

While the two were reclining in their chamber, Venus wishing to discover if the Cat in her change of shape had also altered her habits of life, let down a mouse in the middle of the room.

The Cat, quite forgetting her present condition, started up from the couch and pursued the mouse, wishing to eat it. Venus was much disappointed and again caused her to return to her former shape.

Nature exceeds nurture.

The Cat and the Mice

A CERTAIN HOUSE was overrun with Mice. A Cat, discovering this, made her way into it and began to catch and eat them one by one. Fearing for their lives, the Mice kept themselves close in their holes.

The Cat was no longer able to get at them and perceived that she must tempt them forth by some device. For this purpose she jumped upon a peg, and suspending herself from it, pretended to be dead.

One of the Mice, peeping stealthily out, saw her and said, "Ah, my good madam, even though you should turn into a meal-bag, we will not come near you."

The Cat and the Cock

A CAT caught a Cock, and pondered how he might find a reasonable excuse for eating him. He accused him of being a nuisance to men by crowing in the nighttime and not permitting them to sleep. The Cock defended himself by saying that he did this for the benefit of men, that they might rise in time for their labors.

The Cat replied, "Although you abound in specious apologies, I shall not remain supperless;" and he made a meal of him.

The Charcoal-Burner And The Fuller

A CHARCOAL-BURNER carried on his trade in his own house. One day he met a friend, a Fuller, and entreated him to come and live with him, saying that they should be far better neighbors and that their housekeeping expenses would be lessened.

The Fuller replied, "The arrangement is impossible as far as I am concerned, for whatever I should whiten, you would immediately blacken again with your charcoal."

Like will draw like.

The Cobbler Turned Doctor

A COBBLER unable to make a living by his trade and made desperate by poverty, began to practice medicine in a town in which he was not known. He sold a drug, pretending that it was an antidote to all poisons, and obtained a great name for himself by long-winded puffs and advertisements.

When the Cobbler happened to fall sick himself of a serious illness, the Governor of the town determined to test his skill. For this purpose he called for a cup, and while filling it with water, pretended to mix poison with the Cobbler's antidote, commanding him to drink it on the promise of a reward. The Cobbler, under the fear of death, confessed that he had no knowledge of medicine, and was only made famous by the stupid clamors of the crowd. The Governor then called a public assembly and addressed the citizens: "Of what folly have you been guilty? You have not hesitated to entrust your heads to a man, whom no one could employ to make even the shoes for their feet."

The Fighting Cocks and the Eagle

TWO GAME COCKS were fiercely fighting for the mastery of the farmyard. One at last put the other to flight. The vanquished Cock skulked away and hid himself in a quiet corner, while the conqueror, flying up to a high wall, flapped his wings and crowed exultingly with all his might. An Eagle sailing through the air pounced upon him and carried him off in his talons. The vanquished Cock immediately came out of his corner, and ruled henceforth with undisputed mastery.

Pride goes before destruction.

The Crab and Its Mother

A CRAB said to her son, "why do you walk so one-sided, my child? It is far more becoming to go straight forward." The young Crab replied: "Quite true, dear Mother; and if you will show me the straight way, I will promise to walk in it."

The Mother tried in vain, and submitted without remonstrance to the reproof of her child.

Example is more powerful than precept.

The Crab and the Fox

A CRAB, forsaking the seashore, chose a neighboring green meadow as its feeding ground. A Fox came across him, and being very hungry ate him up.

Just as he was on the point of being eaten, the Crab said, "I well deserve my fate, for what business had I on the land, when by my nature and habits I am only adapted for the sea?"

Contentment with our lot is an element of happiness.

The Crow and the Raven

A CROW was jealous of the Raven, because he was considered a bird of good omen and always attracted the attention of men, who noted by his flight the good or evil course of future events.

Seeing some travelers approaching, the Crow flew up into a tree, and perching herself on one of the branches, cawed as loudly as she could. The travelers turned towards the sound and wondered what it foreboded, when one of them said to his companion, "Let us proceed on our journey, my friend, for it is only the caw of a crow, and her cry, you know, is no omen."

Those who assume a character which does not belong to them, only make themselves ridiculous.

The Crow and the Pitcher

A CROW perishing with thirst saw a pitcher, and hoping to find water, flew to it with delight. When he reached it, he discovered to his grief that it contained so little water that he could not possibly get at it. He tried everything he could think of to reach the water, but all his efforts were in vain.

At last he collected as many stones as he could carry and dropped them one by one with his beak into the pitcher, until he brought the water within his reach and thus saved his life.

Necessity is the mother of invention.

The Mischievous Dog

A DOG used to run up quietly to the heels of everyone he met, and to bite them without notice. His master suspended a bell about his neck so that the Dog might give notice of his presence wherever he went. Thinking it a mark of distinction, the Dog grew proud of his bell and went tinkling it all over the marketplace.

One day an old hound said to him: "Why do you make such an exhibition of yourself? That bell that you carry is not, believe me, any order of merit, but on the contrary a mark of disgrace, a public notice to all men to avoid you as an ill mannered dog."

Notoriety is often mistaken for fame.

The Two Dogs

A MAN had two dogs: a Hound, trained to assist him in his sports, and a Housedog, taught to watch the house. When he returned home after a good day's sport, he always gave the Housedog a large share of his spoil. The Hound, feeling much aggrieved at this, reproached his companion, saying, "It is very hard to have all this labor, while you, who do not assist in the chase, luxuriate on the fruits of my exertions."

The Housedog replied, "Do not blame me, my friend, but find fault with the master, who has not taught me to labor, but to depend for subsistence on the labor of others."

Children are not to be blamed for the faults of their parents.

The Doe and the Lion

A DOE hard pressed by hunters sought refuge in a cave belonging to a Lion.

The Lion concealed himself on seeing her approach, but when she was safe within the cave, sprang upon her and tore her to pieces. "Woe is me," exclaimed the Doe, "who have escaped from man, only to throw myself into the mouth of a wild beast?"

In avoiding one evil, care must be taken not to fall into another.

The Dog and the Hare

A HOUND having started a Hare on the hillside pursued her for some distance, at one time biting her with his teeth as if he would take her life, and at another fawning upon her, as if in play with another dog.

The Hare said to him, "I wish you would act sincerely by me, and show yourself in your true colors. If you are a friend, why do you bite me so hard? If an enemy, why do you fawn on me?"

No one can be a friend if you know not whether to trust or distrust him.

The Dog, the Cock, and the Fox

A DOG and a Cock being great friends, agreed to travel together.

At nightfall they took shelter in a thick wood. The Cock flying up, perched himself on the branches of a tree, while the Dog found a bed beneath in the hollow trunk.

When the morning dawned, the Cock, as usual, crowed very loudly several times. A Fox heard the sound, and wishing to make a breakfast on him, came and stood under the branches, saying how earnestly he desired to make the acquaintance of the owner of so magnificent a voice.

The Cock, suspecting his civilities, said: "Sir, I wish you would do me the favor of going around to the hollow trunk below me, and waking my porter, so that he may open the door and let you in."

When the Fox approached the tree, the Dog sprang out and caught him, and tore him to pieces.

The Dogs and the Fox

SOME DOGS, finding the skin of a lion, began to tear it in pieces with their teeth. A Fox, seeing them, said, "If this lion were alive, you would soon find out that his claws were stronger than your teeth."

It is easy to kick a man that is down.

The Dogs and the Hides

SOME DOGS famished with hunger saw a number of cowhides steeping in a river. Not being able to reach them, they agreed to drink up the river, but it happened that they burst themselves with drinking long before they reached the hides.

Attempt not impossibilities.

The Dog and the Oyster

A DOG, used to eating eggs, saw an Oyster and, opening his mouth to its widest extent, swallowed it down with the utmost relish, supposing it to be an egg.

Soon afterwards suffering great pain in his stomach, he said, "I deserve all this torment, for my folly in thinking that everything round must be an egg."

They who act without sufficient thought, will often fall into unsuspected danger.

The Dog and the Cook

A RICH MAN gave a great feast, to which he invited many friends and acquaintances.

His Dog availed himself of the occasion to invite a stranger Dog, a friend of his, saying, "My master gives a feast, and there is always much food remaining; come and sup with me tonight."

The Dog thus invited went at the hour appointed, and seeing the preparations for so grand an entertainment, said in the joy of his heart, "How glad I am that I came! I do not often get such a chance as this. I will take care and eat enough to last me both today and tomorrow."

While he was congratulating himself and wagging his tail to convey his pleasure to his friend, the Cook saw him moving about among his dishes and, seizing him by his fore and hind paws, bundled him without ceremony out of the window.

He fell with force upon the ground and limped away, howling dreadfully. His yelling soon attracted other street dogs, who came up to him and inquired how he had enjoyed his supper.

He replied, "Why, to tell you the truth, I drank so much wine that I remember nothing. I do not know how I got out of the house."

The Dog and the Shadow

A DOG, crossing a bridge over a stream with a piece of flesh in his mouth, saw his own shadow in the water and took it for that of another Dog, with a piece of meat double his own in size. He immediately let go of his own, and fiercely attacked the other Dog to get his larger piece from him.

He thus lost both: that which he grasped at in the water, because it was a shadow; and his own, because the stream swept it away.

The Eagle and the Jackdaw

AN EAGLE, flying down from his perch on a lofty rock, seized upon a lamb and carried him aloft in his talons.

A Jackdaw, who witnessed the capture of the lamb, was stirred with envy and determined to emulate the strength and flight of the Eagle. He flew around with a great whir of his wings and settled upon a large ram, with the intention of carrying him off, but his claws became entangled in the ram's fleece and he was not able to release himself, although he fluttered with his feathers as much as he could.

The shepherd, seeing what had happened, ran up and caught him. He at once clipped the Jackdaw's wings, and taking him home at night, gave him to his children.

On their saying, "Father, what kind of bird is it?" he replied, "To my certain knowledge he is a Daw; but he would like you to think an Eagle."

The Eagle, the Cat, and the Wild Sow

AN EAGLE made her nest at the top of a lofty oak; a Cat, having found a convenient hole, moved into the middle of the trunk; and a Wild Sow, with her young, took shelter in a hollow at its foot.

The Cat cunningly resolved to destroy this chance-made colony. To carry out her design, she climbed to the nest of the Eagle, and said, "Destruction is preparing for you, and for me too, unfortunately. The Wild Sow, whom you see daily digging up the earth, wishes to uproot the oak, so she may on its fall seize our families as food for her young."

Having thus frightened the Eagle out of her senses, she crept down to the cave of the Sow, and said, "Your children are in great danger; for as soon as you go out with your litter to find food, the Eagle is prepared to pounce upon one of your little pigs."

Having instilled these fears into the Sow, she went and pretended to hide herself in the hollow of the tree. When night came she went forth with silent foot and obtained food for herself and her kittens, but feigning to be afraid, she kept a lookout all through the day.

Meanwhile, the Eagle, full of fear of the Sow, sat still on the branches, and the Sow, terrified by the Eagle, did not dare to go out from her cave. And thus they both, along with their families, perished from hunger, and afforded ample provision for the Cat and her kittens.

The Eagle and the Fox

AN EAGLE and a Fox formed an intimate friendship and decided to live near each other. The Eagle built her nest in the branches of a tall tree, while the Fox crept into the underwood and there produced her young. Not long after they had agreed upon this plan, the Eagle, being in want of provision for her young ones, swooped down while the Fox was out, seized upon one of the little cubs, and feasted herself and her brood.

The Fox on her return, discovered what had happened, but was less grieved for the death of her young than for her inability to avenge them. A just retribution, however, quickly fell upon the Eagle.

While hovering near an altar, on which some villagers were sacrificing a goat, she suddenly seized a piece of the flesh, and carried it, along with a burning cinder, to her nest.

A strong breeze soon fanned the spark into a flame, and the eaglets, as yet unfledged and helpless, were roasted in their nest and dropped down dead at the bottom of the tree. There, in the sight of the Eagle, the Fox gobbled them up.

The Eagle and the Kite

AN EAGLE, overwhelmed with sorrow, sat upon the branches of a tree in company with a Kite.

"Why," said the Kite, "do I see you with such a rueful look?"

"I seek," she replied, "a mate suitable for me, and am not able to find one."

"Take me," returned the Kite, "I am much stronger than you are."

"Why, are you able to secure the means of living by your plunder?"

"Well, I have often caught and carried away an ostrich in my talons."

The Eagle, persuaded by these words, accepted him as her mate.

Shortly after the nuptials, the Eagle said, "Fly off and bring me back the ostrich you promised me." The Kite, soaring aloft into the air, brought back the shabbiest possible mouse, stinking from the length of time it had lain about the fields.

"Is this," said the Eagle, "the faithful fulfillment of your promise to me?" The Kite replied, "That I might attain your royal hand, there is nothing that I would not have promised, however much I knew that I must fail in the performance."

The Farmer and His Sons

A FATHER, being on the point of death, wished to be sure that his sons would give the same attention to his farm as he himself had given it.

He called them to his bedside and said, "My sons, there is a great treasure hid in one of my vineyards." The sons, after his death, took their spades and mattocks and carefully dug over every portion of their land.

They found no treasure, but the vines repaid their labor by an extraordinary and superabundant crop.

The Farmer and the Stork

A FARMER placed nets on his newly-sown plowlands and caught a number of Cranes, which came to pick up his seed. With them he trapped a Stork that had fractured his leg in the net and was earnestly beseeching the Farmer to spare his life.

"Pray save me, Master," he said, "and let me go free this once. My broken limb should excite your pity. Besides, I am no Crane, I am a Stork, a bird of excellent character; and see how I love and slave for my father and mother. Look too, at my feathers —they are not the least like those of a Crane."

The Farmer laughed aloud and said, "It may be all as you say, I only know this: I have taken you with these robbers, the Cranes, and you must die in their company."

Birds of a feather flock together.

The Farmer and the Snake

ONE WINTER a Farmer found a Snake stiff and frozen with cold. He had compassion on it, and taking it up, placed it in his bosom.

The Snake was quickly revived by the warmth, and resuming its natural instincts, bit its benefactor, inflicting on him a mortal wound. "Oh," cried the Farmer with his last breath, "I am rightly served for pitying a scoundrel."

The greatest kindness will not bind the ungrateful.

The Farmer and the Cranes

SOME CRANES made their feeding grounds on some plowlands newly sown with wheat.

For a long time the Farmer, brandishing an empty sling, chased them away by the terror he inspired; but when the birds found that the sling was only swung in the air, they ceased to take any notice of it and would not move.

The Farmer, on seeing this, charged his sling with stones, and killed a great number.

The remaining birds at once forsook his fields, crying to each other, "It is time for us to be off to Liliput: for this man is no longer content to scare us, but begins to show us in earnest what he can do."

If words suffice not, blows must follow.

The Father And His Sons

A FATHER had a family of sons who were perpetually quarreling among themselves.

When he failed to heal their disputes by his exhortations, he determined to give them a practical illustration of the evils of disunion; and for this purpose he one day told them to bring him a bundle of sticks. When they had done so, he placed the faggot into the hands of each of them in succession, and ordered them to break it in pieces. They tried with all their strength, and were not able to do it.

He next opened the faggot, took the sticks separately, one by one, and again put them into his sons' hands, upon which they broke them easily.

He then addressed them in these words: "My sons, if you are of one mind, and unite to assist each other, you will be as this faggot, uninjured by all the attempts of your enemies; but if you are divided among yourselves, you will be broken as easily as these sticks."

The Father and His Two Daughters

A MAN had two daughters, the one married to a gardener, and the other to a tilemaker.

After a time he went to the daughter who had married the gardener, and inquired how she was and how all things went with her. She said, "All things are prospering with me, and I have only one wish, that there may be a heavy fall of rain, in order that the plants may be well watered."

Not long after, he went to the daughter who had married the tilemaker, and likewise inquired of her how she fared; she replied, "I want for nothing, and have only one wish, that the dry weather may continue, and the sun shine hot and bright, so that the bricks might be dried."

He said to her, "If your sister wishes for rain, and you for dry weather, with which of the two am I to join my wishes?"

The Fawn and His Mother

A YOUNG FAWN once said to his Mother, "You are larger than a dog, and swifter, and more used to running, and you have your horns as a defense; why, then, O Mother! Do the hounds frighten you so?"

She smiled, and said: "I know full well, my son, that all you say is true. I have the advantages you mention, but when I hear even the bark of a single dog I feel ready to faint, and fly away as fast as I can."

No arguments will give courage to the coward.

The Fir-Tree and the Bramble

A FIR-TREE said boastingly to the Bramble, "You are useful for nothing at all; while I am everywhere used for roofs and houses."

The Bramble answered: "You poor creature, if you would only call to mind the axes and saws which are about to hew you down, you would have reason to wish that you had grown up a Bramble, not a Fir-Tree."

Better poverty without care, than riches with.

The Flies and the Honey-Pot

A NUMBER of Flies were attracted to a jar of honey which had been overturned in a housekeeper's room, and placing their feet in it, ate greedily. Their feet, however, became so smeared with the honey that they could not use their wings, nor release themselves, and were suffocated. Just as they were expiring, they exclaimed, "O foolish creatures that we are, for the sake of a little pleasure we have destroyed ourselves." Pleasure bought with pains, hurts.

The Fox and the Woodcutter

A FOX, running before the hounds, came across a Woodcutter felling an oak and begged him to show him a safe hiding-place. The Woodcutter advised him to take shelter in his own hut, so the Fox crept in and hid himself in a corner.

The huntsman soon came up with his hounds and inquired of the Woodcutter if he had seen the Fox. He declared that he had not seen him, and yet pointed, all the time he was speaking, to the hut where the Fox lay hidden. The huntsman took no notice of the signs, but believing his word, hastened forward in the chase.

As soon as they were well away, the Fox departed without taking any notice of the Woodcutter: whereon he called to him and reproached him, saying, "You ungrateful fellow, you owe your life to me, and yet you leave me without a word of thanks."

The Fox replied, "Indeed, I should have thanked you fervently if your deeds had been as good as your words, and if your hands had not been traitors to your speech."

The Fox and the Crow

A CROW having stolen a bit of meat, perched in a tree and held it in her beak. A Fox, seeing this, longed to possess the meat himself, and by a wily stratagem succeeded. "How handsome is the Crow," he exclaimed," in the beauty of her shape and in the fairness of her complexion! Oh, if her voice were only equal to her beauty, she would deservedly be considered the Queen of Birds!"

This he said deceitfully; but the Crow, anxious to refute the reflection cast upon her voice, set up a loud caw and dropped the flesh. The Fox quickly picked it up, and thus addressed the Cro "My good Crow, your voice is right enough, but your wit is wanting."

The Fox and the Hedgehog

A FOX swimming across a rapid river was carried by the force of the current into a very deep ravine, where he lay for a long time very much bruised, sick, and unable to move. A swarm of hungry blood-sucking flies settled upon him. A Hedgehog, passing by, saw his anguish and inquired if he should drive away the flies that were tormenting him.

"By no means," replied the Fox; "pray do not molest them." "How is this?" said the Hedgehog; "do you not want to be rid of them?"

"No," returned the Fox, "for these flies which you see are full of blood, and sting me but little, and if you rid me of these which are already satiated, others more hungry will come in their place, and will drink up all the blood I have left."

The Fox and the Monkey

A FOX and a Monkey were traveling together on the same road. As they journeyed, they passed through a cemetery full of monuments. "All these monuments which you see," said the Monkey, "are erected in honor of my ancestors, who were in their day freedmen and citizens of great renown." The Fox replied, "You have chosen a most appropriate subject for your falsehoods, as I am sure none of your ancestors will be able to contradict you."

A false tale often betrays itself.

The Fox and the Lion

WHEN A FOX who had never yet seen a Lion, fell in with him by chance for the first time in the forest, he was so frightened that he nearly died with fear. On meeting him for the second time, he was still much alarmed, but not to the same extent as at first.

On seeing him the third time, he so increased in boldness that he went up to him and commenced a familiar conversation with him.

Acquaintance softens prejudices.

The Fox and the Grapes

A FAMISHED FOX saw some clusters of ripe black grapes hanging from a trellised vine. She resorted to all her tricks to get at them, but wearied herself in vain, for she could not reach them.

At last she turned away, hiding her disappointment and saying: "The Grapes are sour, and not ripe as I thought."

The Fox and the Goat

A FOX one day fell into a deep well and could find no means of escape. A Goat, overcome with thirst, came to the same well, and seeing the Fox, inquired if the water was good. Concealing his sad plight under a merry guise, the Fox indulged in a lavish praise of the water, saying it was excellent beyond measure, and encouraging him to descend.

The Goat, mindful only of his thirst, thoughtlessly jumped down, but just as he drank, the Fox informed him of the difficulty they were both in and suggested a scheme for their common escape. "If," said he, "you will place your forefeet upon the wall and bend your head, I will run up your back and escape, and will help you out afterwards."

The Goat readily assented and the Fox leaped upon his back. Steadying himself with the Goat's horns, he safely reached the mouth of the well and made off as fast as he could.

When the Goat upbraided him for breaking his promise, he turned around and cried out, "You foolish old fellow! If you had as many brains in your head as you have hairs in your beard, you would never have gone down before you had inspected the way up, nor have exposed yourself to dangers from which you had no means of escape."

Look before you leap.

The Fowler and the Viper

A FOWLER, taking his bird-lime and his twigs, went out to catch birds. Seeing a thrush sitting upon a tree, he wished to take it, and fitting his twigs to a proper length, watched intently, having his whole thoughts directed towards the sky. While thus looking upwards, he unknowingly trod upon a Viper asleep just before his feet.

The Viper, turning about, stung him, and falling into a swoon, the man said to himself, "Woe is me! That while I purposed to hunt another, I am myself fallen unawares into the snares of death."

The Two Frogs (1)

TWO FROGS dwelt in the same pool. When the pool dried up under the summer's heat, they left it and set out together for another home.

As they went along they chanced to pass a deep well, amply supplied with water, and when they saw it, one of the Frogs said to the other, "Let us descend and make our abode in this well: it will furnish us with shelter and food."

The other replied with greater caution, "But suppose the water should fail us. how can we get out again from so great a depth?"

Do nothing without a regard to the consequences.

The Two Frogs (2)

TWO FROGS were neighbors. One inhabited a deep pond, far removed from public view; the other lived in a gully containing little water, and traversed by a country road.

The Frog that lived in the pond warned his friend to change his residence and entreated him to come and live with him, saying that he would enjoy greater safety from danger and more abundant food. The other refused, saying that he felt it so very hard to leave a place to which he had become accustomed.

A few days afterwards a heavy wagon passed through the gully and crushed him to death under its wheels.

A willful man will have his way to his own hurt.

The Frogs Asking for a King

THE FROGS, grieved at having no established Ruler, sent ambassadors to Jupiter entreating for a King. Perceiving their simplicity, he cast down a huge log into the lake. The Frogs were terrified at the splash occasioned by its fall and hid themselves in the depths of the pool.

But as soon as they realized that the huge log was motionless, they swam again to the top of the water, dismissed their fears, climbed up, and began squatting on it in contempt.

After some time they began to think themselves ill-treated in the appointment of so inert a Ruler, and sent a second deputation to Jupiter to pray that he would set over them another sovereign. He then gave them an Eel to govern them.

When the Frogs discovered his easy good nature, they sent yet a third time to Jupiter to beg him to choose for them still another King. Jupiter, displeased with all their complaints, sent a Heron, who preyed upon the Frogs day by day till there were none left to croak upon the lake.

The Gamecocks and the Partridge

A MAN had two Gamecocks in his poultry-yard. One day by chance he found a tame Partridge for sale. He purchased it and brought it home to be reared with his Gamecocks.

When the Partridge was put into the poultry-yard, they struck at it and followed it about, so that the Partridge became grievously troubled and supposed that he was thus evilly treated because he was a stranger.

Not long afterwards he saw the Cocks fighting together and not separating before one had well beaten the other. He then said to himself, "I shall no longer distress myself at being struck at by these Gamecocks, when I see that they cannot even refrain from quarreling with each other."

The Gnat and the Lion

A GNAT came and said to a Lion, "I do not in the least fear you, nor are you stronger than I am. For in what does your strength consist? You can scratch with your claws and bite with your teeth an a woman in her quarrels. I repeat that I am altogether more powerful than you; and if you doubt it, let us fight and see who will conquer."

The Gnat, having sounded his horn, fastened himself upon the Lion and stung him on the nostrils and the parts of the face devoid of hair. While trying to crush him, the Lion tore himself with his claws, until he punished himself severely. The Gnat thus prevailed over the Lion, and, buzzing about in a song of triumph, flew away.

But shortly afterwards he became entangled in the meshes of a cobweb and was eaten by a spider. He greatly lamented his fate, saying, "Woe is me! That I, who can wage war successfully with the hugest beasts, should perish myself from this spider, the most inconsiderable of insects!"

The Gnat and the Bull

A GNAT settled on the horn of a Bull, and sat there a long time. Just as he was about to fly off, he made a buzzing noise, and inquired of the Bull if he would like him to go.

The Bull replied, "I did not know you had come, and I shall not miss you when you go away."

Some men are of more consequence in their own eyes than in the eyes of their neighbors.

The Goat and the Goatherd

A GOATHERD had sought to bring back a stray goat to his flock. He whistled and sounded his horn in vain; the straggler paid no attention to the summons. At last the Goatherd threw a stone, and breaking its horn, begged the Goat not to tell his master. The Goat replied, "Why, you silly fellow, the horn will speak though I be silent."

Do not attempt to hide things which cannot be hid.

The Goatherd and the Wild Goats

A GOATHERD, driving his flock from their pasture at eventide, found some Wild Goats mingled among them, and shut them up together with his own for the night.

The next day it snowed very hard, so that he could not take the herd to their usual feeding places, but was obliged to keep them in the fold. He gave his own goats just sufficient food to keep them alive, but fed the strangers more abundantly in the hope of enticing them to stay with him and of making them his own.

When the thaw set in, he led them all out to feed, and the Wild Goats scampered away as fast as they could to the mountains. The Goatherd scolded them for their ingratitude in leaving him, when during the storm he had taken more care of them than of his own herd.

One of them, turning about, said to him: "That is the very reason why we are so cautious; for if you yesterday treated us better than the Goats you have had so long, it is plain also that if others came after us, you would in the same manner prefer them to ourselves."

Old friends cannot with impunity be sacrificed for new ones.

The Goods and the Ills

ALL the Goods were once driven out by the Ills from that common share which they each had in the affairs of mankind; for the Ills by reason of their numbers had prevailed to possess the earth.

The Goods wafted themselves to heaven and asked for a righteous vengeance on their persecutors. They entreated Jupiter that they might no longer be associated with the Ills, as they had nothing in common and could not live together, but were engaged in unceasing warfare; and that an indissoluble law might be laid down for their future protection.

Jupiter granted their request and decreed that henceforth the Ills should visit the earth in company with each other, but that the Goods should one by one enter the habitations of men.

Hence it arises that Ills abound, for they come not one by one, but in troops, and by no means singly: while the Goods proceed from Jupiter, and are given, not alike to all, but singly, and separately; and one by one to those who are able to discern them.

The Grasshopper and the Owl

AN OWL, accustomed to feed at night and to sleep during the day, was greatly disturbed by the noise of a Grasshopper and earnestly besought her to stop chirping.

The Grasshopper refused to desist, and chirped louder and louder the more the Owl entreated. When she saw that she could get no redress and that her words were despised, the Owl attacked the chatterer by a stratagem. "Since I cannot sleep," she said, "on account of your song which, believe me, is sweet as the lyre of Apollo, I shall indulge myself in drinking some nectar which Pallas lately gave me. if you do not dislike it, come to me and we will drink it together."

The Grasshopper, who was thirsty, and pleased with the praise of her voice, eagerly flew up. The Owl came forth from her hollow, seized her, and put her to death.

The Hares and the Foxes

THE HARES waged war with the Eagles, and called upon the Foxes to help them. They replied, "We would willingly have helped you, if we had not known who you were, and with whom you were fighting."

Count the cost before you commit yourselves.

The Hare and the Hound

A HOUND started a Hare from his lair, but after a long run, gave up the chase. A goat-herd seeing him stop, mocked him, saying "The little one is the best runner of the two." The Hound replied, "You do not see the difference between us: I was only running for a dinner, but he for his life."

The Hares and the Frogs

THE HARES, oppressed by their own exceeding timidity and weary of the perpetual alarm to which they were exposed, with one accord determined to put an end to themselves and their troubles by jumping from a lofty precipice into a deep lake below.

As they scampered off in large numbers to carry out their resolve, the Frogs lying on the banks of the lake heard the noise of their feet and rushed helter-skelter to the deep water for safety.

On seeing the rapid disappearance of the Frogs, one of the Hares cried out to his companions: "Stay, my friends, do not do as you intended; for you now see that there are creatures who are still more timid than ourselves."

The Hare and the Tortoise

A HARE one day ridiculed the short feet and slow pace of the Tortoise, who replied, laughing: "Though you be swift as the wind, I will beat you in a race." The Hare, believing her assertion to be simply impossible, assented to the proposal; and they agreed that the Fox should choose the course and fix the goal.

On the day appointed for the race the two started together. The Tortoise never for a moment stopped, but went on with a slow but steady pace straight to the end of the course.

The Hare, lying down by the wayside, fell fast asleep. At last waking up, and moving as fast as he could, he saw the Tortoise had reached the goal, and was comfortably dozing after her fatigue.

Slow but steady wins the race.

The Herdsman and the Lost Bull

A HERDSMAN tending his flock in a forest lost a Bull-calf from the fold. After a long and fruitless search, he made a vow that, if he could only discover the thief who had stolen the Calf, he would offer a lamb in sacrifice to Hermes, Pan, and the Guardian Deities of the forest. Not long afterwards, as he ascended a small hillock, he saw at its foot a Lion feeding on the Calf.

Terrified at the sight, he lifted his eyes and his hands to heaven, and said: "Just now I vowed to offer a lamb to the Guardian Deities of the forest if I could only find out who had robbed me; but now that I have discovered the thief, I would willingly add a full-grown Bull to the Calf I have lost, if I may only secure my own escape from him in safety."

The Hawk, the Kite, and the Pigeons

THE PIGEONS, terrified by the appearance of a Kite, called upon the Hawk to defend them. He at once consented. When they had admitted him into the cote, they found that he made more havoc and slew a larger number of them in one day than the Kite could pounce upon in a whole year.

Avoid a remedy that is worse than the disease.

The Hen and the Golden Eggs

A COTTAGER and his wife had a Hen that laid a golden egg every day. They supposed that the Hen must contain a great lump of gold in its inside, and in order to get the gold they killed it. Having done so, they found to their surprise that the Hen differed in no respect from their other hens. The foolish pair, thus hoping to become rich all at once, deprived themselves of the gain of which they were assured day by day.

Hercules and the Wagoner

A CARTER was driving a wagon along a country lane, when the wheels sank down deep into a rut. The rustic driver, stupefied and aghast, stood looking at the wagon, and did nothing but utter loud cries to Hercules to come and help him.

Hercules, it is said, appeared and thus addressed him: "Put your shoulders to the wheels, my man. Goad on your bullocks, and never more pray to me for help, until you have done your best to help yourself, or depend upon it you will henceforth pray in vain."

Self-help is the best help.

The Horse and the Stag

AT ONE TIME the Horse had the plain entirely to himself. Then a Stag intruded into his domain and shared his pasture.

The Horse, desiring to revenge himself on the stranger, asked a man if he were willing to help him in punishing the Stag. The man replied that if the Horse would receive a bit in his mouth and agree to carry him, he would contrive effective weapons against the Stag. The Horse consented and allowed the man to mount him.

From that hour he found that instead of obtaining revenge on the Stag, he had enslaved himself to the service of man.

The Huntsman and the Fisherman

A HUNTSMAN, returning with his dogs from the field, fell in by chance with a Fisherman who was bringing home a basket well laden with fish. The Huntsman wished to have the fish, and their owner experienced an equal longing for the contents of the game-bag.

They quickly agreed to exchange the produce of their day's sport. Each was so well pleased with his bargain that they made for some time the same exchange day after day.

Finally a neighbor said to them, "If you go on in this way, you will soon destroy by frequent use the pleasure of your exchange, and each will again wish to retain the fruits of his own sport."

Abstain and enjoy.

The Hunter and the Woodman

A HUNTER, not very bold, was searching for the tracks of a Lion. He asked a man felling oaks in the forest if he had seen any marks of his footsteps or knew where his lair was. "I will," said the man, "at once show you the Lion himself."

The Hunter, turning very pale and chattering with his teeth from fear, replied, "No, thank you. I did not ask that; it is his track only I am in search of, not the Lion himself."

The hero is brave in deeds as well as words.

The Jackdaw and the Doves

A JACKDAW, seeing some Doves in a cote abundantly provided with food, painted himself white and joined them in order to share their plentiful maintenance.

The Doves, as long as he was silent, supposed him to be one of themselves and admitted him to their cote. But when one day he forgot himself and began to chatter, they discovered his true character and drove him forth, pecking him with their beaks. Failing to obtain food among the Doves, he returned to the Jackdaws.

They too, not recognizing him on account of his color, expelled him from living with them. So desiring two ends, he obtained neither.

The Jackdaw and the Fox

A HALF-FAMISHED JACKDAW seated himself on a fig-tree, which had produced some fruit entirely out of season, and waited in the hope that the figs would ripen.

A Fox seeing him sitting so long and learning the reason of his doing so, said to him, "You are indeed, sir, sadly deceiving yourself; you are indulging a hope strong enough to cheat you, but which will never reward you with enjoyment."

Jupiter, Neptune, Minerva, and Momus

ACCORDING to an ancient legend, the first man was made by Jupiter, the first bull by Neptune, and the first house by Minerva.

On the completion of their labors, a dispute arose as to which had made the most perfect work. They agreed to appoint Momus as judge, and to abide by his decision. Momus, however, being very envious of the handicraft of each, found fault with all.

He first blamed the work of Neptune because he had not made the horns of the bull below his eyes, so he might better see where to strike. He then condemned the work of Jupiter, because he had not placed the heart of man on the outside, that everyone might read the thoughts of the evil disposed and take precautions against the intended mischief.

And, lastly, he inveighed against Minerva because she had not contrived iron wheels in the foundation of her house, so its inhabitants might more easily remove if a neighbor proved unpleasant. Jupiter, indignant at such inverterate faultfinding, drove him from his office of judge, and expelled him from the mansions of Olympus.

 5

The Kid and the Wolf

A KID standing on the roof of a house, out of harm's way, saw a Wolf passing by and immediately began to taunt and revile him. The Wolf, looking up, said, "Sirrah! I hear thee: yet it is not thou who mockest me, but the roof on which thou art standing."

Time and place often give the advantage to the weak over the strong.

The King's Son and the Painted Lion

A KING, whose only son was fond of martial exercises, had a dream in which he was warned that his son would be killed by a lion. Afraid the dream should prove true, he built for his son a pleasant palace and adorned its walls for his amusement with all kinds of life-sized animals, among which was the picture of a lion.

When the young Prince saw this, his grief at being thus confined burst out afresh, and, standing near the lion, he said: "O you most detestable of animals! Through a lying dream of my father's, which he saw in his sleep, I am shut up on your account in this palace as if I had been a girl: what shall I now do to you?"

With these words he stretched out his hands toward a thorn-tree, meaning to cut a stick from its branches so that he might beat the lion. but one of the tree's prickles pierced his finger and caused great pain and inflammation, so that the young Prince fell down in a fainting fit. A violent fever suddenly set in, from which he died not many days later.

We had better bear our troubles bravely than try to escape them.

The Kingdom of the Lion

THE BEASTS of the field and forest had a Lion as their king. He was neither wrathful, cruel, nor tyrannical, but just and gentle as a king could be.

During his reign he made a royal proclamation for a general assembly of all the birds and beasts, and drew up conditions for a universal league, in which the Wolf and the Lamb, the Panther and the Kid, the Tiger and the Stag, the Dog and the Hare, should live together in perfect peace and amity.

The Hare said, "Oh, how I have longed to see this day, in which the weak shall take their place with impunity by the side of the strong." And after the Hare said this, he ran for his life.

The Kites and the Swans

TEE KITES of olden times, as well as the Swans, had the privilege of song. But having heard the neigh of the horse, they were so enchanted with the sound, that they tried to imitate it; and, in trying to neigh, they forgot how to sing.

The desire for imaginary benefits often involves the loss of present blessings.

The Sick Kite

A KITE, sick unto death, said to his mother: "O Mother! Do not mourn, but at once invoke the gods that my life may be prolonged." She replied, "Alas! My son, which of the gods do you think will pity you? Is there one whom you have not outraged by filching from their very altars a part of the sacrifice offered up to them?"

We must make friends in prosperity if we would have their help in adversity.

The Laborer and the Snake

A SNAKE, having made his hole close to the porch of a cottage, inflicted a mortal bite on the Cottager's infant son. Grieving over his loss, the Father resolved to kill the Snake.

The next day, when it came out of its hole for food, he took up his axe, but by swinging too hastily, missed its head and cut off only the end of its tail. After some time the Cottager, afraid that the Snake would bite him also, endeavored to make peace, and placed some bread and salt in the hole. The Snake, slightly hissing, said: "There can henceforth be no peace between us; for whenever I see you I shall remember the loss of my tail, and whenever you see me you will be thinking of the death of your son." No one truly forgets injuries in the presence of him who caused the injury.

The Lark and Her Young Ones

A LARK had made her nest in the early spring on the young green wheat. The brood had almost grown to their full strength and attained the use of their wings and the full plumage of their feathers, when the owner of the field, looking over his ripe crop, said, "The time has come when I must ask all my neighbors to help me with my harvest."

One of the young Larks heard his speech and related it to his mother, inquiring of her to what place they should move for safety.

"There is no occasion to move yet, my son," she replied; "the man who only sends to his friends to help him with his harvest is not really in earnest."

The owner of the field came again a few days later and saw the wheat shedding the grain from excess of ripeness. He said, "I will come myself tomorrow with my laborers, and with as many reapers as I can hire, and will get in the harvest."

The Lark on hearing these words said to her brood, "It is time now to be off, my little ones, for the man is in earnest this time; he no longer trusts his friends, but will reap the field himself."

Self-help is the best help.

The Lark Burying Her Father

THE LARK (according to an ancient legend) was created before the earth itself, and when her father died, as there was no earth, she could find no place of burial for him. She let him lie uninterred for five days, and on the sixth day, not knowing what else to do, she buried him in her own head. Hence she obtained her crest, which is popularly said to be her father's grave-hillock.

Youth's first duty is reverence to parents.

The Sick Lion

A LION, unable from old age and infirmities to provide himself with food by force, resolved to do so by artifice. He returned to his den, and lying down there, pretended to be sick, taking care that his sickness should be publicly known.

The beasts expressed their sorrow, and came one by one to his den, where the Lion devoured them.

After many of the beasts had thus disappeared, the Fox discovered the trick and presenting himself to the Lion, stood on the outside of the cave, at a respectful distance, and asked him how he was.

"I am very middling," replied the Lion, "but why do you stand without? Pray enter within to talk with me." "No, thank you," said the Fox. "I notice that there are many prints of feet entering your cave, but I see no trace of any returning."

He is wise who is warned by the misfortunes of others.

The Lioness

A CONTROVERSY prevailed among the beasts of the field as to which of the animals deserved the most credit for producing the greatest number of whelps at a birth. They rushed clamorously into the presence of the Lioness and demanded of her the settlement of the dispute.

"And you," they said, "how many sons have you at a birth?" The Lioness laughed at them, and said: "Why! I have only one; but that one is altogether a thoroughbred Lion."

The value is in the worth, not in the number.

The Lion and the Bull

A LION, greatly desiring to capture a Bull, and yet afraid to attack him on account of his great size, resorted to a trick to ensure his destruction. He approached the Bull and said, "I have slain a fine sheep, my friend; and if you will come home and partake of him with me, I shall be delighted to have your company." The Lion said this in the hope that, as the Bull was in the act of reclining to eat, he might attack him to advantage, and make his meal on him.

The Bull, on approaching the Lion's den, saw the huge spits and giant caldrons, and no sign whatever of the sheep, and, without saying a word, quietly took his departure.

The Lion inquired why he went off so abruptly without a word of salutation to his host, who had not given him any cause for offense.

"I have reasons enough," said the Bull. "I see no indication whatever of your having slaughtered a sheep, while I do see very plainly every preparation for your dining on a bull."

The Lion and the Three Bulls

THREE BULLS for a long time pastured together. A Lion lay in ambush in the hope of making them his prey, but was afraid to attack them while they kept together.

Having at last by guileful speeches succeeded in separating them, he attacked them without fear as they fed alone, and feasted on them one by one at his own leisure.

Union is strength.

The Lion and the Shepherd

A LION, roaming through a forest, trod upon a thorn. Soon afterward he came up to a Shepherd and fawned upon him, wagging his tail as if to say, "I am a suppliant, and seek your aid."

The Shepherd boldly examined the beast, discovered the thorn, and placing his paw upon his lap, pulled it out; thus relieved of his pain, the Lion returned into the forest.

Sometime after, the Shepherd, being imprisoned on a false accusation, was condemned "to be cast to the Lions" as the punishment for his imputed crime. But when the Lion was released from his cage, he recognized the Shepherd as the man who healed him, and instead of attacking him, approached and placed his foot upon his lap.

The King, as soon as he heard the tale, ordered the Lion to be set free again in the forest, and the Shepherd to be pardoned and restored to his friends.

The Lion And The Mouse

A LION was awakened from sleep by a Mouse running over his face. Rising up angrily, he caught him and was about to kill him, when the Mouse piteously entreated, saying: "If you would only spare my life, I would be sure to repay your kindness."

The Lion laughed and let him go. It happened shortly after this that the Lion was caught by some hunters, who bound him by strong ropes to the ground. The Mouse, recognizing his roar, came and gnawed the rope with his teeth, and set him free, exclaiming:

"You ridiculed the idea of my ever being able to help you, not expecting to receive from me any repayment of your favor; now you know that it is possible for even a Mouse to confer benefits on a Lion."

The Lion, Jupiter, and the Elephant

THE LION wearied Jupiter with his frequent complaints. "It is true, O Jupiter!" he said, "that I am gigantic in strength, handsome in shape, and powerful in attack. I have jaws well provided with teeth, and feet furnished with claws, and I lord it over all the beasts of the forest, and what a disgrace it is, that being such as I am, I should be frightened by the crowing of a cock."

Jupiter replied, "Why do you blame me without a cause? I have given you all the attributes which I possess myself, and your courage never fails you except in this one instance."

On hearing this the Lion groaned and lamented very much and, reproaching himself with his cowardice, wished that he might die. As these thoughts passed through his mind, he met an Elephant and came close to hold a conversation with him. after a time he observed that the Elephant shook his ears very often, and he inquired what was the matter and why his ears moved with such a tremor every now and then.

Just at that moment a Gnat settled on the head of the Elephant, and he replied, "Do you see that little buzzing insect? if it enters my ear, my fate is sealed. I should die presently."

The Lion said, "Well, since so huge a beast is afraid of a tiny gnat, I will no more complain, nor wish myself dead. I find myself, even as I am, better off than the Elephant."

The Lion, the Wolf, and the Fox

A LION, growing old, lay sick in his cave. All the beasts came to visit their king, except the Fox. The Wolf therefore, thinking that he had a capital opportunity, accused the Fox to the Lion of not paying any respect to him who had the rule over them all and of not coming to visit him.

At that very moment the Fox came in and heard these last words of the Wolf. The Lion roaring out in a rage against him, the Fox sought an opportunity to defend himself and said, "And who of all those who have come to you have benefited you so much as I, who have traveled from place to place in every direction, and have sought and learnt from the physicians the means of healing you?"

The Lion commanded him immediately to tell him the cure, when he replied, "You must flay a wolf alive and wrap his skin yet warm around you."

The Wolf was at once taken and flayed; whereon the Fox, turning to him, said with a smile, "You should have moved your master not to ill, but to good, will."

The Lion, the Bear, and the Fox

A LION and a Bear seized a Kid at the same moment, and fought fiercely for its possession. When they had fearfully lacerated each other and were faint from the long combat, they lay down exhausted with fatigue.

A Fox, who had gone round them at a distance several times, saw them both stretched on the ground with the Kid lying untouched in the middle. He ran in between them, and seizing the Kid scampered off as fast as he could.

The Lion and the Bear saw him, but not being able to get up, said, "Woe be to us, that we should have fought and belabored ourselves only to serve the turn of a Fox."

It sometimes happens that one man has all the toil, and another all the profit.

The Lion, the Mouse, and the Fox

A LION, fatigued by the heat of a summer's day, fell fast asleep in his den. A Mouse ran over his mane and ears and woke him from his slumbers. He rose up and shook himself in great wrath, and searched every corner of his den to find the Mouse.

A Fox seeing him said: "A fine Lion you are, to be frightened of a Mouse."

"'It's not the Mouse I fear," said the Lion; "I resent his familiarity and ill-breeding."

Little liberties are great offenses.

The Lion, the Fox, and the Ass

THE LION, the Fox and the Ass entered into an agreement to assist each other in the chase. Having secured a large booty, the Lion on their return from the forest asked the Ass to allot his due portion to each of the three partners in the treaty.

The Ass carefully divided the spoil into three equal shares and modestly requested the two others to make the first choice. The Lion, bursting out into a great rage, devoured the Ass. Then he requested the Fox to do him the favor to make a division.

The Fox accumulated all that they had killed into one large heap and left to himself the smallest possible morsel. The Lion said, "Who has taught you, my very excellent fellow, the art of division? You are perfect to a fraction." He replied, "I learned it from the Ass, by witnessing his fate." Happy is the man who learns from the misfortunes of others.

The Lion in Love

A LION demanded the daughter of a woodcutter in marriage. The Father, unwilling to grant, and yet afraid to refuse his request, hit upon this expedient to rid himself of his importunities. He expressed his willingness to accept the Lion as the suitor of his daughter on one condition: that he should allow him to extract his teeth, and cut off his claws, as his daughter was fearfully afraid of both.

The Lion cheerfully assented to the proposal. But when the toothless, clawless Lion returned to repeat his request, the Woodman, no longer afraid, set upon him with his club, and drove him away into the forest.

The Old Lion

A LION, worn out with years and powerless from disease, lay on the ground at the point of death. A Boar rushed upon him, and avenged with a stroke of his tusks a long-remembered injury.

Shortly afterwards the Bull with his horns gored him as if he were an enemy. When the Ass saw that the huge beast could be assailed with impunity, he let drive at his forehead with his heels.

The expiring Lion said, "I have reluctantly brooked the insults of the brave, but to be compelled to endure such treatment from thee, a disgrace to Nature, is indeed to die a double death."

 6

The Man and His Two Sweethearts

A MIDDLE-AGED MAN, whose hair had begun to turn gray, courted two women at the same time. One of them was young, and the other well advanced in years.

The elder woman, ashamed to be courted by a man younger than herself, made a point, whenever her admirer visited her, to pull out some portion of his black hairs. The younger, on the contrary, not wishing to become the wife of an old man, was equally zealous in removing every gray hair she could find. Thus it came to pass that between them both he very soon found that he had not a hair left on his head.

Those who seek to please everybody MIDDLE-AGED please nobody.

The Man Bitten by a Dog

A MAN who had been bitten by a Dog went about in quest of someone who might heal him. A friend, meeting him and learning what he wanted, said, "If you would be cured, take a piece of bread, and dip it in the blood from your wound, and go and give it to the Dog that bit you."

The Man who had been bitten laughed at this advice and said, "Why? If I should do so, it would be as if I should beg every Dog in the town to bite me."

Benefits bestowed upon the evil-disposed increase their means of injuring you.

The Man and His Wife

A MAN had a Wife who made herself hated by all the members of his household. Wishing to find out if she had the same effect on the persons in her father's house, he made some excuse to send her home on a visit to her father.

After a short time she returned, and when he inquired how she had got on and how the servants had treated her, she replied, "The herdsmen and shepherds cast on me looks of aversion."

He said, "O Wife, if you were disliked by those who go out early in the morning with their flocks and return late in the evening, what must have been felt towards you by those with whom you passed the whole day!"

Straws show how the wind blows.

The Man and the Lion

A MAN and a Lion traveled together through the forest. They soon began to boast of their respective superiority to each other in strength and prowess.

As they were disputing, they passed a statue carved in stone, which represented "a Lion strangled by a Man."

The traveler pointed to it and said: "See there! How strong we are, and how we prevail over even the king of beasts."

The Lion replied: "This statue was made by one of you men. If we Lions knew how to erect statues, you would see the Man placed under the paw of the Lion."

One story is good, till another is told.

The Man and the Satyr

A MAN and a Satyr once drank together in token of a bond of alliance being formed between them.

One very cold wintry day, as they talked, the Man put his fingers to his mouth and blew on them. When the Satyr asked the reason for this, he told him that he did it to warm his hands because they were so cold.

Later on in the day they sat down to eat, and the food prepared was quite scalding. The Man raised one of the dishes a little towards his mouth and blew in it.

When the Satyr again inquired the reason, he said that he did it to cool the meat, which was too hot. "I can no longer consider you as a friend," said the Satyr, "a fellow who with the same breath blows hot and cold."

The Man, the Horse, the Ox, and the Dog

A HORSE, Ox, and Dog, driven to great straits by the cold, sought shelter and protection from Man. He received them kindly, lighted a fire, and warmed them. He let the Horse make free with his oats, gave the Ox an abundance of hay, and fed the Dog with meat from his own table.

Grateful for these favors, the animals determined to repay him to the best of their ability. For this purpose, they divided the term of his life between them, and each endowed one portion of it with the qualities which chiefly characterized himself.

The Horse chose his earliest years and gave them his own attributes: hence every man is in his youth impetuous, headstrong, and obstinate in maintaining his own opinion. The Ox took under his patronage the next term of life, and therefore man in his middle age is fond of work, devoted to labor, and resolute to amass wealth and to husband his resources.

The end of life was reserved for the Dog, wherefore the old man is often snappish, irritable, hard to please, and selfish, tolerant only of his own household, but averse to strangers and to all who do not administer to his comfort or to his necessities.

The Master and His Dogs

A CERTAIN MAN, detained by a storm in his country house, first of all killed his sheep, and then his goats, for the maintenance of his household. The storm still continuing, he was obliged to slaughter his yoke oxen for food.

On seeing this, his Dogs took counsel together, and said, "It is time for us to be off, for if the master spare not his oxen, who work for his gain, how can we expect him to spare us?"

He is not to be trusted as a friend who mistreats his own family.

Mercury and the Sculptor

MERCURY ONCE DETERMINED to learn in what esteem he was held among mortals. For this purpose he assumed the character of a man and visited in this disguise a Sculptor's studio having looked at various statues, he demanded the price of two figures of Jupiter and Juno. When the sum at which they were valued was named, he pointed to a figure of himself, saying to the Sculptor, "You will certainly want much more for this, as it is the statue of the Messenger of the Gods, and author of all your gain." The Sculptor replied, "Well, if you will buy these, I'll fling you that into the bargain."

Mercury and the Workmen

A WORKMAN, felling wood by the side of a river, let his axe drop by accident into a deep pool. Being thus deprived of the means of his livelihood, he sat down on the bank and lamented his hard fate.

Mercury appeared and demanded the cause of his tears. After he told him his misfortune, Mercury plunged into the stream, and, bringing up a golden axe, inquired if that were the one he had lost. On his saying that it was not his, Mercury disappeared beneath the water a second time, returned with a silver axe in his hand, and again asked the Workman if it were his.

When the Workman said it was not, he dived into the pool for the third time and brought up the axe that had been lost. The Workman claimed it and expressed his joy at its recovery.

Mercury, pleased with his honesty, gave him the golden and silver axes in addition to his own. The Workman, on his return to his house, related to his companions all that had happened.

One of them at once resolved to try and secure the same good fortune for himself. He ran to the river and threw his axe on purpose into the pool at the same place, and sat down on the bank to weep.

Mercury appeared to him just as he hoped he would; and having learned the cause of his grief, plunged into the stream and brought up a golden axe, inquiring if he had lost it.

The Workman seized it greedily, and declared that truly it was the very same axe that he had lost. Mercury, displeased at his knavery, not only took away the golden axe, but refused to recover for him the axe he had thrown into the pool.

The Mouse, the Frog, and the Hawk

A MOUSE who always lived on the land, by an unlucky chance formed an intimate acquaintance with a Frog, who lived for the most part in the water. The Frog, one day intent on mischief, bound the foot of the Mouse tightly to his own.

Thus joined together, the Frog first of all led his friend the Mouse to the meadow where they were accustomed to find their food. After this, he gradually led him towards the pool in which he lived, until reaching the very brink, he suddenly jumped in, dragging the Mouse with him.

The Frog enjoyed the water amazingly, and swam croaking about, as if he had done a good deed. The unhappy Mouse was soon suffocated by the water, and his dead body floated about on the surface, tied to the foot of the Frog.

A Hawk observed it, and, pouncing upon it with his talons, carried it aloft. The Frog, being still fastened to the leg of the Mouse, was also carried off a prisoner, and was eaten by the Hawk.

Harm hatch, harm catch.

The Mice and the Weasels

THE WEASELS and the Mice waged a perpetual war with each other, in which much blood was shed. The Weasels were always the victors. The

Mice thought that the cause of their frequent defeats was that they had no leaders set apart from the general army to command them, and that they were exposed to dangers from lack of discipline.

They therefore chose as leaders Mice that were most renowned for their family descent, strength, and counsel, as well as those most noted for their courage in the fight, so that they might be better marshaled in battle array and formed into troops, regiments, and battalions.

When all this was done, and the army disciplined, and the herald Mouse had duly proclaimed war by challenging the Weasels, the newly chosen generals bound their heads with straws, that they might be more conspicuous to all their troops. Scarcely had the battle begun, when a great rout overwhelmed the Mice, who scampered off as fast as they could to their holes.

The generals, not being able to get in on account of the ornaments on their heads, were all captured and eaten by the Weasels.

The more honor the more danger.

The Town Mouse and the Country Mouse

A COUNTRY MOUSE invited a Town Mouse, an intimate friend, to pay him a visit and partake of his country fare.

As they were on the bare plowlands, eating there wheat-stocks and roots pulled up from the hedgerow, the Town Mouse said to his friend, "You live here the life of the ants, while in my house is the horn of plenty. I am surrounded by every luxury, and if you will come with me, as I wish you would, you shall have an ample share of my dainties." The Country Mouse was easily persuaded, and returned to town with his friend.

On his arrival, the Town Mouse placed before him bread, barley, beans, dried figs, honey, raisins, and, last of all, brought a dainty piece of cheese from a basket. The Country Mouse, being much delighted at the sight of such good cheer, expressed his satisfaction in warm terms and lamented his own hard fate.

Just as they were beginning to eat, someone opened the door, and they both ran off squeaking, as fast as they could, to a hole so narrow that two could only find room in it by squeezing.

They had scarcely begun their repast again when someone else entered to take something out of a cupboard, whereupon the two Mice, more frightened than before, ran away and hid themselves.

At last the Country Mouse, almost famished, said to his friend: "Although you have prepared for me so dainty a feast, I must leave you to enjoy it by yourself. It is surrounded by too many dangers to please me. I prefer my bare plowlands and roots from the hedgerow, where I can live in safety, and without fear."

The Milk-Woman and Her Pail

A FARMER'S daughter was carrying her Pail of milk from the field to the farmhouse, when she fell a-musing. "The money for which this milk will be sold, will buy at least three hundred eggs.

The eggs, allowing for all mishaps, will produce two hundred and fifty chickens. The chickens will become ready for the market when poultry will fetch the highest price, so that by the end of the year I shall have money enough from my share to buy a new gown. In this dress I will go to the Christmas parties, where all the young fellows will propose to me, but I will toss my head and refuse them every one."

At this moment she tossed her head in unison with her thoughts, when down fell the milk pail to the ground, and all her imaginary schemes perished in a moment.

The Miller, His Son, and Their Ass

A MILLER and his son were driving their Ass to a neighboring fair to sell him. They had not gone far when they met with a troop of women collected round a well, talking and laughing.

"Look there," cried one of them, "did you ever see such fellows, to be trudging along the road on foot when they might ride?" The old man hearing this, quickly made his son mount the Ass, and continued to walk along merrily by his side.

Presently they came up to a group of old men in earnest debate. "There," said one of them, "it proves what I was a-saying. What respect is shown to old age in these days? Do you see that idle lad riding while his old father has to walk? Get down, you young scapegrace, and let the old man rest his weary limbs."

Upon this the old man made his son dismount, and got up himself. In this manner they had not proceeded far when they met a company of women and children: "Why, you lazy old fellow," cried several tongues at once, "how can you ride upon the beast, while that poor little lad there can hardly keep pace by the side of you?" The good-natured Miller immediately took up his son behind him. They had now almost reached the town.

"Pray, honest friend," said a citizen, "is that Ass your own?"

"Yes," replied the old man.

"O, one would not have thought so," said the other, "by the way you load him. Why, you two fellows are better able to carry the poor beast than he you."

"Anything to please you," said the old man; "we can but try."

So, alighting with his son, they tied the legs of the Ass together and with the help of a pole endeavored to carry him on their shoulders over a bridge near the entrance to the town.

This entertaining sight brought the people in crowds to laugh at it, till the Ass, not liking the noise nor the strange handling that he was subject to, broke the cords that bound him and, tumbling off the pole, fell into the river.

Upon this, the old man, vexed and ashamed, made the best of his way home again, convinced that by endeavoring to please everybody he had pleased nobody, and lost his Ass in the bargain.

The Dancing Monkeys

A PRINCE had some Monkeys trained to dance. Being naturally great mimics of men's actions, they showed themselves most apt pupils, and when arrayed in their rich clothes and masks, they danced as well as any of the courtiers.

The spectacle was often repeated with great applause, till on one occasion a courtier, bent on mischief, took from his pocket a handful of nuts and threw them upon the stage.

The Monkeys at the sight of the nuts forgot their dancing and became (as indeed they were) Monkeys instead of actors. Pulling off their masks and tearing their robes, they fought with one another for the nuts.

The dancing spectacle thus came to an end amidst the laughter and ridicule of the audience.

The Monkeys and Their Mother

THE MONKEY, it is said, has two young ones at each birth. The Mother fondles one and nurtures it with the greatest affection and care, but hates and neglects the other.

It happened once that the young one which was caressed and loved was smothered by the too great affection of the Mother, while the despised one was nurtured and reared in spite of the neglect to which it was exposed.

The best intentions will not always ensure success.

The Monkey and the Dolphin

A SAILOR, bound on a long voyage, took with him a Monkey to amuse him while on shipboard. As he sailed off the coast of Greece, a violent tempest arose in which the ship was wrecked and he, his Monkey, and all the crew were obliged to swim for their lives.

A Dolphin saw the Monkey contending with the waves, and supposing him to be a man (whom he is always said to befriend), came and placed himself under him, to convey him on his back in safety to the shore.

When the Dolphin arrived with his burden in sight of land not far from Athens, he asked the Monkey if he were an Athenian. The latter replied that he was, and that he was descended from one of the most noble families in that city. The Dolphin then inquired if he knew the Piraeus (the famous harbor of Athens).

Supposing that a man was meant, the Monkey answered that he knew him very well and that he was an intimate friend. The Dolphin, indignant at these falsehoods, dipped the Monkey under the water and drowned him.

The Monkey and the Camel

THE BEASTS of the forest gave a splendid entertainment at which the Monkey stood up and danced. Having vastly delighted the assembly, he sat down amidst universal applause.

The Camel, envious of the praises bestowed on the Monkey and desiring to divert to himself the favor of the guests, proposed to stand up in his turn and dance for their amusement.

He moved about in so utterly ridiculous a manner that the Beasts, in a fit of indignation, set upon him with clubs and drove him out of the assembly.

It is absurd to ape our betters.

The Mountain in Labor

A MOUNTAIN was once greatly agitated. Loud groans and noises were heard, and crowds of people came from all parts to see what was the matter. While they were assembled in anxious expectation of some terrible calamity, out came a Mouse.

Don't make much ado about nothing.

The Mules and the Robbers

TWO MULES well-laden with packs were trudging along. One carried panniers filled with money, the other sacks weighted with grain. The Mule carrying the treasure walked with head erect, as if conscious of the value of his burden, and tossed up and down the clear-toned bells fastened to his neck. His companion followed with quiet and easy step. All of a sudden Robbers rushed upon them from their hiding-places, and in the scuffle with their owners, wounded with a sword the Mule carrying the treasure, which they greedily seized while taking no notice of the grain. The Mule which had been robbed and wounded bewailed his misfortunes.

The other replied, "I am indeed glad that I was thought so little of, for I have lost nothing, nor am I hurt with any wound."

The North Wind and the Sun

THE NORTH WIND and the Sun disputed as to which was the most powerful, and agreed that he should be declared the victor who could first strip a wayfaring man of his clothes.

The North Wind first tried his power and blew with all his might, but the keener his blasts, the closer the Traveler wrapped his cloak around him, until at last, resigning all hope of victory, the Wind called upon the Sun to see what he could do.

The Sun suddenly shone out with all his warmth. The Traveler no sooner felt his genial rays than he took off one garment after another, and at last, fairly overcome with heat, undressed and bathed in a stream that lay in his path.

Persuasion is better than Force.

The Oak and the Reeds

A VERY LARGE OAK was uprooted by the wind and thrown across a stream. It fell among some Reeds, which it thus addressed: "I wonder how you, who are so light and weak, are not entirely crushed by these strong winds."

They replied, "You fight and contend with the wind, and consequently you are destroyed; while we on the contrary bend before the least breath of air, and therefore remain unbroken, and escape."

Stoop to conquer.

The Oak and the Woodcutters

THE WOODCUTTER cut down a Mountain Oak and split it in pieces, making wedges of its own branches for dividing the trunk.

The Oak said with a sigh, "I do not care about the blows of the axe aimed at my roots, but I do grieve at being torn in pieces by these wedges made from my own branches."

Misfortunes springing from ourselves are the hardest to bear.

The Olive-Tree and the Fig-Tree

THE OLIVE-TREE ridiculed the Fig-Tree because, while she was green all the year round, the Fig-Tree changed its leaves with the seasons.

A shower of snow fell upon them, and, finding the Olive full of foliage, it settled upon its branches and broke them down with its weight, at once despoiling it of its beauty and killing the tree. But finding the Fig-Tree denuded of leaves, the snow fell through to the ground, and did not injure it at all.

The Ox and the Frog

AN OX drinking at a pool trod on a brood of young frogs and crushed one of them to death.

The Mother coming up, and missing one of her sons, inquired of his brothers what had become of him. "He is dead, dear Mother; for just now a very huge beast with four great feet came to the pool and crushed him to death with his cloven heel."

The Frog, puffing herself out, inquired, "if the beast was as big as that in size." "Cease, Mother, to puff yourself out," said her son, "and do not be angry; for you would, I assure you, sooner burst than successfully imitate the hugeness of that monster."

The Oxen and the Butchers

THE OXEN once upon a time sought to destroy the Butchers, who practiced a trade destructive to their race. They assembled on a certain day to carry out their purpose, and sharpened their horns for the contest. But one of them who was exceedingly old (for many a field had he plowed) thus spoke: "These Butchers, it is true, slaughter us, but they do so with skillful hands, and with no unnecessary pain. If we get rid of them, we shall fall into the hands of unskillful operators, and thus suffer a double death: for you may be assured, that though all the Butchers should perish, yet will men never want beef."

Do not be in a hurry to change one evil for another.

The Oxen and the Axle-Trees

A HEAVY WAGON was being dragged along a country lane by a team of Oxen. The Axle-trees groaned and creaked terribly; whereupon the Oxen, turning round, thus addressed the wheels: "Hullo there! Why do you make so much noise? We bear all the labor, and we, not you, ought to cry out."

Those who suffer most cry out the least.

The Owl and the Birds

AN OWL, in her wisdom, counseled the Birds that when the acorn first began to sprout, to pull it all up out of the ground and not allow it to grow. She said acorns would produce mistletoe, from which an irremediable poison, the bird-lime, would be extracted and by which they would be captured.

The Owl next advised them to pluck up the seed of the flax, which men had sown, as it was a plant which boded no good to them.

And, lastly, the Owl, seeing an archer approach, predicted that this man, being on foot, would contrive darts armed with feathers which would fly faster than the wings of the Birds themselves.

The Birds gave no credence to these warning words, but considered the

Owl to be beside herself and said that she was mad. But afterwards, finding her words were true, they wondered at her knowledge and deemed her to be the wisest of birds.

Hence it is that when she appears they look to her as knowing all things, while she no longer gives them advice, but in solitude laments their past folly.

The Panther and the Shepherds

A PANTHER, by some mischance, fell into a pit. The Shepherds discovered him, and some threw sticks at him and pelted him with stones, while others, moved with compassion towards one about to die even though no one should hurt him, threw in some food to prolong his life. At night they returned home, not dreaming of any danger, but supposing that on the morrow they would find him dead. The Panther, however, when he had recruited his feeble strength, freed himself with a sudden bound from the pit, and hastened to his den with rapid steps.

After a few days he came forth and slaughtered the cattle, and, killing the Shepherds who had attacked him, raged with angry fury. Then they who had spared his life, fearing for their safety, surrendered to him their flocks and begged only for their lives.

To them the Panther made this reply: "I remember alike those who sought my life with stones, and those who gave me food aside, therefore, your fears. I return as an enemy only to those who injured me."

The Peasant and the Apple-Tree

A PEASANT had in his garden an Apple-Tree which bore no fruit but only served as a harbor for the sparrows and grasshoppers. He resolved to cut it down, and taking his axe in his hand, made a bold stroke at its roots. The grasshoppers and sparrows entreated him not to cut down the tree that sheltered them, but to spare it, and they would sing to him and lighten his labors. He paid no attention to their request, but gave the tree a second and a third blow with his axe.

When he reached the hollow of the tree, he found a hive full of honey. Having tasted the honeycomb, he threw down his axe, and looking on the tree as sacred, took great care of it.

Self-interest alone moves some men.

The Peacock and the Crane

A PEACOCK spreading its gorgeous tail mocked a Crane that passed by, ridiculing the ashen hue of its plumage and saying, "I am robed, like a king, in gold and purple and all the colors of the rainbow; while you have not a bit of color on your wings."

"True," replied the Crane; "but I soar to the heights of heaven and lift up my voice to the stars, while you walk below, like a cock, among the birds of the dunghill."

Fine feathers don't make fine birds.

The Philosopher, the Ants, and Mercury

A PHILOSOPHER witnessed from the shore the shipwreck of a vessel, of which the crew and passengers were all drowned. He inveighed against the injustice of Providence, which would for the sake of one criminal perchance sailing in the ship allow so many innocent persons to perish. As he was indulging in these reflections, he found himself surrounded by a whole army of Ants, near whose nest he was standing. One of them climbed up and stung him, and he immediately trampled them all to death with his foot.

Mercury presented himself, and striking the Philosopher with his wand, said, "And are you indeed to make yourself a judge of the dealings of Providence, who hast thyself in a similar manner treated these poor Ants?"

The Thirsty Pigeon

A PIGEON, oppressed by excessive thirst, saw a goblet of water painted on a signboard. Not supposing it to be only a picture, she flew towards it with a loud whir and unwittingly dashed against the signboard, jarring herself terribly. Having broken her wings by the blow, she fell to the ground, and was caught by one of the bystanders.

Zeal should not outrun discretion.

The Two Pots

A RIVER carried down in its stream two Pots, one made of earthenware and the other of brass. The Earthen Pot said to the Brass Pot, "Pray keep at a distance and do not come near me, for if you touch me ever so slightly, I shall be broken in pieces, and besides, I by no means wish to come near you."

Equals make the best friends.

The Raven and the Swan

A RAVEN saw a Swan and desired to secure for himself the same beautiful plumage. Supposing that the Swan's splendid white color arose from his washing in the water in which he swam, the Raven left the altars in the neighborhood where he picked up his living, and took up residence in the lakes and pools. But cleansing his feathers as often as he would, he could not change their color, while through want of food he perished.

Change of habit cannot alter Nature.

The Salt Merchant and His Ass

A PEDDLER drove his Ass to the seashore to buy salt. His road home lay across a stream into which his Ass, making a false step, fell by accident and rose up again with his load considerably lighter, as the water melted the sack.

The Peddler retraced his steps and refilled his panniers with a larger quantity of salt than before. When he came again to the stream, the Ass fell down on purpose in the same spot, and, regaining his feet with the weight of his load much diminished, brayed triumphantly as if he had obtained what he desired.

The Peddler saw through his trick and drove him for the third time to the coast, where he bought a cargo of sponges instead of salt. The Ass, again playing the fool, fell down on purpose when he reached the stream, but the sponges became swollen with water, greatly increasing his load. And thus his trick recoiled on him, for he now carried on his back a double burden.

The Seagull and the Kite

A SEAGULL having bolted down too large a fish, burst its deep gullet-bag and lay down on the shore to die. A Kite saw him and exclaimed: "You richly deserve your fate; for a bird of the air has no business to seek its food from the sea."

Every man should be content to mind his own business.

The Serpent and the Eagle

A SERPENT and an Eagle were struggling with each other in deadly conflict. The Serpent had the advantage, and was about to strangle the bird.

A countryman saw them, and running up, loosed the coil of the Serpent and let the Eagle go free. The Serpent, irritated at the escape of his prey, injected his poison into the drinking horn of the countryman.

The rustic, ignorant of his danger, was about to drink, when the Eagle struck his hand with his wing, and, seizing the drinking horn in his talons, carried it aloft.

The Shepherd's Boy and the Wolf

A SHEPHERD-BOY, who watched a flock of sheep near a village, brought out the villagers three or four times by crying out, "Wolf! Wolf!" and when his neighbors came to help him, laughed at them for their pains. The Wolf, however, did truly come at last. The Shepherd-boy, now really alarmed, shouted in an agony of terror: "Pray, do come and help me; the Wolf is killing the sheep;" but no one paid any heed to his cries, nor rendered any assistance. The Wolf, having no cause of fear, at his leisure lacerated or destroyed the whole flock.

There is no believing a liar, even when he speaks the truth.

The Shepherd and the Sheep

A SHEPHERD driving his Sheep to a wood, saw an oak of unusual size full of acorns, and spreading his cloak under the branches, he climbed up into the tree and shook them down.

The Sheep eating the acorns inadvertently frayed and tore the cloak. When the Shepherd came down and saw what was done, he said, "O you most ungrateful creatures! You provide wool to make garments for all other men, but you destroy the clothes of him who feeds you."

The She-Goats and Their Beards

THE SHE-GOATS having obtained a beard by request to Jupiter, the He-Goats were sorely displeased and made complaint that the females equaled them in dignity.

"Allow them," said Jupiter, "to enjoy an empty honor and to assume the badge of your nobler sex, so long as they are not your equals in strength or courage."

It matters little if those who are inferior to us in merit should be like us in outside appearances.

The Shipwrecked Man and the Sea

A SHIPWRECKED MAN, having been cast upon a certain shore, slept after his buffetings with the deep. After a while he awoke, and looking upon the Sea, loaded it with reproaches.

He argued that it enticed men with the calmness of its looks, but when it had induced them to plow its waters, it grew rough and destroyed them. The Sea, assuming the form of a woman, replied to him: "Blame not me, my good sir, but the winds, for I am by my own nature as calm and firm even as this earth; but the winds suddenly falling on me create these waves, and lash me into fury."

The Sick Stag

A SICK STAG lay down in a quiet corner of its pasture-ground. His companions came in great numbers to inquire after his health, and each one helped himself to a share of the food which had been placed for his use; so that he died, not from his sickness, but from the failure of the means of living.

Evil companions bring more hurt than profit.

The Stag in the Ox-Stall

A STAG, roundly chased by the hounds and blinded by fear to the danger he was running into, took shelter in a farmyard and hid himself in a shed among the oxen.

An Ox gave him this kindly warning: "O unhappy creature! Why should you thus, of your own accord, incur destruction and trust yourself in the house of your enemy?" The Stag replied: "Only allow me, friend, to stay where I am, and I will undertake to find some favorable opportunity of effecting my escape."

At the approach of the evening the herdsman came to feed his cattle, but did not see the Stag; and even the farm-bailiff with several laborers passed through the shed and failed to notice him. The Stag, congratulating himself on his safety, began to express his sincere thanks to the Oxen who had kindly helped him in the hour of need. One of them again answered him: "We indeed wish you well, but the danger is not over.

There is one other yet to pass through the shed, who has as it were a hundred eyes, and until he has come and gone, your life is still in peril." At that moment the master himself entered, and having had to complain that his oxen had not been properly fed, he went up to their racks and cried out: "why is there such a scarcity of fodder? There is not half enough straw for them to lie on.

Those lazy fellows have not even swept the cobwebs away." While he thus examined everything in turn, he spied the tips of the antlers of the Stag peeping out of the straw. Then summoning his laborers, he ordered that the Stag should be seized and killed.

The Stag, the Wolf, and the Sheep

A STAG asked a Sheep to lend him a measure of wheat, and said that the Wolf would be his surety.

The Sheep, fearing some fraud was intended, excused herself, saying, "The Wolf is accustomed to seize what he wants and to run off; and you, too, can quickly outstrip me in your rapid flight. How then shall I be able to find you, when the day of payment comes?"

Two blacks do not make one white.

The Stag at the Pool

A STAG overpowered by heat came to a spring to drink. Seeing his own shadow reflected in the water, he greatly admired the size and variety of his horns, but felt angry with himself for having such slender and weak feet.

While he was thus contemplating himself, a Lion appeared at the pool and crouched to spring upon him. The Stag immediately took to flight, and exerting his utmost speed, as long as the plain was smooth and open kept himself easily at a safe distance from the Lion. But entering a wood he became entangled by his horns, and the Lion quickly came up to him and caught him.

When too late, he thus reproached himself: "Woe is me! How I have deceived myself! These feet which would have saved me I despised, and I gloried in these antlers which have proved my destruction."

What is most truly valuable is often underrated.

The Swallow and the Crow

THE SWALLOW and the Crow had a contention about their plumage. The Crow put an end to the dispute by saying, "Your feathers are all very well in the spring, but mine protect me against the winter."

Fair weather friends are not worth much.

 8

The Thief and His Mother

A BOY stole a lesson-book from one of his schoolfellows and took it home to his Mother. She not only abstained from beating him, but encouraged him.

He next time stole a cloak and brought it to her, and she again commended him. The Youth, advanced to adulthood, proceeded to steal things of still greater value. At last he was caught in the very act, and having his hands bound behind him, was led away to the place of public execution.

His Mother followed in the crowd and violently beat her breast in sorrow, whereupon the young man said, "I wish to say something to my Mother in her ear." She came close to him, and he quickly seized her ear with his teeth and bit it off.

The Mother upbraided him as an unnatural child, whereon he replied, "Ah! If you had beaten me when I first stole and brought to you that lesson-book, I should not have come to this, nor have been thus led to a disgraceful death."

The Thief and the Innkeeper

A THIEF hired a room in a tavern and stayed a while in the hope of stealing something which should enable him to pay his reckoning.

When he had waited some days in vain, he saw the Innkeeper dressed in a new and handsome coat and sitting before his door. The Thief sat down beside him and talked with him.

As the conversation began to flag, the Thief yawned terribly and at the same time howled like a wolf. The Innkeeper said, "why do you howl so fearfully?"

"I will tell you," said the Thief, "but first let me ask you to hold my clothes, or I shall tear them to pieces. I know not, sir, when I got this habit of yawning, nor whether these attacks of howling were inflicted on me as a judgment for my crimes, or for any other cause; but this I do know, that when I yawn for the third time, I actually turn into a wolf and attack men."

With this speech he commenced a second fit of yawning and again howled like a wolf, as he had at first. The Innkeeper, hearing his tale and believing what he said, became greatly alarmed and, rising from his seat, attempted to run away.

The Thief laid hold of his coat and entreated him to stop, saying, "Pray wait, sir, and hold my clothes, or I shall tear them to pieces in my fury, when I turn into a wolf." At the same moment he yawned the third time and set up a terrible howl.

The Innkeeper, frightened lest he should be attacked, left his new coat in the Thief's hand and ran as fast as he could into the inn for safety. The Thief made off with the coat and did not return again to the inn.

Every tale is not to be believed.

The Tortoise and the Eagle

A TORTOISE, lazily basking in the sun, complained to the sea-birds of her hard fate, that no one would teach her to fly. An Eagle, hovering near, heard her lamentation and demanded what reward she would give him if he would take her aloft and float her in the air.

"I will give you," she said, "all the riches of the Red Sea." "I will teach you to fly then," said the Eagle; and taking her up in his talons he carried her almost to the clouds suddenly he let her go, and she fell on a lofty mountain, dashing her shell to pieces. The Tortoise exclaimed in the moment of death: "I have deserved my present fate; for what had I to do with wings and clouds, who can with difficulty move about on the earth?"

If men had all they wished, they would be often ruined.

The Thieves and the Cock

SOME THIEVES broke into a house and found nothing but a Cock, whom they stole, and got off as fast as they could.

Upon arriving at home they prepared to kill the Cock, who thus pleaded for his life: "Pray spare me; I am very serviceable to men. I wake them up in the night to their work."

"That is the very reason why we must the more kill you," they replied; "for when you wake your neighbors, you entirely put an end to our business."

The safeguards of virtue are hateful to those with evil intentions.

The Three Tradesmen

A GREAT CITY was besieged, and its inhabitants were called together to consider the best means of protecting it from the enemy.

A Bricklayer earnestly recommended bricks as affording the best material for an effective resistance. A Carpenter, with equal enthusiasm, proposed timber as a preferable method of defense.

Upon which a Currier stood up and said, "Sirs, I differ from you altogether: there is no material for resistance equal to a covering of hides; and nothing so good as leather."

Every man for himself.

The Boasting Traveler

A MAN who had traveled in foreign lands boasted very much, on returning to his own country, of the many wonderful and heroic feats he had performed in the different places he had visited. Among other things, he said that when he was at Rhodes he had leaped to such a distance that no man of his day could leap anywhere near him as to that, there were in Rhodes many persons who saw him do it and whom he could call as witnesses.

One of the bystanders interrupted him, saying: "Now, my good man, if this be all true there is no need of witnesses. Suppose this to be Rhodes, and leap for us."

The Two Travelers and the Axe

TWO MEN were journeying together. One of them picked up an axe that lay upon the path, and said, "I have found an axe." "Nay, my friend," replied the other, "do not say 'I,' but 'We' have found an axe."

They had not gone far before they saw the owner of the axe pursuing them, and he who had picked up the axe said, "We are undone." "Nay," replied the other, "keep to your first mode of speech, my friend; what you thought right then, think right now. Say 'I,' not 'We' are undone."

He who shares the danger ought to share the prize.

The Seaside Travelers

SOME TRAVELERS, journeying along the seashore, climbed to the summit of a tall cliff, and looking over the sea, saw in the distance what they thought was a large ship. They waited in the hope of seeing it enter the harbor, but as the object on which they looked was driven nearer to shore by the wind, they found that it could at the most be a small boat, and not a ship.

When however it reached the beach, they discovered that it was only a large faggot of sticks, and one of them said to his companions, "We have waited for no purpose, for after all there is nothing to see but a load of wood."

Our mere anticipations of life outrun its realities.

The Traveler and Fortune

A TRAVELER wearied from a long journey lay down, overcome with fatigue, on the very brink of a deep well.

Just as he was about to fall into the water, Dame Fortune, it is said, appeared to him and waking him from his slumber thus addressed him: "Good Sir, pray wake up: for if you fall into the well, the blame will be thrown on me, and I shall get an ill name among mortals; for I find that men are sure to impute their calamities to me, however much by their own folly they have really brought them on themselves."

Everyone is more or less master of his own fate.

The Travelers and the Plane-Tree

TWO TRAVELERS, worn out by the heat of the summer's sun, laid themselves down at noon under the widespreading branches of a Plane-Tree.

As they rested under its shade, one of the Travelers said to the other, "What a singularly useless tree is the Plane! It bears no fruit, and is not of the least service to man."

The Plane-Tree, interrupting him, said, "You ungrateful fellows! Do you, while receiving benefits from me and resting under my shade, dare to describe me as useless, and unprofitable?"

Some men underrate their best blessings.

The Traveler and His Dog

A TRAVELER about to set out on a journey saw his Dog stand at the door stretching himself. He asked him sharply: "Why do you stand there gaping? Everything is ready but you, so come with me instantly." The Dog, wagging his tail, replied: "O, master! I am quite ready; it is you for whom I am waiting."

The loiterer often blames delay on his more active friend.

The Widow and the Sheep

A CERTAIN poor widow had one solitary Sheep. At shearing time, wishing to take his fleece and to avoid expense, she sheared him herself, but used the shears so unskillfully that with the fleece she sheared the flesh.

The Sheep, writhing with pain, said, "Why do you hurt me so, Mistress? What weight can my blood add to the wool? If you want my flesh, there is the butcher, who will kill me in an instant; but if you want my fleece and wool, there is the shearer, who will shear and not hurt me."

The least outlay is not always the greatest gain.

The Wild Ass and the Lion

A WILD ASS and a Lion entered into an alliance so that they might capture the beasts of the forest with greater ease. The Lion agreed to assist the Wild Ass with his strength, while the Wild Ass gave the Lion the benefit of his greater speed.

When they had taken as many beasts as their necessities required, the Lion undertook to distribute the prey, and for this purpose divided it into three shares. "I will take the first share," he said, "because I am King: and the second share, as a partner with you in the chase: and the third share (believe me) will be a source of great evil to you, unless you willingly resign it to me, and set off as fast as you can."

Might makes right.

The Old Woman and the Wine-Jar
AN OLD WOMAN found an empty jar which had lately been full of prime old wine and which still retained the fragrant smell of its former contents. She greedily placed it several times to her nose, and drawing it backwards and forwards said, "O most delicious! How nice must the Wine itself have been, when it leaves behind in the very vessel which contained it so sweet a perfume!"

The memory of a good deed lives.

The Wolf and the Sheep
A WOLF, sorely wounded and bitten by dogs, lay sick and maimed in his lair. Being in want of food, he called to a Sheep who was passing, and asked him to fetch some water from a stream flowing close beside him. "For," he said, "if you will bring me drink, I will find means to provide myself with meat." "Yes," said the Sheep, "if I should bring you the draught, you would doubtless make me provide the meat also."

Hypocritical speeches are easily seen through.

The Wolves and the Sheep
"WHY SHOULD there always be this fear and slaughter between us?" said the Wolves to the Sheep. "Those evil-disposed Dogs have much to answer for. They always bark whenever we approach you and attack us before we have done any harm. If you would only dismiss them from your heels, there might soon be treaties of peace and reconciliation between us." The Sheep, poor silly creatures, were easily beguiled and dismissed the Dogs, whereupon the Wolves destroyed the unguarded flock at their own pleasure.

The Wolf in Sheep's Clothing
ONCE UPON A time a Wolf resolved to disguise his appearance in order to secure food more easily. Encased in the skin of a sheep, he pastured with the flock deceiving the shepherd by his costume. In the evening he was shut up by the shepherd in the fold; the gate was closed, and the entrance made thoroughly secure. But the shepherd, returning to the fold during the night to obtain meat for the next day, mistakenly caught up the Wolf instead of a sheep, and killed him instantly.

Harm seek, harm find.

The Wolves and the Sheepdogs

THE WOLVES thus addressed the Sheepdogs: "Why should you, who are like us in so many things, not be entirely of one mind with us, and live with us as brothers should? We differ from you in one point only. We live in freedom, but you bow down to and slave for men, who in return for your services flog you with whips and put collars on your necks. They make you also guard their sheep, and while they eat the mutton throw only the bones to you. If you will be persuaded by us, you will give us the sheep, and we will enjoy them in common, till we all are surfeited." The Dogs listened favorably to these proposals, and, entering the den of the Wolves, they were set upon and torn to pieces.

The Wolf and the Fox

AT ONE TIME a very large and strong Wolf was born among the wolves, who exceeded all his fellow-wolves in strength, size, and swiftness, so that they unanimously decided to call him "Lion." The Wolf, with a lack of sense proportioned to his enormous size, thought that they gave him this name in earnest, and, leaving his own race, consorted exclusively with the lions.

An old sly Fox, seeing this, said, "May I never make myself so ridiculous as you do in your pride and self-conceit; for even though you have the size of a lion among wolves, in a herd of lions you are definitely a wolf."

The Wolf and the Shepherd

A WOLF followed a flock of sheep for a long time and did not attempt to injure one of them. The Shepherd at first stood on his guard against him, as against an enemy, and kept a strict watch over his movements. But when the Wolf, day after day, kept in the company of the sheep and did not make the slightest effort to seize them, the Shepherd began to look upon him as a guardian of his flock rather than as a plotter of evil against it; and when occasion called him one day into the city, he left the sheep entirely in his charge. The Wolf, now that he had the opportunity, fell upon the sheep, and destroyed the greater part of the flock. When the Shepherd returned/ to find his flock destroyed, he exclaimed: "I have been rightly served; why did I trust my sheep to a Wolf?"

The Wolf and the Horse

A WOLF coming out of a field of oats met a Horse and thus addressed him: "I would advise you to go into that field. It is full of fine oats, which I have left untouched for you, as you are a friend whom I would love to hear enjoying good eating."

The Horse replied, "If oats had been the food of wolves, you would never have indulged your ears at the cost of your belly."

Men of evil reputation, when they perform a good deed, fail to get credit for it.

The Wolf and the Lion

ROAMING BY the mountainside at sundown, a Wolf saw his own shadow become greatly extended and magnified, and he said to himself, "Why should I, being of such an immense size and extending nearly an acre in length, be afraid of the Lion? Ought I not to be acknowledged as King of all the collected beasts?"

While he was indulging in these proud thoughts, a Lion fell upon him and killed him. He exclaimed with a too late repentance, "Wretched me! This overestimation of myself is the cause of my destruction."

The Wolf and The Lamb

WOLF, meeting with a Lamb astray from the fold, resolved not to lay violent hands on him, but to find some plea to justify to the Lamb the Wolf's right to eat him.

He thus addressed him: "Sirrah, last year you grossly insulted me."

"Indeed," bleated the Lamb in a mournful tone of voice, "I was not then born."

Then said the Wolf, "You feed in my pasture."

"No, good sir," replied the Lamb, "I have not yet tasted grass."

Again said the Wolf, "You drink of my well."

"No," exclaimed the Lamb, "I never yet drank water, for as yet my mother's milk is both food and drink to me."

Upon which the Wolf seized him and ate him up, saying, "Well! I won't remain supperless, even though you refute every one of my imputations."

The tyrant will always find a pretext for his tyranny.

The Wolf and the Crane

A WOLF who had a bone stuck in his throat hired a Crane, for a large sum, to put her head into his mouth and draw out the bone.

When the Crane had extracted the bone and demanded the promised payment, the Wolf, grinning and grinding his teeth, exclaimed: "Why, you have surely already had a sufficient recompense, in having been permitted to draw out your head in safety from the mouth and jaws of a wolf."

In serving the wicked, expect no reward, and be thankful if you escape injury for your pains.

The Wolf, the Fox, and the Ape

A WOLF accused a Fox of theft, but the Fox entirely denied the charge. An Ape undertook to adjudge the matter between them.

When each had fully stated his case the Ape announced this sentence: "I do not think you, Wolf, ever lost what you claim; and I do believe you, Fox, to have stolen what you so stoutly deny."

The dishonest, if they act honestly, get no credit.